DUFF HART-DAVIS

THE
WAR THAT
NEVER WAS

arrow books

Published by Arrow Books 2012

2 4 6 8 10 9 7 5 3 1

First published in Great Britain in 2011 by
Century
Random House, 20 Vauxhall Bridge Road,
London SW1V 2SA

www.randomhouse.co.uk

Addresses for companies within The Random House Group Limited can be found at: www.
randomhouse.co.uk/offices.htm

The Random House Group Limited Reg. No. 954009

A CIP catalogue record for this book
is available from the British Library

ISBN 9780099553298

The Random House Group Limited supports The Forest Stewardship Council (FSC®), the
leading international forest certification organisation. Our books carrying the FSC label are
printed on FSC® certified paper. FSC is the only forest certification scheme endorsed by
the leading environmental organisations, including Greenpeace. Our paper procurement
policy can be found at www.randomhouse.co.uk/environment

Typeset in Bembo by Palimpsest Book Production Limited,
Falkirk, Stirlingshire

Printed and bound by CPI Group (UK) Ltd, Croydon CR0 4YY

For Jan Johnson
and her family

CONTENTS

Author's Note

It was Jim Johnson who first suggested that I should write this book. He and I talked over the possibility some time during the 1990s, but he decided that it was still too soon to tell the story of the unattributable campaign waged by his private army in the Yemen from 1963 to 1967. Then in 2006 he made contact again, and I went to see him at his cottage in Wiltshire, where I met Tony Boyle, who had worked as his second-in-command during the war. At my behest Jim and Tony began to talk about their operation, and I recorded their conversation. But after an hour or so I stopped them and said, 'This is ridiculous. I've never been to the Yemen, and I know hardly any of the people who were involved. Tony was there throughout and is familiar with every aspect of the story. Far better that *he* should write the book.'

So it was agreed, and he began work. He already had in his possession files containing reports, cables, radio messages and correspondence generated during the war, and over the next two years he went to great lengths to amass further material, seeking out the diaries, tapes and logbooks of survivors, and collecting relevant published books. He drafted some parts of the story, concentrating on Aden (where he himself had worked at the outset) and on the Emirates of the South Arabian Federation. In his mind were all the details of the ultra-secret Israeli parachute-drops of weapons and ammunition, which he himself (a former fast-jet pilot) had organised.

Then, alas, in May 2008 Tony died suddenly of a heart-attack at the age of only seventy-three, and in due course I was asked to take the book over. Jim outlived him by less than two months, dying on 20 July 2008 after a long illness, aged eighty-three.

It should be emphasised that the campaign in the Yemen was *not* an official SAS operation. On the contrary: it was entirely unofficial, it had no name and it was denied by the British Government. Although most of the men who took part had been in 21 SAS (the territorial regiment) or 22 SAS (in which personnel serve full-time) all were either on leave or had been granted leave of absence from the regiment for the duration of their tours. The regiment did not organise the campaign, and Her Majesty's Government (hereafter known as 'HMG') did not pay for it.

In most of the narrative I have used Christian names, for the mercenary force was so small that this was how its members knew each other. I am enormously indebted to Tony Boyle for his painstaking research, and to the executors of his estate for entrusting me with the papers that he assembled. These led me to numerous survivors of the operation, among them Fiona Allen (formerly Fraser), David Bailey, Mick Facer, Philip Horniblow, Alastair Macmillan, Jack Miller, Bernard Mills, Frank Smith and Kerry Stone, all of whom I should like to thank for their cooperation. I am most grateful to Nahum Admoni, Brian Cluer, Sultan Ghalib al-Qu'aiti, John Harding, David Harrington, James Nash, Arieh Oz and Stephen Walton

(Archivist at the Imperial War Museum, Duxford), for help of various kinds; and to the following for permission to publish extracts from family books and papers: Ben Cooper, Alexander Kennedy, Jack Miller, Christl Pearson, Xan Smiley and Michael Woodhouse. I owe particular thanks to Jim's widow, Jan, and to his children, Rupert and Lottie, for entrusting me with their family memories.

Sources

Much of the material in this narrative is taken from the archive of reports, letters, diaries, logbooks and other documents amassed by Jim Johnson and Tony Boyle during the covert operation in the Yemen. The papers are still in private hands; and because they had not been numbered or indexed at the time of writing, it was not possible to give individual references for passages quoted.

Other primary sources

The National Archives (formerly the Public Record Office) at Kew. Records available under the 30-year rule include documents with the following prefixes:

CAB	Cabinet Office
CO	Colonial Office
DEFE	Ministry of Defence
FO	Foreign Office
MINT	Mint
PREM	Prime Minister's Office
WO	War Office

Imperial War Museum, Duxford

Papers of Lieutenant Colonel Neil (Billy) McLean. Many of these are duplicated in the Johnson/Boyle private archive.

Dramatis Personae

With approximate ages (if known) in 1963

The Saudis
generally in Riyadh (the capital) or Jeddah

HRH King Saud bin Abdul Aziz 61 Deposed, November 1964.

Prince (later King) Feisal bin Abdul Aziz al-Saud 59
Code name *Burns*
The King's half-brother, the Crown Prince and Prime Minister. Became King, November 1964.

Prince Sultan bin Abdul Aziz 35 *Tourist, Seymour* Minister of Defence.

Kemal Adham 34 Cambridge-educated Head of Security, brother-in-law of Feisal.

Prince Mohamed Sudairi Governor of Jizan. The Sudairis were one of the most powerful Saudi families.

The Yemeni Royalists

Imam Mohamed al–Badr 36 *Baby, Duncan, Dickens, Infant* Head of the ruling Hamid ud Din family. Deposed in a coup orchestrated by Nasser, September 1962 Escaped into the mountains of the north-west. Spent first years of the war in caves at El Qara. Did no fighting, exercised little control.

Yahya al-Hirsi The Imam's father-in-law, secretary and boozing companion. Short and thickset. Sandhurst-trained, he had defected from the State Forces of 'Lahej, in the Aden Protectorate. As a commoner, he was despised by other members of the royal family.

Prince Hassan bin Yahya 56 Uncle of the Imam. Declared King after the coup, but formally relinquished the throne and was made Crown Prince and Prime Minister, operating from a cave.

Prince Mohamed bin Hussein 28 *AA* Nephew of the old Imam. Quiet-spoken, gentle, with a youthful look. Good English. Educated in Cairo, then Yemeni Ambassador in Germany. Commander of the First National Army, in the Jauf, the eastern sector. The best and most inspiring of the Yemeni leaders. Showed great courage at the battle of Wadi Humeidat, April 1965. Highly ambitious. Hoped to become the next Imam.

Prince Abdullah bin Hassan 26 *Gardener, Abbey* Educated at the American University in Beirut. Effective

Commander of the Second National Army, in the Khowlan, the central mountains. Assassinated, July 1969.

Ahmed al-Siyaghi A commander, and an adroit politician. Deputy Prime Minister. Killed late in 1963.

Gassim Monassir Aggressive and effective military leader. Not a member of the royal family.

Nagi al-Ghadr *Nail, Pipsqueak* Another effective commander in the Khowlan. Paramount sheikh of the Bakil tribes. Suspected of having been bribed by the Egyptians.

Sayid Ahmed al-Shami 39 *Sammy* Yemeni Foreign Minister. Strong supporter of the mercenaries. Mainly in London, but often in Saudi Arabia.

BEIHAN

Sherif Hussein *Whiskers* The ruler. Well disposed towards the British.

The Egyptians and Yemeni Republicans

Gamal Abdel Nasser 45 *Christie* President of Egypt. Organiser of Yemen revolution. Backed by Soviet Union and (at first) the United States.

Colonel Abdullah al-Sallal 46 Commander of the Royal Guard in Sana'a, but leader of the 1962 revolution. Became Nasser's puppet in Sana'a.

The British

Lieutenant Colonel Jim Johnson 39 *Jay* Underwriter at Lloyd's. Former Commanding Officer of 21 (Territorial) SAS. Leader of the British Field Liaison Force. Mainly based in London, but many trips to Jeddah, Aden, Tel Aviv, Teheran, Paris, etc.

Flight Lieutenant Tony Boyle 28 *Tea or T* Former RAF fast-jet pilot. ADC to the Governor of Aden, then second-in-command to Jim Johnson in London. Numerous trips to Tel Aviv, Jeddah, Aden, the Yemen. Organiser of the Israeli air-drops.

Lieutenant Colonel Johnny Cooper 41 *Abdullah bin Nasser* The first of the mercenaries into the Yemen, and the most active throughout the war.

Colonel David Smiley 47 *Grin* Retired professional soldier. Made independent reconnaissance trips to the Yemen. Became Field Commander of the mercenary force in April 1965.

Major Bernard Mills 31 *Bee, Baptist, Sayf* Professional soldier. First tour as a mercenary in the Khowlan, second in the Jauf. Planned the key battle of Wadi Humeidat, April 1965.

Jack Miller 20s Worked with Prince Abdullah bin Hassan and the Imam. Kept extensive diary.

Rupert France 40s *Franco* The mercenaries' radio anchor man, first in Aden, then in Nuqub (in Beihan), then in Jeddah.

Liam McSweeney 40s *Mac* Former wrestler. Became radio anchor man in Aden.

Cyril Weavers 35 Radio operator and technician.

Chris Sharma 20s *Mansoor* Spent much time advising the Imam.

David Bailey 24 *Damson or Dandy* Three six-month tours. Regarded the whole thing as a great adventure.

David Walter 20s *Daoud bin Qasim* In the Jauf, then with the Imam.

Jimmy Knox 20s Former miner. Radio operator, worked with Bernard Mills.

Alastair Macmillan 35 *Mimic* Three tours: one at El Qara, with the Imam, two in the Khowlan.

Frank Smith 20s *Squire, then Spearmint* Tours in Wadi Heera-a'an.

Kerry Stone 26 *Kudu* Tours at Sirwah, Wadi Heera'an and Beit Obeidi.

Mick Facer 35 *Fathom* Mechanic, based at Najran in Saudi Arabia, but travelled through Yemen repairing vehicles. Known to the French as Fat Hom.

Duncan Pearson 27 *Gassim* Tour at Gara, in the Khowlan.

Advisers

Lieutenant Colonel Neil (Billy) Mclean 44 *Berber*
Conservative MP, well-known politician. Travelled indefatigably in the Yemen and to Saudi Arabia and Jordan, in
support of the Royalists.

Colonel John Woodhouse 41 Outstanding commander of
22 SAS. One of the founders of the mercenary force.
Immediately after his retirement in 1965, made a tour of
the Yemen.

Colonel David Stirling 47 Wartime founder of the SAS.
Prime mover in the initial despatch of mercenaries to the
Yemen in 1963.

1

Clubmen Unite

In the spring of 1963 Colonel Jim Johnson was working in London as an underwriter at Lloyd's. A tall, dark, good-looking man, always immaculately dressed, with a silk handkerchief protruding from the breast pocket of his suit, he lived in Chelsea with his wife Judy (a former Wren), their two children and two budgerigars, and as he strode off in the morning towards the King's Road carrying a briefcase, he looked every inch the city executive and club man. That summer he was awarded the OBE, for 'classified reasons', and later became an ADC to the Queen. Yet his smooth, conventional appearance concealed exceptional determination and a liking for adventure, which, at the age of thirty-nine, had by no means burnt out.

As a boy he had spent time in Ceylon, where his father Paul and his Australian mother Dorothy were tea-planters; but he either did not know, or else concealed, details of his father's career. In the 1930s, when he was eight or so, the family went to live for a couple of years in Florence,[1] and Paul seems to have worked in some branch of intelligence. Jim's most burning memory from the time in Italy was of the occasion on which he found the maid swinging a cat against the wall. Incensed, he picked up a tapestry-covered brick and slugged her with it. The girl fell to the floor and lay still – whereupon he raced upstairs to his mother and blurted out, 'I've killed her!' Three local policemen quickly appeared wearing magnificent tricorn hats, which impressed Jim enormously – and later in life he claimed that he was arrested for attempted murder. Whether or not this was an invention, he was forced to visit the maid in hospital and present her with a lace handkerchief in atonement.

Sometime in the late 1930s the family returned to England, and for a while they lived in London. Then, on 2 September 1939, they suddenly moved to Letchworth Garden City (in Jim's memory 'a ghastly place'), where IBM was making primitive forms of computer equipment. Because this was relatively close to the top-secret, code-breaking establishment at Bletchley Park, Jim surmised that during the war his father was employed there on the Enigma project, although never a word was said about it.

His school career – at St Edmund's, Hindhead, and then Westminster – was undistinguished. He had no interest in sport, and never shone on the playing field; nor did he manage to win a place at university, although he would have liked to do so. Then, as a junior officer in the 2nd (Armoured) Battalion of the Welsh Guards during the Second World War, he had a disappointing time, in that, much as he wanted to fight, he never had a chance to become involved. In the spring of 1944, during the run-up to D-Day, he fell off a tank while training on Salisbury Plain and broke a leg. During the preparations for the Rhine crossing he went down with jaundice and had to spend months in hospital.

In 1945, with the war in Europe over, he volunteered for a Guards' Division that was being formed to join the campaign against the Japanese. The new unit, dressed in American kit, began training at Warminster, and was due to go on for further training in Florida; but in August the atom bombs on Hiroshima and Nagasaki put an end to the scheme. In 1947, feeling he had not got enough money to become a regular officer, Jim resigned his commission and went into Lloyd's.

He soon started to do well in the City, but missed the army – so he went to see Lieutenant Colonel Brian Franks, a wartime commander of the SAS, who was starting up the territorial regiment, 21 SAS, and applied to join. Franks said he was besieged by experienced Special Forces officers and didn't need any more: only if Johnson was prepared to come in as an other-rank, on a year's probation, would he be accepted. Jim therefore joined as a trooper, did a parachute course, went on to command a squadron, and from January 1960 to December 1962 commanded the regiment as a Territorial Army officer. Then he retired and returned to Lloyd's full-time.

Men who served with him or under him conceived the highest admiration for his qualities as a leader. One young officer described Jim as being 'of no mean originality and wit'; all praised his unfailingly even temper, his sense of humour and, above all, his easy authority. Naturally ebullient, he had a wonderful talent for cheering people up. But he also had a tough streak: a colleague once overheard Judy tell a potential recruit, not entirely in jest, 'Don't join 21 SAS. The Colonel's a bastard. Take the soft option – join the Marine Commandos.' Another former colleague remembered that 'he could make blistering remarks' if someone had transgressed; but he had an exceptional ability to delegate and to trust his subordinates – and then, if they made mistakes, to back them up and shoulder responsibility. He also had a very clear vision of how things ought to be done, and hence the ability to take decisions quickly.

One of his recruits for the Yemen operation found Jim's passion for taking on seemingly impossible tasks infectious. In the middle of the campaign, when the man asked, 'Why, against international laws and Queen's Regulations, are we involved?', Jim replied, 'It's not in spite of the rules. It's *because of* the bloody rules. When it's over, we'll write a new page for Regimental SOPs [Standard Operating Procedures].'[2] Many of the mercenaries felt that they were members of *Beni* Johnson – Family Johnson; a few, when they wrote, addressed him as 'Colonel', but to most he was simply Jim; and so few people were involved that Christian names, or cover names, were used throughout. Just as the men conceived a fierce loyalty to their commander, so he returned their commitment, always doing his best to make sure they were well looked after and not let down.

Throughout the campaign Judy gave him unstinting support. Not only was she intelligent and well read, but being herself a colonel's daughter, she understood the pressure under which Jim was working, and moreover she was always forthright, telling him not what she imagined he wanted to hear, but what she herself thought. In the words of their daughter Lottie, 'They really were soulmates.'[3] Judy might pretend that she did not dare go down to the basement of their house in Sloane Avenue, for fear of what she might find there, but in fact she knew exactly what was going on. Strange men were constantly coming and going at all hours of the day and night – once a mercenary who was suffering from malaria borrowed her fur coat to contain his shuddering. Another time a man arrived at the front door and announced that he had brought some equipment: taking him for a mercenary, Judy directed him to the basement, where he was disconcerted to find several men servicing sub-machine guns. His alarm was not surprising, for he was a Hoover salesman.

For more than eight centuries the Mutawakkilite Kingdom of the Yemen, stretching from the eastern shore of the Red Sea to the borders of Saudi Arabia, had been ruled by a succession of Imams, or priest-kings, belonging to the Hamid ud Din family; but in September 1962 a *coup d'état* had driven the last of them, Imam Mohamed al-Badr, from his palace in the capital, and he had taken refuge in the mountains. The revolution had been precipitated by the intrigues of Gamal Abdel Nasser, President of Egypt, who was being strongly backed by the Soviet Union in his attempt to gain control of the Arabian peninsula.

Nasser, at that stage, was eager to throw his weight behind revolution wherever it happened, in his attempt to unify a socialist Arab world against the forces of reaction. Principal among these, in his eyes, was Britain. Relations between Britain and Egypt had never recovered since the Suez conflict of 1956, which left Nasser virulently opposed to British influence in South Arabia.[4] Now his aim was to take over the Yemen, and then the port and city of Aden, one of the last bastions of imperialism in the Arab world.

A British Crown colony since 1838, Aden in 1962 had a rapidly growing population of 220,000, a large proportion of which comprised immigrant labour. The third-busiest port in the world, blessed with the best natural harbour in southern Arabia, it was an important deep-water bunkering station for ships on their way to and from India, the Far East and Australasia, and was handling more than 5,000 vessels a year. It was also an important strategic military and naval base,

housing a busy RAF airfield at Khormaksar and the headquarters of British Middle East Command, with defence
responsibilities from Kuwait to East Africa, and was a vital
link in the military chain to Singapore and Hong Kong.
Nasser naturally wanted to secure this rich prize; yet his
further ambitions were even more alarming: to infiltrate Saudi
Arabia from its western and southern underbelly, seize the
oilfields, gain control of the entire Persian Gulf and finally
annihilate Israel. 'The road to Tel Aviv,' he was fond of
pronouncing, 'lies via the Gulf and Riyadh.'[5]

Immediately after the Yemeni revolution of 1962, pressure
not to recognise the new regime was put on the British
Government from several quarters. Two days after the coup,
the uncle of the deposed Imam, fifty-six year-old Prince
Hassan bin Yahya, who had been in America serving as the
Yemeni delegate to the United Nations, arrived in London
and called on the Foreign Secretary, Lord Home,[6] in search
of help. With his piercing black eyes, fine white beard and
pale-blue, ankle-length robe, he cut a striking figure: one
observer described him as 'wrinkled and gnarled as an old
olive tree'.[7] But he got no satisfaction. Another early visitor
to London was King Hussein, the young ruler of Jordan, who
met the Minister for Aviation, Julian Amery,[8] and through
him urged the British not to recognise the Republican regime.

HMG dithered. On 23 October 1962 the Foreign Secretary reported to the Cabinet that 'the general situation was
disturbing', and the Cabinet approved recognition of the
Republican regime 'in principle'.[9] Then in November HMG
was alarmed by reports that the regime intended to declare
war on Saudi Arabia, and that recognition of it 'might undermine our whole position in the area'.[10] At the same time the
Government was trying to dissuade the Americans from

recognising the Republicans; but the United States Administration, under President Kennedy, was apparently unable to appreciate the depth of Nasser's mendacity or the risks that he posed. Distracted as it was by the war in Vietnam, the White House failed to realise that he was cleverly playing East against West: the Americans naively hoped that if the West supported his policies, Nasser might be prised away from the Soviet Bloc (which was supplying him with weapons and technology) and become a bulwark against the spread of communism. The Americans therefore did recognise the revolutionary regime – and they also greatly increased the shipments of surplus wheat which they had been sending Egypt since 1954.

With the London Government apparently in a state of paralysis on the issue, Jim Johnson quickly spotted the potential for some kind of covert intervention. One night in November 1962 he and Judy went to dinner with their friends Philip Horniblow and his wife Binnie. Horniblow – a doctor and former army officer – had been Chief Medical Officer to the Kuwait Army during the 1950s, and had later joined 21 SAS as a trooper. He thus had useful military experience and good knowledge of the Middle East; he also spoke some Arabic.[11] During the evening Jim mentioned that he had been approached by 'influential people', inside and outside the Conservative Government, with the idea of starting a clandestine operation, and suggested to his host that, if anything developed, he might take part.

One of the 'influential people' to whom Jim referred was Amery – a man of wide military and political experience, who had served in Albania, Egypt, Africa and China during the Second World War, was a passionate enthusiast for Empire and was said, because of his aristocratic background, to have been born with a silver grenade in his mouth. He was also a key member of the Suez Group, the backbench coterie formed when Nasser was shaping to take control of the Canal in the 1950s, and was dedicated to the maintenance of British power in the Middle East. Another was Duncan Sandys,[12] who in 1963 was Secretary of State for the Colonies.

Yet by far the most articulate advocate of intervention in the Yemen was Lieutenant Colonel Neil McLean, DSO (always known as 'Billy'), the Conservative Member of Parliament for Inverness and friend of many leading politicians.[13] A big, tough Scottish Highlander, who slicked his hair back with pomade, he too had seen much irregular action during the Second World War, commanding a guerrilla unit in Abyssinia and organising partisan resistance in Albania. In the eyes of some friends he had a touch of Buchan's Sandy Arbuthnot about him, for he frequented London clubs, had a habit of going off without warning to distant parts of the globe and tended to reappear with his face deeply tanned.[14]

Now, at the age of forty-three, he was a well-known figure in British politics, had numerous friends in Whitehall and contacts at the highest level in the Middle East, and was exceptionally persuasive in diplomatic negotiation. One contemporary described him as 'a master of deception, a consummate practitioner of Balkan politics'.[15] With the Yemen in turmoil – but no one in London sure exactly what was happening there – he set off to find out, on the first of many reconnaissance visits, in October 1962.

By then the situation in the Yemen was becoming extremely dangerous and unpleasant. Nasser was pouring troops, tanks and artillery into the country, and pilots of the Egyptian Air Force, flying Russian MiG 17 fighters and Ilyushin Il-28 jet bombers (known as Beagles), were indiscriminately bombing and strafing the mountain villages around which the tribes loyal to the Imam were holding out.[16] The Royalists were not only disorganised, and desperately short of weapons and ammunition: they had no form of communication beyond human runners, and lacked medical facilities of any kind – the standard remedy for injuries and illnesses, even a persistent headache, being branding on the stomach, chest, legs or arms with a red-hot iron, a treatment known as *woosam*, which was thought to let the evil out.

Pressure was growing not only on the Yemeni Royalists, but also on the independent states along the country's southern border, which Britain, in 1959, had begun to combine into the South Arabian Federation. MiG fighter-bombers flying from Sana'a, the Yemeni capital, had started to launch raids on Beihan, the Sultanate some 200 miles north-east of Aden. Trouble was brewing also in the Radfan – the mountainous region due north of Aden, and much closer than Beihan. Tribesmen were crossing into the Yemen, joining the Republican forces for a few months and being given rifles and ammunition, which they then brought home. This meant that dissidents in the Radfan were becoming steadily better armed – and at the same time leaders trained by the Egyptians were infiltrating the country from the Yemen, to organise subversion more effectively – developments that threatened the British aim of keeping the Federation a coherent and secure entity.

The British were uncomfortably divided in their views about how to tackle the problem. The newly declared Yemen Arab Republic (YAR) had broken off diplomatic relations with HMG. The Foreign Office, heavily influenced by America, wished to recognise the Republican regime. On the other hand, the Colonial Office, alarmed by the number of insurgents filtering into Aden from the Yemen, vigorously opposed Foreign Office policy for the region, and was supported in its views by the Prime Minister (Harold Macmillan), the Colonial Secretary (Duncan Sandys), the Aviation Minister (Julian Amery) and even the Foreign Secretary, Lord Home (in direct opposition to the Foreign Office, of which he was the head).

What could be done to bolster the Imam? MI6, the Secret Intelligence Service, would have liked to mount some under-cover campaign, but after the Second World War the organisation had been stripped of its special operations capability and was powerless to start anything of that kind. Macmillan's attitude was defeatist: he told one visiting diplomat that he was 'reminded of the Bonny Prince Charlie conflict in the Scotland of 1745; the Highlanders were more attractive, but one knew that the Lowlanders would win in the end'.[17]

It so happened that the Conservative Government was falling into a state of disarray and indecision, shaken by two major political scandals. The first had been provoked by John Profumo, the Secretary of State for War, who had had an association with Christine Keeler, a London showgirl whom he met at Cliveden, the Astor family's grand house above the Thames in Buckinghamshire. Fuel was added to the flames of gossip by the fact that Keeler had also been involved with Yevgeny Ivanov, a naval attaché at the Soviet Embassy in London. In March 1963, after months of rumours, Profumo told the House of Commons that there had been 'no impropriety whatever' in his relationship with Keeler, threatening to sue anyone who repeated allegations outside the House; but the press and television remained agog.

The second scandal threatened another prominent member of the Government: Duncan Sandys. When the 11th Duke

of Argyll sued his wife Margaret for divorce on the grounds
of rampant infidelity, claiming that she had slept with eighty-
two men, he produced, as part of his evidence, Polaroid photographs of her, naked except for a three-strand pearl necklace,
fellating a man whose head had been cut out of the picture.
The identity of the 'headless man' had not been certainly
established, but persistent rumour claimed that it was Sandys.

With the Government's resolve weakened by these tremors,
it became clear to McLean and other advocates of action
that Britain would not back the Yemeni Royalists with any
official or overt support; but moves to provide them with
clandestine assistance were afoot. Mossad, the Israeli intelligence service, had approached George Young, former deputy
head of MI6, asking him to find someone who would run
an unattributable guerrilla war against the Republicans, and
Young had introduced McLean to Brigadier Dan Hiram, a
former artillery officer and now the Israeli defence attaché,
who agreed to supply weapons and money (Israel's aim being
to detain Nasser's troops in the Yemen for as long as possible).

In London, Jim Johnson had many friends in high places,
military, political and social. Among them was Colonel David
Stirling, at 6 feet 4 inches a legendary and literally towering
figure in the SAS, which he himself had founded in 1942
during the war in the Western Desert.[18] He had a discon-
certing habit of talking out of one corner of his mouth, so
that listeners often failed to catch what he had said; but he
was also immensely determined, and if he thought that something ought to be done, he made sure that it was. Now forty-
seven, he was, as always, full of ideas, and looking for people
to translate them into action.

When he saw that no official move would be made to
help the Yemeni Royalists, he arranged (with the connivance

of Home and Amery) for Billy McLean to meet Brian Franks
(then Colonel Commandant of the SAS) at White's Club in
St James's Street – and it was Franks who suggested that Jim
Johnson might be the person to organise some deniable under-
cover operation.

As Jim himself recalled, he and Judy were sitting in their
drawing room at about nine o'clock one evening when the
telephone rang. It was Franks, calling from White's. He said,
'May I come round and have a glass of brandy?' – and Jim
replied, 'Of course.' Round he came, and as he sat down he
said that he had just come from a meeting with Alec Home,
Julian Amery, David Stirling and Billy McLean at White's.
'Don't believe the Americans about the Yemen,' said Franks.
'They don't understand the Middle East. The resistance under
the Imam is terrific.'

He explained briefly how the Royalists had taken to the
mountains, but were being bombed and strafed by Russian
aircraft based on the air-strip at Sana'a. 'Would you like to
go in and burn all these aeroplanes?' he suggested.

'Well, yes,' Jim replied nonchalantly. 'I've nothing particular to do in the next few days. I might have a go.'[19]

He never proposed to carry out the assignment himself –
but he quickly got down to work. Through Amery he met
Sayid Ahmed al-Shami, Foreign Minister of the Yemen and
the most politically astute of the Royalist leaders, who was
in London seeking help.[20] Money seemed to be the least of
the problems. Shami, who spoke English reasonably well, but
could not write it, produced a cheque book and told Jim to
make out a cheque for £5,000 (worth £150,000 in today's
values). Shami then signed the cheque, and they took it to
the Hyde Park Hotel (where Franks was Chairman of the
Board) and asked Salvatore, the Manager, to cash it for them.

He was astonished. 'What do you need all this money for?' he demanded.

'My daughter's getting married,' Jim told him (his daughter Lottie was then eight).

'But you can't possibly spend that amount on a wedding.'

'Never mind!'

Salvatore agreed to cash the cheque and keep the money in the hotel safe, handing it out as it was needed.

In search of saboteurs who would blow up the aircraft at Sana'a, Jim was naturally inclined to look for recruits among former members of the SAS. The first man he approached – in characteristic fashion, by inviting him to have a drink at the Cadogan Hotel – was Major Bernard Mills, a professional soldier home on inter-tour leave from Oman, where he was commanding the first Arab company in the Muscat Regiment. Not only had Mills known Jim in the SAS: he also spoke Arabic – an essential requirement for the job being proposed.

Much as he liked the sound of the Yemen operation, Mills declined to take it on, for the time being, at any rate: he was still in the process of forming the Arab company, and felt he must return to Oman to finish the job. But he suggested a man who would be ideal for the task: Lieutenant Colonel Johnny Cooper, a seasoned campaigner then in his early forties, tall and thin, almost as dark and wiry as an Arab, with a shock of black hair, described by the explorer Ranulph Fiennes as 'a sinewy major with sun-blackened skin and the features of a Greek bandit'.[21] As a corporal during the Second World War, Johnny had been Stirling's driver, navigator and bodyguard in the desert,[22] and was expert at blowing up aircraft, having spent months engaged in that agreeable occupation.

In 1963 Johnny was serving as second-in command of the Muscat Regiment of the Sultan of Oman's armed forces and, since he spoke Arabic, was a natural candidate for the new enterprise. Out went a telegram from Stirling: 'Join me Aden soonest possible'. Johnny replied with a radio message: there was no commercial air service between Muscat and Aden, but he could catch the weekly plane to Bahrain. Another cable from Stirling: 'Meet me soonest Speedbird Hotel Bahrain'.

Realising that some secret operation was in the offing, Colonel Hugh Oldman, commander of the Sultan's armed forces, arranged for a telegram to be sent to Johnny saying that his mother was dying and that he was being granted two weeks' compassionate leave. Released by this swift manoeuvre, Johnny took the plane for Bahrain.[23]

Stirling was not entirely fit, having recently suffered a minor stroke; so to look after him during the journey to the Middle East, Jim appointed Philip Horniblow as his baggage handler and medical assistant. When the two boarded the Comet at Heathrow, Horniblow became apprehensive, because his charge's hand-luggage was bulging with weapons and Stirling was, in his view, the 'most insecure man' he had ever known – that is, he had no thought for security, but was inclined to repeat confidential information in the wrong places, and to do whatever came into his head. He demonstrated this last propensity when they arrived in Aden, by walking off the aeroplane and disappearing through the perimeter fence of the airfield without going near customs.

Horniblow, somewhat baffled, booked into a hotel and awaited further instructions. Stirling went to stay with the Governor, Sir Charles Johnston, an old friend. That night, pleading exhaustion, Johnston went to bed early and left Stirling in the care of his young ADC, Flight Lieutenant Tony Boyle (then twenty-eight), a former fast-jet pilot on secondment from the RAF.

Over a whisky-and-soda, as they sat on the terrace in the warm tropical night, watching the lights of ships easing their way in and out of the harbour, Stirling told Boyle that, with the authority of two Government ministers (Amery and Sandys) and the knowledge of the Prime Minister (Macmillan), a group of former SAS soldiers was about to be infiltrated into the Yemen. Should the operation go wrong, it would be denied by the British Government. Stirling asked Tony to see the men through Aden airport without any documentation, and to arrange their onward journey.

The conversation left the ADC in a dilemma: was his boss, the Governor, aware of this secret mission – or had Stirling deliberately not mentioned it to him, on the grounds that the less he knew about it, the easier it would be for him to deny it? Whichever way, next morning Tony decided to say nothing, but to do as he had been asked; and in due course it became obvious that Johnston knew exactly what was happening.[24] When the mercenary operation expanded, Tony kept the MI6 resident in Aden informed of developments – and as the resident's weekly meetings with the Governor passed off without provoking any explosion, the ADC knew he had made the right decision.

Next day Stirling and Horniblow went on to Bahrain, where Horniblow met Johnny Cooper, but told him only that he was to lead an operation in a Middle Eastern country 'to obtain military information of vital interest'.[25] The project had been initiated in England, but Frenchmen were also being recruited into the team as a smokescreen.

Reaching London on 3 June 1963, Johnny went straight

to meet Jim Johnson, who briefed him with his plans, such as they were. His most urgent need was to find more Arabic-speakers, and on the same evening he, Johnny and Stirling flew to Paris. At a meeting on the rue de la Fronquenelle in the home of Prince Michel Bourbon de Parme,[26] they sat round a table into the early hours of the morning with senior Government officials from both Britain and France. Also present was Colonel Roger Faulques, then thirty-nine, a former Legionnaire who had fought in Indochina, been imprisoned by the Vietminh and handed back to the French so seriously wounded that his captors thought he was about to die. Cooper was briefed to lead a reconnaissance party of two French and four British soldiers into the north Yemen, to establish the strength of the Royalist resistance.[27]

Jim quickly set about finding more men. Through Colonel John Woodhouse, then commanding 22 SAS at Hereford, he recruited Sergeant Geordie Dorman, a veteran of the campaign in Malaya and a skilled mortar expert; Corporal Chigey, an experienced medical orderly; and a firearms expert, Trooper Richardson – all of whom were, in Woodhouse's own words, 'permitted to be absent without leave'. Secrecy cloaked the proceedings from the start. Because this was a clandestine operation, the men were released from the regiment unofficially; and when Johnny went to pick them up, he collected them after dark from various places around Hereford, in a hire-car that Jim had laid on. That same evening they were joined in London by two Arabic-speaking volunteers from the Deuxième Bureau – the French intelligence service – who, because Air France flights had been grounded by a strike, were driven from Paris in an official staff car. Jim had meanwhile begun badgering friendly armourers for weapons, ammunition and explosives – including plastic explosive and Schmeisser sub-machine guns – which he stored temporarily in the basement of his London house in Sloane Avenue.

Then on 5 June (Johnny's birthday) a political bombshell exploded in Westminster. In the Commons, Profumo admitted that he had lied to the House, and resigned from the Government and from politics. His revelation not only finished his own public career: it also severely damaged the reputation of Harold Macmillan, who was judged to have handled the matter ineffectually, and it made other leading Conservative politicians exceedingly nervous.

The immediate result was a telephone call from Sandys (described by Jim as 'that shit'), telling Stirling to cancel the Yemen expedition. Stirling rang Jim and said, 'I'm sorry. We're going to have to call it off. There's heavy pressure from the Minister, who's worried about his own reputation.'

Far from standing his men down and going to bed, Jim had what he described as 'a rather restless night'. Reckoning that no one in the Colonial Office or the White House (SIS headquarters) would take action before the day-shift came on at 0900 the next morning, and without telling anybody in authority what he was doing, he telephoned one airline after another in search of seats on overnight flights to Aden. He booked the Frenchmen onto the direct Comet flight, which staged through Rome and Tripoli, and found places for three of the British on an Alitalia departure. Johnny he booked onto another flight to Tripoli, which also went via Rome. He himself drove the volunteers to the terminal (then in the Cromwell Road, west London) and saw them off.

The plan was that all members of the team would unite in Tripoli and carry on to Aden together aboard the Comet – and this they did, but not before the British contingent had had a narrow escape at Tripoli airport. As they collected their luggage to check in for the next leg, one of their bulging suitcases burst open, releasing rolls of plastic explosive done up in paper: luckily the substance had a smell like that of almonds, and as the Libyan security guards helped to repack it, Johnny explained that he was a marzipan salesman, taking samples to various Arab potentates.

In London, after breakfast, Jim rang Stirling and said, 'I'm most frightfully sorry, but I can't stop them. They've already gone.'

When the Comet landed in Aden and the other passengers disembarked, the mercenaries sat tight. Tony Boyle had arranged for a DC3 of Aden Airways to pull up alongside the stand on which the jet came to a stop. He himself was absent on duty in the Federation, but he had asked James Nash, a senior Political Officer, to meet the team. Nash prudently kept away, but deputed a local assistant, Mohamed Affara, who signalled the newcomers to dash across to the Dakota when it came alongside. In a few seconds they were on board for the forty-minute flight to Beihan.

There they changed into Arab dress – a shirt, a calf-length skirt or kilt called a *futa*, with a large, curved, two-sided dagger known as a *jambiya* carried in a sheath in the middle of a broad belt,[28] and a *mar-arraga*, or skull cap, on the head. Thus accoutred, they set off with a train of 150 camels carrying weapons and ammunition to the Royalist strongholds in the mountains. As an article in the *Daily Telegraph* later remarked, 'Nothing had happened like this since Colonel Lawrence played hide-and-seek with the Turks on the Hejaz railway [in 1916–17].'[29]

And so some nine months after Nasser's invasion, the British Field Liaison Force, or BFLF, came into being. Thus – in utterly unorthodox fashion – was launched an operation, directed for the most part by two men and a girl from a civilian office in London, which ran for four years, caused Nasser immense aggravation and had a profound effect on the Six-Day War of 1967, when Israel inflicted a humiliating defeat on Egypt after less than a week's combat.

Jim Johnson soon became so heavily involved that he had to step down temporarily from Lloyd's. As the pressure built up, he got Paul Paulson, MI6 Controller for the Middle East and Africa, to ask his chairman to grant him leave of absence. 'When do you want him?' asked the chairman. 'Tomorrow,' was the answer – and that was that. Jim cleared his desk and vanished, but on his frequent trips abroad he still masqueraded as an insurance broker, and if anyone remarked on his suntan, he simply said that he had been on holiday.

Nasser lost more than 20,000 men in the Yemen, and came to look on the campaign there as his Vietnam. At one stage he claimed that 800 mercenaries were at large in the mountains, whereas the true figure was more like forty, and of these the majority were French or Belgian, and Jim's men on the ground numbered no more than twelve at any one time. His private army was so small that its members were known and addressed by their Christian names (Johnny, Chris, Rupert) or by their cover pseudonyms (Abdullah, Mansoor, Franco).

Jim's motives were purely patriotic. His aim was not to earn a fortune, but to remove a hostile power – the Soviet-backed Egyptians – from the Yemen: like Julian Amery, he strongly believed that Britain should safeguard its interests in the Middle East and keep communist influence out. He himself never fought in the war that he ran. He travelled immense distances, flying repeatedly to Saudi Arabia and Aden (usually with a pistol in a shoulder-holster under his jacket), sometimes to Israel and Iran, and he made one foray into the Yemen itself. Yet although he never fired a shot in anger, he directed the operation with such skill, cunning, patience and tenacity that Nasser, becoming exasperated, recognised Jim as his principal adversary in London, and told a diplomat visiting Cairo that if ever the Colonel felt like coming to Egypt, he would be granted seven years' free accommodation in any one of the Government's special institutions.

2

Nasser's Wiles

The revolution in the Yemen, provoked by Egyptian intrigues, took place on 20 September 1962. Some Egyptian historians have suggested that the uprising was spontaneous, but the extraordinary 'Confession' obtained by Billy McLean from Imam al-Badr, during the course of conversations in his cave headquarters, reveals that Nasser had been manoeuvring to undermine the ancient regime for at least four years before that.[1] Had the Americans realised how treacherous he was, and how accomplished a liar, they would surely never have backed his puppet government in Sana'a.

Nasser was actively planning to disrupt the Yemen as early as 1958, when he summoned Crown Prince al-Badr, son of the ruler, to a meeting in Damascus. There Nasser and other prominent Egyptians spent twenty-four hours discussing with the Crown Prince plans for disrupting Saudi Arabia and gaining control of the Arab world. The first stage of this plan was to be a coup against al-Badr's father, Imam Ahmed, after which Nasser would use the Yemen as a base for further subversive operations in Arabia and the Persian Gulf. In Cairo, on his way home, al-Badr was intercepted by Nasser, who offered him £50,000 in sterling, 25,000 Egyptian pounds and two cases of pistols if he would overthrow his father in a *coup d'état*.

Al-Badr appeared to accept the offer, but was either unable or unwilling to carry out his side of the bargain; yet Nasser was relentless in his efforts to take over the Yemen. Later in 1958 he summoned the Crown Prince to Baghdad for further plotting, then invited him to Alexandria and had him driven to a house four hours out in the desert. When al-Badr arrived, Nasser was waiting, and they spent the whole night discussing plans for the fomentation of revolution in Saudi Arabia. In Cairo, Nasser introduced him to some Algerians, who offered him commandos and saboteurs, to be placed under his orders in the Yemen if he would implement plans for the conquest of Arabia.

Deeply involved though he was with the Russians – whose principal aim was to open up commercial opportunities in East Africa – Nasser slyly advised al-Badr to improve his relations with Britain and the Americans so that he should not be branded a Soviet agent. At the same time, he told al-Badr to invite the Russian Navy to visit the Yemen. The old Imam Ahmed, meanwhile, had become suspicious about the number of Chinese workers who had been admitted to the country and forbade his son to have any more dealings with communist countries.

All the while Nasser was inciting the people of the Yemen and other Arab countries to rise against their rulers and band together in a United Arab Republic (UAR). Exploiting the millions of small, battery-operated transistor radios that had flooded the Arab world, he broadcast interminable speeches over Cairo radio (*Sawt al Arab* – Voice of the Arabs), exhorting the citizens to unite and regain their lost pride and glory. From every shop, house and taxi in Arabia, from every camel-driver in the Yemen, his ceaseless, ranting propaganda urged the people to rebel. To the tribesmen he was a great popular hero; but he was a nightmare figure to their leaders, for they knew that if he managed to sweep the Yemen into the UAR, they would lose their power and position.

With the old Imam absent in Rome for medical treatment, Nasser again ordered al-Badr to engineer a revolution against his father, and arranged for large, unmarked crates of Chinese weapons to be sent into the Yemen. He told al-Badr that the boxes (alleged to contain material for the construction of the road between Sana'a and the Red Sea port of Hodeidah, on which the Chinese were working) should be allowed through customs without examination, but that, if their contents were discovered, it should be put about that the weapons were for use against the British in Aden.

When the boxes arrived in the spring of 1962 and were taken from Hodeidah to Sana'a in ten lorries, the Egyptians spread rumours that a revolution was impending, and Nasser sent al-Badr a telegram telling him to kill his father. Defying the great bully once again, the Crown Prince confessed all the intrigues to his father, who forgave him, but ordered him to give a full account of Nasser's chicanery to King Saud of Saudi Arabia and King Hussein of Jordan. This convinced the Saudis that, if Nasser managed to take over the Yemen, they would be next in line.

Nasser's most active pawns in the Yemen were two army officers, the first of whom was the short, swarthy and blue-jowled Colonel Abdullah al-Sallal, who had spent seven years in gaol, much of the time chained to the wall, accused of plotting against the old Imam. Once he had been an urban charcoal-seller, but now he was the recently appointed Commander of the Royal Guard. The second conspirator was a young lieutenant, Ali Abdul al-Moghny. Each had been preparing separate plots, but in the event both merged into one.

On 18 September 1962 Imam Ahmed died, having survived twelve attempts on his life. A grotesque figure, as a boy he had deliberately made his eyeballs bulge by tightening a cord around his neck in order to render his appearance more formidable. On Fridays he had personally supervised the public decapitation of enemies in the main square of Sana'a; he kept 100 slaves in his three palaces, was reputed to have eaten a whole sheep at a sitting, and through his gluttony had, by the end, increased his weight to some 350 pounds.

Many citizens were surprised to hear that he had died in his bed – but on the day after his death, at a great ceremony in Sana'a, his son was elected the sixty-sixth Imam of the Yemen. On that same day Nasser sent al-Badr an ultimatum ordering him to declare immediate union with Egypt, and to make a speech attacking the British in Aden. Al-Badr refused, saying that he wanted to remain neutral, like Switzerland.

In neither Eastern nor Western eyes did the new Imam cut a distinguished figure. From the British point of view, it was unfortunate that when he visited England in 1957 he had been received so coolly that he turned for support to other patrons, principally Egypt, Russia and China.

A big, heavy man, taller (at six feet) than most of his subjects, he was now in his late thirties; travels in Europe and America had given him a taste for drink and drugs, and he had undergone cures for alcohol and morphine addiction. On his accession, however, he began to show some spirit: in a speech from the throne he announced an amnesty for political prisoners and exiles, promised economic development and outlined the creation of a forty-strong advisory council.

His initiatives proved futile, for Nasser's agents were poised to strike, and an army of occupation was already on the move. The day after the new Imam's accession – and four days before the coup – four Egyptian ships, the *Nile*, the *al-Wadi*, the *Cleopatra* and the *Sudan*, sailed from Egypt and headed down the Gulf of Suez towards the Red Sea. The 3,000 soldiers on board had been told they were going to Algeria, but in fact they were bound for Yemen's main port, Hodeidah.[2]

On the evening of 26 September, after a Cabinet meeting, the new Imam was walking along a corridor towards his private apartments on the third floor of the Dar el Basha'ir Palace – 'the House of Good Omen' – in Sana'a when he heard a click behind him. Turning, he saw Hussein al-Sukairi, the Guard Commander, holding a sub-machine gun. Either the weapon had misfired or his assailant had deliberately given him a warning. With a yell, he dived through the door into his private rooms.

Outside, the rebels had surrounded the palace with tanks. Now, through loudspeakers, they broadcast a demand that the royal bodyguard surrender the ruler. At midnight all the lights went out and the telephone wires were cut. The bodyguard opened fire, as did the Imam himself, with a machine gun through a window – whereupon the attackers responded with the tanks' main armament and blew the top floor of the palace to pieces; but because the tanks could not depress their guns sufficiently, the lower storeys remained relatively intact. The Imam's men then doused some sacks of sand with petrol, crept out into the garden, put the sacks on the tanks and set them on fire. Within seconds the crews were flushed into the open, and the Imam, his father-in-law, Yahya al-Hirsi, and their retainers gunned them down with rifles and sub-machine guns.

The rebels announced that the Imam had been killed, but in fact he managed to slip out of the palace and lie low for most of the next day in a nearby house, where he changed into borrowed army uniform; then, at nightfall, he made away on foot, and after a gruelling journey through his kingdom towards the north-west, gathering tribesmen as he went, and with many skirmishes fought on the way, reached Jizan, the Saudi town on the coast of the Red Sea, just outside the Yemen border, which had electric light, internal telephones, a telegraph link to Jeddah and an air-strip on the sea shore. There he gave a press conference at which he forecast, with some accuracy, that his country would become 'the grave-yard of the Egyptian army'.

On the run again, the Imam crossed back into the Yemen and took refuge in the high, harsh mountains of the north. His enemies later claimed that he had evaded capture in Sana'a by enveloping himself in a woman's burqa, but this may have been an invention designed to discredit him. Many of his relations and former government ministers were less fortunate: almost fifty people were shot or knifed to death in the square at Sana'a, and their bodies dragged through the streets or hung in chains from buildings, before being left for the stray dogs that infested the city. It is thought that alto-gether more than 500 tribal and national leaders were slaugh-tered in the aftermath of the coup.

When it became clear that the Imam was alive, his uncle, Prince Hassan bin Yahya, who had been declared King, formally relinquished the throne and was made Crown Prince and Prime Minister. Armed with a radio telephone, money and weapons supplied by the Saudi Army, he set up a makeshift headquarters in a mountain cave near Sa'ada, the most northerly town in the Yemen.

Landing in their thousands at Hodeidah, the Egyptian soldiers quickly took control of the flat coastal plain, 40 miles wide, known as the Tihamah (literally 'hot lands'). They then had to wind their way through the 90-odd miles of the Western Highlands, along the country's one metalled road (atrociously built by the Chinese), which twisted for much of the way though narrow wadis (valleys or canyons), offering ideal points for ambushes or the creation of avalanches. To the east of those first mountain ranges the invaders occupied Sana'a, an ancient city of tower-houses, lying in an oblong plateau more than 6,000 feet above sea-level. From there the troops spread out, establishing separate garrisons a short distance to the north, and further to the south; but they scarcely ventured into the country's tremendous central massif, where the jagged peaks and ridges rose to 12,000 feet – and it was from these mountains that the Royalists mounted their most effective resistance.

In Aden, on the morning after the attack, four smartly dressed Arabs appeared in Tony Boyle's office, announcing themselves as members of the Yemeni royal family. Their leader, wearing a black suit and tie, introduced himself in good English as Prince Abdurrahman bin Yahya, the Deputy Prime Minister of the Yemen. The group, six strong in all, had been on their way to Sana'a, but, finding there were only three seats on the first plane that morning, had decided to wait for the next flight and repaired to the Crescent Hotel. There they had heard of the coup over the radio, and swiftly changed their plans. Had they caught the plane and landed in the capital, they would almost certainly have been shot out of hand. As it was, they spent the morning in Government House, telephoning the heir to the throne in New York and planning to launch a counter-attack on the rebels from Saudi Arabia.

The Yemen Airlines aircraft that would have taken the royal party to their doom in Sana'a had never left Aden. Boyle tried again and again to persuade the pilot to fly the royal party to Jeddah; but the man was so frightened about what might happen to his family that he refused. The royals then cabled King Saud in Riyadh, asking him to send a private aircraft to collect them; back came the answer that no plane was available, and that they must wait for the next scheduled flight in two days' time. The Yemenis also asked for support from London, in the form of arms and ammunition, but after consultation between Charles Johnston and the Foreign Office their request was rejected – in Boyle's view, a disastrous mistake by HMG. It seemed to him that if the British had acted swiftly, at that critical moment, they could have snuffed out the rebellion in short order. But Whitehall's policy was a passive one of non-intervention: when the Royalists captured four Russians and handed them over, far from calling a press conference and exhibiting the prisoners, as they might have done to advantage, the British put an embargo on their appearance in Aden and sent them back to Moscow.

Writing home prophetically, Boyle told his parents how Aden had suddenly changed from the 'happy-go-lucky' place they had seen when visiting earlier in the year:

At first sight it is the same, but under the surface nationalism, intrigue and intimidation are boiling up into a situation which could well become explosive – and disastrous to our interests in this part of the world.

Tony Boyle was no run-of-the mill airman. Not only had

his father, Sir Dermot Boyle, been Marshal of the Royal Air
Force, but he himself had won the sword of honour at Cran-
well, and had flown Hunter jets in Britain and delta-winged
Javelin all-weather fighter-bombers in Britain and Germany.
A thoughtful and efficient man, he also had a keen sense of
humour and was naturally gregarious. One of his attractions
among fellow expatriates was that he had with him in Aden
his father's yacht, *Chuff*, a 26-foot Fairey Marine Atalanta.[3]
Someone had persuaded the RAF to fly the boat out, and
short voyages to beaches along the coast were much enjoyed.
Tony also harboured a streak of eccentricity, manifest in later
life when he became a farmer and at one stage took a deep
interest in the manufacture of a friend's trebuchet – a medieval
siege-engine – with which he managed to throw a dead sow
340 yards.

In the RAF his appetite for adventure had once led him to
fly a Javelin beyond recommended limits in a privately arranged
and highly illegal twenty-minute dogfight with a friend in a
Hunter. During the contest he found he could outmanoeuvre
the Hunter easily enough, but only by ignoring the bleeper
which warned that his aircraft's speed was dangerously low, and
by not easing his turns until the klaxon warned of an imminent stall. As he walked away from the aircraft after landing, his
navigator told him that if that ever happened again, he would
ask for a change of pilot – to which Tony replied that, as a
result of the experiment, the navigator would be much safer
in his hands, should they ever come up against a real foe.[4]

Tony had naturally hoped to make his whole career in the
RAF, and it was a severe blow to him when persistent migraine
headaches curtailed his flying career; but through his posting
to Aden he found a challenging new form of employment.

*   *   *

In October 1962, a month after the revolution, Billy McLean went off on a fact-finding tour at the suggestion of King Hussein of Jordan, who paid for his trip. He called first at Amman, the Jordanian capital, where he discussed the situation with several ambassadors, most usefully the Italian diplomat Amandeo Ghia, who had worked in the Yemen earlier and had been in Sana'a on the day of the coup. From Ghia came the news that the Yemeni Air Force consisted of only three old DC3 Dakotas, two six-seater Air Commanders, two helicopters and twenty-nine Russian Yak 28s (piston-engined fighter-bombers), which had been grounded for years and were covered in tarpaulins (as one Yemeni remarked, if you looked under the tarpaulins, 'mouses jumped out').

It was a striking illustration of McLean's personal standing that he spent the night of 22 October in Riyadh as a guest of King Saud. After the Suez debacle in 1956, Saudi Arabia had broken off diplomatic relations with Britain; but now the King felt strongly that Britain should help the Imam – if possible, openly with air support, but, failing that, clandestinely. Saud suggested that aircraft could be painted with the Imam's insignia and Yemeni markings, and flown by volunteer pilots from Turkey and elsewhere.

On the night of 25 October Tony Boyle was just going to bed in Aden when he got a call from air-traffic control saying that an aircraft purporting to be King Hussein's private jet was only 20 miles out and asking permission to land. What were they to do? Forced to make an immediate decision, Tony said, 'Allow it in' – and it was lucky he did, for, having driven rapidly to the airport, he found that the plane was being flown by King Saud's air adviser, Squadron Leader Erik Bennett[5], and on board was Billy McLean.

From Government House in Aden on 26 October McLean

despatched a secret telegram to Duncan Sandys, Secretary of
State for the Colonies, reporting his conversations in Riyadh:

> King Saud said that the Egyptian military intervention
> in the Yemen was the first phase of a wider plot by
> Nasser in which the Russians were also involved. The
> aim is to disrupt Saudi Arabia, the Aden Protectorate[6]
> and the Gulf Sheikhdoms, and later Jordan and Syria.
> Unless the Egyptians are checked, there will be an imme-
> diate and serious threat to security in the whole of the
> Arabian Peninsula. HMG should therefore not recog-
> nise the rebel government of [Colonel Abdullah al-Sallal]
> [Nasser's puppet in Sana'a], but give all possible support
> to the Imam.[7]

In a separate report McLean confirmed that Prince Feisal
(King Saud's half-brother and Prime Minister) could not
understand why HMG did nothing to support the Royalists
in the Yemen or to oppose the Egyptian intervention there:

> HMG must know that Nasser intends to push the British
> out of Aden and the Persian Gulf and that he would
> probably be helped in this by both the Russians and
> the Americans. Prince Feisal said he himself had been
> under the strongest American pressure to discontinue
> his efforts to oppose Sallal and the Egyptians in the
> Yemen but he had not yet given in and did not intend
> to do so.[8]

In Aden, McLean planned a trip through the Yemen, travelling by Land Rover, camel and on foot from south-east to
north-west. As one friend and colleague remarked, in wildest

Arabia 'he turned himself into a brigand with the London
sleekness stripped away'.[9] At Harib, a village of only about
twenty houses, surrounded by a 12-foot mud wall to keep out
the ever-drifting desert sand, he met the Yemeni Royalist Deputy
Prime Minister, Ahmed al-Siyaghi, who 'talked well and convinc-
ingly' and impressed his visitor with his 'intelligence, toughness
and his skill in dealing with the tribes'. McLean described how
he was taken to the house in the middle of the village where
Siyaghi had set up his headquarters:

> It was surrounded by hundreds of soldiers all armed to
> the teeth, some with machine guns as well as rifles,
> lounging around, many of them chewing qat.[10] I was
> taken up to the guest room of the house where Siyaghi
> was holding court. The room soon filled up with chiefs
> and notables, some of whom had come in that day to
> offer their allegiance to the Imam. Their tribesmen fired
> several hundred rounds of ammunition into the air to
> stress the importance of the occasion.[11]

Siyaghi explained that although there was heavy fighting
in the west, close to Sana'a, the east of the country was still
in the hands of the tribes, and the various Royalist armies
were commanded by uncles or cousins of the Imam. McLean
saw plenty of evidence of foreign intervention, including
identity cards taken from thirty-five dead Egyptian parachutists
killed in airborne attacks (many of them picked off by sharp-
shooters before they reached the ground, others knifed as
they struggled to release their harnesses); he also met a
wounded Egyptian paratrooper who said that Nasser had told
him and his companions that they were being sent to the
Yemen to fight the British.

At the end of his tour McLean crossed into Saudi Arabia at Najran — a prosperous oasis of date palms, with impressive, well-spaced mud-built houses — and immediately despatched a cable to Duncan Sandys, via Riyadh. There the message was decoded and translated from English to Arabic; it was then encoded again and sent to Amman, where King Hussein himself rendered it back into English and passed it to the British Ambassador. Notwithstanding all these switches, the cable reached Sandys in time for the Cabinet meeting of 31 October.

Meanwhile McLean had returned by air to Riyadh, where he had another audience with the monarch on 30 October. In a record of his conversation with the King, he left a memorable picture of Saud, then sixty, who sat on a leopard-skin chair wearing dark glasses and talking slowly in a deep voice. His 'huge yellow hands hung relaxed over the arms of his chair', but when he talked they shook strongly, as if he was in the advanced stages of Parkinson's disease. He had 'a nervous gesture of adjusting his head-dress when discussing a tricky point' and frequently took off his glasses to reveal pale, watery eyes. 'Strangely enough, he has a strong and deep laugh.'

Also present at the audience was the King's younger brother, Prince Feisal, the Prime Minister. He, too, had a striking appearance, 'like a rather elderly peregrine or some desert bird of prey'; but McLean thought his eyes and face, with his dark eyebrows and pointed beard, 'very intelligent and expressive', and found that he grasped ideas quickly. Compared with the King, Feisal seemed 'very modern'. He also knew the Yemen well, for he had led forces into the country in the 1930s.[12]

Both Saudi leaders favoured the idea of providing air support for the Imam. Their own air force was grounded, because the King did not trust the pilots or mechanics, or any officer trained in Egypt; but Feisal made practical suggestions for deploying Jordanian Hunter fighter-bombers from the air-base at Taif, the Saudi summer capital in the mountains behind Jeddah. Ideally, he would like them to bomb Sana'a's radio and airfield.

McLean returned to London heartened by these exchanges – and found that his telegram from Najran had proved timely, for at a critical moment it had persuaded Lord Home, the Foreign Secretary, to hold out against American demands that Britain should back the Republican rebels. The fact that HMG held firm cleared the way for Britain and Saudi Arabia to resume diplomatic relations, and in November the Saudis showed their increasing disgust with Nasser by breaking off relations with Egypt.

McLean's reports from the front line had a powerful effect on the debate, because he bypassed the Foreign Office and took them straight to the Prime Minister, Macmillan. Moreover, he received support from the previous Prime Minister, Sir Anthony Eden, who was still recuperating in the West Indies from the illness that had precipitated his departure from office after the fiasco of Suez. 'You are, of course, absolutely right,' Eden told McLean in a letter from Friendship Bay, on St Vincent, 'and I am glad that Alec Home and FO are standing firm against recognition . . . To follow US in appeasement this time would finally put paid to our position in Arabia and the Gulf.'[13]

On 6 December the Imam sent a dignified letter to President Kennedy, protesting 'with the utmost vigour' against American support for the rebels. 'Shortly after the mutiny,' he wrote:

Egyptian arms and equipment arrived by ship which must have left Egypt before its outbreak. This confirms other evidence we have that the mutiny was plotted by Egypt . . . The pretext used to justify this aggression was that the Egyptian forces were to defend the Yemen against the armies of Saudi Arabia, Jordan and Britain. This is completely false. No foreign troops other than Egyptian have entered my country, and none are here now.[14]

In spite of this appeal, the United States formally recognised Sallal's regime on 19 December 1962. During that month Duncan Sandys flew to Aden, but his visit seemed merely to emphasise the futility of HMG's policy. 'He is a so-and-so,' Tony Boyle reported in a letter home. 'We had thirty-six hours of chaos while he went round probing and suggesting.' News of the war was more cheerful: 'The Egyptians are getting short shrift from the Royalists. When they are caught they have their noses, ears and lips removed, and are then sent back to the Republican rebel leader naked!'[15] Nasser, by now, was well aware of the identity of his opponents in Britain, and at the end of December he sent Billy a printed official card, extending his 'best wishes for the New Year'.

More and more the Royalists were looking to Britain for help. Early in April 1963 Prince Abdullah wrote an impassioned letter to Macmillan, addressing him as 'His Highness the Prime Minister of the United Kingdom', and beginning 'May God prolong your days'. He described how the Egyptians were strengthening their position in the Khowlan, and planning to attack both Jizan (in Saudi Arabia) in the north and Beihan, outside the Yemen's southern frontier. Several times he pleaded for military help, now that Nasser had 'opened the gates of the Middle East to the evils of red Communism'.[16]

In April McLean was back in the Yemen, this time going in by Land Rover from the north. From the Red Sea port of Jizan, with its ancient Turkish fort standing out on a prominent hill, he was driven to Mabta, a day's march short of the Imam's latest headquarters on Jebel El Qara, some 80 miles to the north of Sana'a, in the north-west of the country (*jebel* means 'mountain').

Having travelled until midnight, he awoke in the morning to find himself in a tented camp at the foot of mountains crowned with medieval castles and fortified villages:

Kilted and turbaned tribesmen, festooned with bandoliers, pistols and hand grenades, and with enormous curved daggers stuck in their belts, swarmed round the Imam's tent, chanting battle songs and firing salvoes from their rifles, while a couple of anti-aircraft guns fired occasional bursts into the air.[17]

In another secret report he described his arrival:

We were tired and hungry after travelling all night, and so greatly enjoyed our breakfast of tinned Egyptian beans, mixed with raw onions and submerged in olive oil and vinegar, into which we dipped huge flaps of toasted unleavened bread, followed by honey, washed down in unnumerable [*sic*] cups of very sweet tea.[18]

The camp at Mabta turned out to be pleasant and comfortable. There were tents with electric light, a refrigerator and even an air-conditioner in McLean's tent. Above the camp was a waterfall, with a pool for washing in, and the food was plain but plentiful. After a day's delay, waiting for mules, he

set out with escorts for EL Qara, climbing a steep escarpment for the first three hours and being stopped several times
by villagers who insisted on bringing them coffee, tea, yoghurt
and bread soaked in sesame oil. At the top of the escarpment
they turned off the main track and made a detour to the
village of Al-Kowma, which the Egyptians had bombed with
poison gas.

In the middle of March, Egyptian aircraft had dropped
what the local people called two *qunbula sahriya* – magic
bombs – on the village. One had exploded with a kind of
soft pop; the other did not burst, but gave off blue-black
fumes and smoke. Six children, aged three to eight, were
killed, and twenty-two men, women and children injured. A
secret report, drawn up by the Prime Minister's secretary,
Ibrahim al-Khibsi,[19] gave gruesome details of the fatalities:

1 Mohamed Ali Massaoud, eight years old. Died two
   hours after vomiting blood and his skin and flesh
   falling off when he scratched.
2 His brother, Hussein Ali Massaoud, two years old.
   Sleeping in a nearby house when bomb fell. Vomited
   blood and died after 2½ hours.
3 Abdullah bin Ali bin Nasser, five years old. His body
   swelled up, vomited blood and skin, and flesh fell
   off when he scratched it. Died after four days. He
   could not swallow, and when given water or milk,
   it came out through his nose.[20]

When McLean reached Al-Kowma, six weeks had elapsed
since the raid, and heavy rain had fallen; even so, 20 or 30
yards from the bombs' impact point he became aware of
'an unusual, unpleasant and pungent smell . . . rather like a

sweet-sour musty chloroform mixed with a strong, sour odour of geranium plant'.[21] Many of the surviving children had sores and scars; some adults had red eyes, and complained of comparative loss of vision. Cows had lost their coats, their udders were covered with scabs, and they had ceased to give milk.

From Al-Kowma the party descended steeply several thousand feet into a valley, then climbed even more steeply up the escarpment on the other side on a well-made path of marble slabs, constructed (McLean was told) by the Imam's great-grandfather, who had been lord of the nearby medieval castle of Washha.

The tall stone houses of El Qara, with their flat roofs and empty eye-sockets of windows, crowned the ridge of a mountain, and the Imam's bombproof cave was at the foot of the cliffs below. He was sharing his accommodation with the short, thickset al-Hirsi, who was not only his secretary, but also his father-in-law. Earlier, Hirsi had defected with the state funds from Lahej (west of Aden) to the Yemen, and the Imam had married his daughter as a second wife. McLean described him as the Imam's 'most intimate confidant and former boozing companion'. Clearly, Hirsi had become indispensable to the ruler; but many Yemenis told McLean how much they disliked him, because they thought he exercised an evil influence, and they resented the fact that the Imam trusted him rather than them.[22]

Outside the cave there was always a milling crowd of supplicants and tribal leaders clamouring to present their *warraqas* – chits, or requests scribbled on scraps of paper – and offering their allegiance in exchange for rifles and gold. McLean thought the Imam 'an amiable young man', with an easy-going manner and a ready sense of humour; but he also felt that the ruler, though brave, 'lacked the ability to apply himself seriously to any task other than political plots or personal intrigues'. He slept late and spent the afternoon and half the night signing chits, writing letters and chewing *qat*, so that it was generally not until far into the night that he became free for serious talks. Never once during the four days that McLean was present did he leave his cave.

'Despite the Imam's personal faults,' McLean reported, 'his name carries fantastic prestige among the tribes. He is also lavish with his money which endears him even more to the tribesmen.' Later McLean recorded that he had been:

> amazed at the respect, affection and love the Yemenis hold for the Imam and the institution of the Imamate. The Imam's position is something like that of a spiritual pope who is also a temporal king. On the one hand, the Yemenis are very fierce in their insistence that the Imam and the princes must fight the Jihad, or holy war. I have been told many times of tribesmen who have come to the Imam and said, 'We will die together with you fighting the Jihad . . . but if you leave us, we will kill you, for this is a fight to the death.'[23]

And yet, as the war went on, it became increasingly clear that the Imam was neither directing strategy nor exercising command over his scattered armies. He was naturally indolent, and far too fond of alcohol to make an effective military leader. Decisions were left to individual princes, who spent most of their time widely separated from each other by the rugged nature of the environment, and had (at first) only the most primitive form of communication in the form of human runners, so that messages often took days to reach their destination. The result was that the Royalists never managed to organise concerted action − and this was the principal reason for the war lasting so long.

Attempts to render the Royalists assistance were veiled in secrecy. While McLean was moving around in the Yemen, Tony Boyle had visited Beihan and seen Sherif Hussein's son, Emir Saleh, who told him that money had arrived from Feisal, as well as 50,000 rounds of .303 ammunition. But when the Sherif proposed to spend the money on Mauser ammunition and send it all to Abdullah bin Hassan, Tony emphasised that 'this must not get to the ears of the British authorities, as, if it did, they would be unlikely to provide any further assistance.'

In 1963 the Yemen was still in most respects medieval. Outside two or three cities there were no roads, no telephones, no electricity, no medical facilities, no piped water, no schools. The country was closed to foreigners, so that 99 per cent of its inhabitants lived in ignorance of the outside world. If Ronald Bailey, until 1962 the British Consul in Taiz (the country's second city), wanted to go for a walk, he first had to obtain permission from the Imam, which could take two weeks to arrive. If permission was eventually granted, he was obliged to perambulate carrying an open umbrella, to demonstrate that he was a person of importance, so that people would treat him with respect.

When someone gave the old Imam an aeroplane, he had it taken to pieces and stored the parts in different caves so that nobody could steal it.

His authority, based on Islamic law, was tempered only by the main tribes, and by the decisions of the Ulem'ma, a body of respected elders. The principal unit of population was the

tribe – a military and political as well as a social group. A tribe
was split into clans, the clans into sections, and each section
into a number of families. Within the tribe, the members looked
to a chief (sheikh), who acted as judge or mediator to settle
inter-tribal disputes.

During the next ten days McLean made his way right through
the Yemen and met other Royalist leaders in their mountain
strongholds: sometimes driving, more often riding camels or
walking, he frequently had to take cover from Egyptian air-
raids, and once was machine-gunned by a helicopter before
he emerged into Beihan. Always a man for detail, he jotted
down some logistics of Yemeni transport:

Camel loads
A good camel can carry up to 300 lbs on flat or about
    250 lbs in hills.
Average speed of camel on flat 3 mph. In hills 2 mph.
    Average daily journey twenty miles.
Rifles weigh 9 lbs – therefore 20–30 rifles [per camel].
Average 24 on flat, 20 in hills.
Ammo box 600 rounds = ? lbs.
Average camel load – two boxes = 1,200 rounds ? lbs.
Donkey – One box ammo, 10–20 rifles.[24]

Perhaps his most important discovery was that all the
Royalist armies were severely short of arms and ammunition. Rifles were highly prized by the tribesmen – for rifle-
shooting was the national sport. Proud owners habitually
carried their weapons fully loaded, with a round in the
chamber, the safety-catch off, and the barrel aligned hori-
zontally backwards or forwards over one shoulder: a contin-

uous hazard to anyone in close proximity. The commonest type of rifle was the British Lee Enfield Mk 4 .303, dating from the First World War; but still more popular were the even-older .300 Mausers, made in 1903 or 1904 for the Shah of Iran, which in spite of their age were excellent long-range weapons. As one of the British mercenaries remarked, 'Even if you failed to kill a man at 1,000 yards with one of them, you could give him a very nasty fright.' Because they had a little engraving of the sun on the action, the Mausers were known as *abu ashams*, father of the sun. One Lee Enfield fetched 140 Maria Theresa silver dollars (known as 'MTD's and each worth about seven shillings, or £10 in today's terms), and a Mauser up to 380.

As a result of constant practice, the standard of marksmanship among the tribesmen was extremely high: many of them, firing over open sights, could hit a Maria Theresa dollar at 50 yards. But there was always a risk that when new consignments of rifles came into the country, half of them would disappear and be hoarded, sold or bartered away as a form of currency, rather than used against the enemy. Heavier weapons included bazookas (shoulder-held anti-tank rocket-launchers), 57mm and 75mm recoilless anti-tank rifles, which also fired rockets, and various types of mortar (3-inch and 81mm), which launched bombs in a high parabola. The Egyptian infantry had Kalashnikov automatic rifles – essentially close-quarter weapons, good up to 300 yards – and various heavy weapons also of Russian manufacture, including machine guns, T-34 tanks and artillery.

In London McLean's message to the politicians was the same: that the Royalists urgently needed support from the West; but the Americans were putting pressure on both Jordan and

Saudi Arabia to back Sallal's regime. In March 1963, determined to strengthen his knowledge of the situation, he set
out yet again for the Middle East – a journey that he described
in a Top Secret report.

In Riyadh he stayed with Prince Feisal, who was then
engaged in a power-struggle with his half-brother, the King,
but felt most strongly that HMG should give help to the
Royalists, and suggested that 'the British could do this secretly
in ways that they knew how to use better than anyone else'.

In the Yemen McLean paid a brief visit to the Imam, who
had temporarily gone to ground in caves on the side of a
steep valley at Shadda, near Hijla, in the north-west. There
McLean found him living 'in the greatest possible squalor
and confusion, but . . . almost completely safe from air
attacks'.[25] According to the ruler, the position in the north
and west was stronger than ever, but elsewhere the Egyptians
had cut some of the Royalists' supply routes, and were threatening to isolate elements of their forces in the east, where
there was a desperate shortage of ammunition.

On his way back through Riyadh, McLean saw Feisal again,
and after a conversation noted that the Prince had agreed to
send 10,000 gold sovereigns to Sherif Hussein, the *de facto*
ruler of Beihan – '5,000 immediately by air and 5,000 overland' – for Prince Abdullah bin Hassan, Commander of the
Royalist Second National Army in the Khowlan. Feisal also
agreed to spend up to £50,000 financing an operation by
the BFLF, 'but not through Saudi Arabia'.[26]

A stout, middle-aged man with a bushy beard, Sherif
Hussein became known to the BFLF by the code name
'Whiskers', and was described by one journalist as 'an old
roaring lion of a man'. Dynastic complexities meant that his
eldest son, Emir Saleh, was the nominal ruler of Beihan, but

in fact it was Whiskers who took the decisions. Saleh might happily tell the British that they should be bombing the Egyptian forces in the Yemen, just as the Americans were bombing the enemy in North Vietnam – but he had no executive power.

Over the years the Sherif proved a staunch ally of Britain. Although a clever man, he was not educated, and occasionally became recalcitrant and devious; but he gave invaluable help by granting the mercenaries the use of various houses, and letting them, their arms and ammunition pass through his territory on their way into the south-east corner of Yemen. War materials and gold came through in great quantities from Saudi Arabia: Sultan Ghalib al-Qu'aiti, the young ruler of the Hadhramaut (one of the states in the Aden Protectorate) remembered sitting on a small hill one evening and seeing columns of vehicles crawling across the desert, for hours on end. By discreetly milking the convoys, the Sherif made a great deal of money, and became so rich that he was able to present King Feisal with a Rolls-Royce. His own policy was certainly robust: whenever Republican Yemenis came across the border and blew up a house belonging to his own people, he would riposte by sending in a gang to blow up two of theirs.

If the Royalists were in trouble, things were not going well for the Republicans, either. At a press conference in Sana'a, Sallal had inadvertently given the impression that he was no more than a puppet, completely dominated by the Egyptians;[27] and when he visited his outlying garrison at Marib, in the south-east of the Yemen, to bang the drum, all the tribesmen had disappeared from the town, so that he found himself addressing 150 Egyptian soldiers, to whom he made the futile proclamation: 'The revolution in Arabia is imminent, and all Arab countries will be Republican.' Reports of food shortages in Sana'a seemed to be substantiated by the fact that he had two cows killed, loaded them onto his truck and drove them to the capital.[28]

The Saudis were becoming ever more eager to get the Egyptians out of the Yemen, and at the end of April Feisal signed a Disengagement Agreement, whereby he would stop sending supplies to the Royalists if Nasser would withdraw his troops in phases and cease attacking Yemeni villages from the air. Nasser's reaction was typical: having got this agreement, at the end of June he increased the number of troops in the Egyptian Expeditionary Force from 23,000 to 32,000 and resumed the bombing and strafing.

Back in London, McLean again pressed his cause. If the Royalist regime was to be saved, and Nasser thwarted, urgent action was needed – and so it was that HMG, lacking the resolution to send in the SAS, looked the other way when SAS officers past and present – Johnson, Stirling, Woodhouse and Franks – went into action, and Jim's tiny private army slipped quietly into being.

All four instigators were formidable characters, and none more so than Woodhouse. With his slender, gangling figure and a bit of a stoop, he did not cut an immediately impressive figure; but he was an enormously professional soldier, and in the words of a fellow officer, he was 'steel to the core . . . an outstanding leader who always drove himself to his limits, put the welfare of his men above his own, and expected the highest standards from everyone'.[29] The recent successes of the SAS in Malaya and Oman had been due in no small measure to his leadership and dedication.

In May 1963, via the Governor's Office in Aden, McLean had sent a message to one of the Royalist princes, saying that 'a group of Englishmen in no way connected with the British Government will be coming out here'. When they came, the note said, they would need support, and the writer emphasised that silence would be essential, 'as the scheme could not be condoned by the Govt, and would have to fall through if HMG heard about it'. On 5 May Tony Boyle passed on the information verbally in an interview with Emir Saleh of Beihan, asking for his help to infiltrate men into the Yemen, and on the 10th he did the same with the Emir's father, Whiskers, or (more properly) Sherif Hussein.

In another secret report McLean suggested that the poison-gas bombs that devastated Al-Kowma might have been dropped in an attempt to kill the Imam, and that the pilot of the aircraft hit the wrong target, misled by the fact that Kowma had a white mosque, as did El Qara. It was not long, however, before the Egyptians resorted to similar tactics on three other villages south of the town of Sa'ada; no one was killed in these attacks, but some fifty people were blinded or scorched and left with skin peeling off.

Secrecy was all as Johnny Cooper and his companions set out from Beihan into the hinterland, to establish contact with Prince Abdullah bin Hassan, Commander of the Second National Army, at his headquarters in the Khowlan, the towering mountain country east of Sana'a, and to ascertain the strength of the occupying Egyptian forces.

After the brief flight from Aden to Beihan, they drove on to Nuqub, only 15 miles from the Yemeni border. There they were issued with Arab clothes and joined a train of some 150 camels carrying weapons, ammunition and other supplies. Each man had escape money in the form of thirty gold sovereigns sewn into a belt. (Other mercenaries, thinking a belt too obvious, stowed the money in a kind of home-made sporran, under the *futa* – the theory being that any tribesman searching them would hesitate to fumble in that area, for fear of appearing to make homosexual advances.)

After one night in the home of the Sherif, the pioneers crossed the border at dusk next day and set off on a long penetration march. Because Egyptian MiG 17 fighters and Ilyushin 28 fighter-bombers were liable to appear suddenly overhead at any time during daylight, the caravan moved only at night: before dawn the camels were unloaded and let loose to graze on whatever scrub they could find, and the humans camouflaged themselves among rocks or scattered bushes. The newcomers became terribly sore in the backside from the unaccustomed, lurching gait of their mounts, and found it less painful to walk than to ride. The biggest obstacle on the route was the town of Marib, which rises out of the flat desert on a mound. Once it was the capital of the great Sabaean empire, and reputedly the birthplace of Bilqis, the legendary Queen of Sheba; now the Egyptian garrison had mined the tracks around it to prevent parties of this very kind getting past; but the Royalist guides knew the mine-fields well and had no difficulty leading the camels through in single file.[30]

The mercenaries were travelling the ancient incense trail, moving at the same pace, and on the same route, as the cara-vans that had once transported frankincense and myrrh from Oman and the Hadhramaut right through the Yemen towards the Phoenician ports of Tyre and Sidon and the lucrative markets in the north.[31] Demand for the oriental aromatics remained strong for centuries: in the time of the Pharaohs, Egyptians burnt incense during religious and sacrificial cere-monies, and used myrrh as medicine and for embalming; but it was the Romans' passion for the exotically scented resins that brought the Yemen lasting prosperity. Such was the volume of traffic, on foot or by camel, that on some steep slopes broad steps had been cut out of the rock to facilitate progress. In antiquity the land round Marib was very fertile, thanks to irrigation from the colossal dam built on the River Adhanat in the ninth century BC, which survived until the barrage collapsed in about AD 570. Fifteen centuries after that disaster, the area's prosperity had long since vanished, and now Marib was nothing but one old Turkish fort and a collection of four- and five-storey mud houses surrounded by a high mud wall in the middle of a wind-blown, silty desert, dotted with a few tamarisk trees.

At the end of a marathon trek Cooper's little gang reached the Prince's headquarters outside the village of Gara, only a few miles east of Sana'a, but separated from the capital by ferociously steep mountain country, and 3,000 feet above it. The travellers received a noisy welcome, as the tribesmen loosed off volleys of precious ammunition skywards and the Prince came riding to meet them on a mule at the head of his troops.

The younger son of the Prime Minister, Abdullah bin Hassan was a serious and gentle young man of twenty-six who spoke some English, having been educated in Beirut and having worked under his father in New York, in the Yemeni delegation to the UN.[32] He was described by the journalist Sanche de Gramont as an unlikely-looking guerrilla sheikh, small-boned and delicate, with 'the aquiline features and large sloe eyes of a Byzantine icon'.[33] His temporary home was a cave, but, as de Gramont recorded, he was making the best of things:

His manservant is always at his side and sleeps at his feet. Every night the manservant inflates a pneumatic mattress for the prince and massages his feet with aromatic oils. In the morning he brings an incense burner laden with sandalwood, and the prince stands over it and lets the fragrant fumes rise through his clothing.[34]

Hassan loyally supported the Imam; he had a high reputation for bravery among his own people – and he was far from effete. On the night of the coup he, too, had escaped from the palace in Sana'a, and after an arduous three-week trek through the mountains had reached Harib, picking up tribesmen as he went. Near Marib he managed to ambush an Egyptian convoy of eleven armoured cars and personnel carriers. When the Royalists opened fire with their rifles, the Egyptians panicked, leapt from their vehicles and tried to flee – but, as Hassan later recounted, 'There was nowhere for them to go, and we shot them all.'[35]

Now he had been expecting Johnny Cooper and his companions; he was glad to see them, and agreed that they should start carrying out reconnaissance sorties immediately. These were what Johnny described as only short expeditions: 5- to 10-mile hikes designed to acclimatise themselves to the high altitude. A terrific walker himself, he stretched all his followers to the limit; and he quickly saw that although the Egyptians were well established in the low ground around Sana'a, they were reluctant to venture further afield or to climb the mountains.

After just two days he sent an enthusiastic report to Johnson and Stirling, entrusting his handwritten letter to a Frenchman who was returning to Aden:

We cannot get at Sana'a, as a full-blown war is now in the making and the route to our targets almost impossible at present. So they [the tribesmen] are fighting with heavy weapons on selected targets in support. They have been strafed by Yaks, napalmed by Ilyushins, machine-gunned by ground forces. All are excellent and our doc has done wonders. Only an hour ago we were strafed, and he is tending a wounded soldier now . . . The powers that be here are most impressed with our efforts to help, and I believe just our arrival here has made the entire project worthwhile and your added grey hairs honourable.

Will keep at it, have no worry, but my Arabic has been stretched to the limit, still no interpreter.[36] We could all write a book on this place and its people, with a large appendix on Egyptians – Wogs blast 'em . . .[37]

My cave is comfortable but come the morn I move – the strafing is getting closer. Thank God they have no pilots of any quality . . . It is a wonderful, hard, exciting and frustrating life – Johnny.

He was certainly enjoying himself – but he was also being pursued by demons from his past. He knew that Colonel Waterfield, the Military Secretary in Oman, who controlled the money for contract officers, was determined to end his term with the Sultan's armed forces, even though his own former Commanding Officer, Colonel Oldman, was doing all he could to protect his position. In his report to London, Johnny appealed to Johnson and Stirling for help:

I must stay on to honour our contract. Be it on my head. But if you can write to Col. Oldman (who knows all) and stress national or anti-Nasser importance, and [say] that I will leave here without fail on 10 July . . . and will forfeit all the time against my leave in September. If I am sacked by Waterfall, that is my lookout.

Sacked he was – though not until September – by a sharp letter from Waterfield, who sent copies to every address he had (five in all), in the hope of catching him:

My dear Cooper, I am instructed to inform you that your service with the Sultan's Armed Forces has been terminated with effect from 6th June, 1963, in view of your unauthorised departure and absence from the Sultanate. I am further instructed to say that you may not return to the Sultanate. Please inform me what is to be done with your heavy baggage.

For the time being, Johnny was beyond reach. In spite of the problems of communication, he and his colleagues began to give the tribesmen basic training in guerrilla warfare. The Yemenis' normal form of attack was to rush forward, barefoot and screaming, brandishing their *jambiyas* or firing rifles (if they had any), and to overrun an enemy position, seizing more weapons as they went through. Johnny now began to instil more sophisticated techniques, particularly that of fire and movement, in which one section puts down covering fire while the other advances. Another major advance was the use of Bren guns – light machine guns fitted with bipods – which, with their 28-round magazines, could maintain a far higher rate of fire than rifles. The Arabs had a natural aptitude for shooting and soon, with their the new weapons, were organised into small fire-sections of five or seven men apiece.

One morning three Il–28s – twin-engined jet bombers, with cannons fore and aft – dropped bombs and strafed the village of Gara with 20mm rockets. Behind them came piston-engined Yaks, fighter aircraft agile enough to fly right down into the wadis and machine-gun any target that presented itself. The attack caused no casualties, because the people had withdrawn into caves; but the raid no doubt sharpened Johnny's appetite for a scrap, and after only a few days he devised a plan 'to tickle up the opposition': he would get the Prince's men to lay mines, thereby provoking the Egyptians to attack, and so lead them into a chosen killing ground.

He set up the ambush in Wadi Thoul, between Abdullah's headquarters and Sana'a, at a point where the rising valley split into a Y on a steep slope. The arms of the Y petered out into unassailably steep little ravines, but between them was an area of level ground some 50 yards across. This Johnny designated the killing zone, and he marked it out with little cairns of stones. Above it, looking down, he placed three gun-sections in camouflaged spots protected by rocks, with 'funk holes' behind, into which the riflemen could withdraw 'when the real shit came in'. His own report gave a vivid idea of the action – and of the enemy's incompetence:

At about 0900 hours the Egyptians moved into the wadi in great strength, with a parachute battalion up front and a force of T-34 tanks and light artillery bringing up the rear. They were still unaware of our presence further up the wadi, and were nosing around. Half-way up the wadi the tanks and artillery pulled up and the infantry advanced in extended order, packed shoulder to shoulder.

They were carrying a lot of heavy clobber, and were dragging heavy Soviet machine guns along on wheels.

As the enemy reached the markers, our men opened up with devastating effect, knocking down the closely-packed infantry like ninepins. Panic broke out in the ranks behind, and then their tanks opened fire, but their shells were exploding not on our positions, but among their own men. The light artillery also joined in, and most of the casualties they took during the ten-minute firefight were from their own guns.

For the rest of the day the Egyptians kept fire on the top of our hill, but we were well covered in our funk holes. The bodies that had fallen on the killing ground – we counted some eighty-five afterwards – were left where they had fallen and by nightfall the whole Egyptian force had left the wadi, returning to Sana'a with a very bloody nose indeed.[38]

Johnny's second offensive was almost as successful: a mortar attack launched at dawn on an Egyptian garrison on top of a hill, encircled by barbed wire and mines, and overlooked by a still higher hill. It was, in his eyes, 'a beautiful target'. After an approach march with camels carrying the mortar and ammunition, Geordie Dorman – an expert at this form of warfare – got the range with his second round, and followed up rapidly with thirty more bombs:

Observed from the top, the panic was fantastic. It was obvious that the enemy thought they had been attacked by a force of infantry, as they started to blaze away in all directions. It was quite some time before their artillery started to follow up the wadi behind, but such was their state of turmoil that by then we were three or four miles away. They even kept on shelling the wrong valley for the whole of the rest of the day.[39]

Another engagement, on the night of 6–7 July, elicited the approval of Kim d'Estainville, one of the French mercenaries, who later told Tony Boyle that 'when the tribesmen fight . . . they are jolly good'. When the Egyptians launched a heavy attack with T-34 tanks and artillery (Kim reported), the Royalists showed 'very high fire control' in letting them come on; then, for once, the enemy 'sent infantry up the hills', and again revealed a fatal ignorance of basic tactics:

Like on a promenade [he meant 'parade'] those troops were not in proportion to the artillery, tanks and air forces engaged. Anyhow they met with disaster. We saw and counted forty bodies on two hills . . . and for the following week the Royalists ate Egyptian rations, carrying round automatic rifles, six radio sets (Russian), five calibre .30 machine guns and four bazookas.

In spite of these successes, the Yemenis were curiously disinclined to give the mercenaries a free hand in the fighting. As Kim recorded:

We tried several times to use bazookas against the tanks – crazily exposed by the Egyptians, but each time [got] opposition from our [own] side – they seem terribly reluctant to engage us directly [that is, to let us take a direct part]. We therefore keep up with wounded and try what we can to repair guns and teach etc.

Johnny – who now styled himself Abdullah bin Nasser – was in his element; the violently steep nature of the mountainsides meant that the environment was ideal for cutting roads, sections of which would fall away for hundreds of feet if an explosive charge was detonated at the right point. He himself spent several nights climbing down precipitous slopes on exploratory sorties, to determine which spots were most vulnerable; but his brief was to return to England as soon as possible and present the BFLF with an Egyptian ORBAT, or order of battle. In a short time he had obtained such excellent results from the tribesmen that Abdullah bin Hassan was reluctant to let him go; but Johnny promised he would return and, leaving the two Frenchmen *in situ*, he and his British companions walked back the way they had come, to the border of Beihan and Nuqub, whence they were flown to Aden and the United Kingdom.[40]

In a three-page report for Jim he summed up his experiences. The attack on Sana'a airfield, which they had adumbrated at the first meeting in Paris a year earlier, had proved to be 'a pipe dream', although within a few months it might become a reality. In fact, Abdullah bin Hassan – keen as he was to rout the invading forces – had advised *against* an attack, on the grounds that even if they managed to destroy a few planes, the Egyptians would quickly fly more in; he would rather Jim sent out men to train the various Royalist tribal armies.

Johnny reported that his first deployment had turned into a reconnaissance, and at the same time a military mission to advise Abdullah bin Hassan on tactics – and it had proved '100 per cent successful'. Corporal Chigey had dealt with thirty major cases of wounded soldiers, and lost only one: a 'great effort'. Overall, Johnny reckoned, 'We honoured our agreement with Feisal, and created a great feeling of trust between the Royalists and the British & French.' Having seen both the Egyptian Air Force and the Army in action, he reckoned them 'fourth rate in all departments', and recorded that some Egyptians working for the Yemenis in the outstations were being paid in food only. At the end of his report he added a warning for anyone who followed in his footsteps:

Entry to Jebel Sihan area takes between five and eight days, when fit! One has to be prepared to ride camels for eight hours the first night and ten hours the second. The towns of Marib, Sirwah and el Argoub en route are garrisoned and need to be passed with care, as tanks and mobile patrols are active. Water is scarce en route. We nearly came unstuck the last day of our exit near Harib, not a funny experience as a *khamseen* [sand storm] was blowing.

'So much,' he concluded, 'now depends on support given to Abdullah bin Hassan by the other armies.'

3

Mountain Warriors

On his return to London in the autumn of 1963 Johnny was extensively debriefed by Stirling and Johnson, and his report made it clear that the scope for action in the Yemen was enormous. Jim therefore at once began arranging for him to return; but it was also evident that the Royalists urgently needed better communications, so he despatched Johnny to Kent to collect radio equipment. To give him some semblance of cover, he was provided with a 16mm movie camera and tripod – the idea being that he could pose as a cameraman, and also with luck obtain footage of Egyptian bombing attacks on the mountain villages.

Meanwhile, the French mercenaries sent in useful information about Sana'a and its surroundings. The town was relatively low down, laid out in the centre of a long plateau – but even that was 6,000 feet above sea-level. It then had about 120,000 inhabitants, and was dominated by a high mountain 2 kilometres to the east. Sallal's house and the Egyptian headquarters were well guarded, but the cantonments outside the town were practically unprotected, and had no defence works or barbed wire. Soldiers were walking out unarmed, and lorries were leaving unescorted. The radio station was also lightly guarded – 'One could easily reach the radio from outside the town' – and several little hills that 'descend with a gentle inclination towards Sana'a ... could easily be used for night approaches'.

On the Al-Adeni military airfield half a mile south-west of the town there were twelve Russian helicopters, twelve Yaks and eighteen transport planes, but no jet fighters. It was thought that some twenty MiG 17s were stationed at the new airport being built by the Russians 15 miles to the north, and that about 1,000 Egyptians were working there. All the aircraft were marked with the green Yemeni star. The road from Sana'a to Hodeidah, on the coast, was of special interest to the mercenary force, since it offered rich opportunities for mining and ambushes. Along its 137 miles, which took a Land Rover nearly six hours to negotiate, there were only seven or eight Egyptian garrisons, and many weak points – not least the pass 6 miles from Hodeidah, which overlooked the inland plateau and was dominated by peaks to north and south, but was not guarded.

To someone as combative as Johnny Cooper, all this looked very enticing. As soon as possible he flew from London to Aden, and he described his return to the Khowlan as 'uneventful'. This time, though, he acted as a gold-carrier. Behind his riding camel came another, attached by a rope, loaded with bags of sovereigns and half-sovereigns to pay Abdullah bin Hassan's soldiers. Ahead of his group went a decoy caravan, its camels carrying bags that looked as if they contained gold, but in fact were full of stones. His journey took nine days, for two of which he had to wait in the neighbourhood of Marib while trouble with the camel-men was sorted out.

At the Prince's headquarters in the caves at Gara he was

reunited with two of the Frenchmen from the Deuxième Bureau, Philippe Camus and Tony de St Paul. Together they built a stone radio shack on the mountain at one end of the village, near the grape vines, some 200 yards from the house in which they lived. The radio station was tucked in against a rock, with a co-axial aerial run out across the hillside; as they were 9,000 feet above sea-level, they got excellent reception from Aden, and were delighted with their position. They began to make regular contact with Tony Boyle, who kept the MI6 resident in Aden informed of their activities.

When not devising new ways of discomfiting the enemy, Johnny spent much time doing medical work, which he found enjoyable and satisfying. Like all former SAS personnel, he had had some medical training, and now found unlimited opportunities for practising his skills.

Together with a boy of about fifteen called Ahmed, he set up an al-fresco surgery under a tree in a nearby wadi, where he worked from 9 a.m. to 11 a.m. daily; and as word went out, men, women and children came from miles in search of treatment. Eye complaints were their most common affliction, but he also treated one bad case of phosphor burns from a bomb, and one gunshot wound in the knee. Because none of the patients had ever been given antibiotics before, a single shot of penicillin usually had a miraculously swift effect on ailments such as boils or skin infections.

So accustomed were the people to *woosam* – cure by burning – that they believed any remedy, to do good, must be accompanied by pain. This meant that every patient had to be injected, no matter what was wrong with him or her, even if it was only a headache; fortunately young Ahmed soon became adept at driving a needle into arms, legs or backsides. The Frenchmen were doing similar work in nearby villages, and between them, by the middle of August, the mercenaries had treated more than 100 patients. As the American author Dana Adams Schmidt remarked of the Yemenis, 'Much as they were given to shouting for every other reason, they accepted physical affliction with little protest.'[1]

The mercenaries found that some of the tribesmen had a genetic quirk that caused an extra thumb to grow out of the joint where a normal thumb joins the wrist. Each appendage had a nail, skin and two knuckles, but no muscles or tendons, so that it resembled a claw. Men with the deformities were interested in the idea of having them removed, and said that although there was some feeling in them, they were not as sensitive as their normal thumbs and fingers.

The halcyon days at Gara did not last long. Some informer probably told the Republicans that Europeans had arrived on the scene, for early one morning two Russian-built transport planes banked over their caves and dropped silvery cylinders, which burst open as they hit the ground, releasing a white cloud that filled the bottom of the wadi. Johnny, who had gone down lower to answer a call of nature, ran back up, to find dozens of tribesmen staggering out of the first cave, holding their eyes and shouting for help. Half an hour later he discovered Philippe up at the radio station, sitting beside the radio shack saying quietly that he was blind. Around the spot where one of the bombs had landed the ground was coated with a black, gooey substance that was still giving off vapour:

Helping Philippe back down to where Tony was waiting, we tried to do our best for him, but the only thing we had in the first-aid pack was a bottle of Optrex. This was of no use whatsoever, and slowly his eyelids closed, leaving him totally blind ... There were dozens of tribesmen in the same predicament, and we could do little to relieve their agony. Abdullah arranged for them to be evacuated, and I asked him for a caravan to take Philippe and Tony down to Nuqub so that he could be given treatment in a hospital in France ... His courage in sitting backwards astride a camel for two weeks, blind and not knowing what was going on around him, was a great tribute to the Deuxième Bureau.[2]

The departure of the Frenchmen left Johnny on his own – and so he remained for months, an exceptionally resilient survivor in an exceptionally uncomfortable environment. During the day, to avoid the Egyptian bombing and strafing raids, he would leave his flea-ridden cave and walk out into the mountains to watch the air activity from afar. His food consisted mainly of *khubs* (unleavened bread baked round hot stones and issued to all every morning), sometimes accompanied by a ration of 'vile-tasting tough meat stew', made from a recently slaughtered cow or goat.

Later he discovered one of the strange anomalies that prevailed in the civil war: once a week a tradesman came up with his donkey from enemy-occupied Sana'a, bringing goods that had been ordered, and presumably paying Egyptians or Republicans some tribute to let him through. He brought material for clothes, petrol for the generator, flour and dried fruit. Johnny's regular order was for golden syrup, which always seemed to be available, and he laced his *khubs* with that, or with a mixture of honey and olive oil. There was always a danger that food might have been poisoned – but presumably the tradesman wanted to preserve his own livelihood, and the risk seemed small.

Radio contact with Aden was intermittent and tediously slow (all messages being transmitted in Morse and in code) and whenever Johnny found a reliable courier, he made tape-recordings or scribbled long situation reports in pencil. Far from feeling depressed by his solitary existence, he wrote in his diary on 19 August, 'Feeling fit and well now and more settled to my lonely life of no English speakers. Shaved and fed well today.'

His daily tasks consisted of checking local armament stores, cleaning, servicing and repairing weapons, forming a team to collect reliable intelligence, and training men to lay mines at key points on the roads that the Egyptians used for supplying their outposts. Had the roads been asphalted, the task would have been much harder; but the dusty, sandy surfaces of the tracks were ideal for the purpose – easily dug up, and easily restored to their normal appearance after a mine had been laid. Knowing his Arabs, Johnny would display five gold sovereigns in front of a prospective mine-layer, give him two of them, and tell him that he would have the other three if he laid the mine and it went off satisfactorily. He would also pay a second crew to monitor the results. Most of the mines were of American origin, left over from the Second World War and still in boxes bearing the hand-shake symbol of the Lend-Lease programme.

His other main occupation was ministering to the sick and wounded. The fact that he had adequate medical supplies was due to the energy of the redoubtable Lady Birdwood, who, under the auspices of the Yemen Relief Committee, assembled a large consignment and had it sent to Aden. Later in her life she became notorious for her strident campaign against the 'blasphemy and filth' being shown on stage and television, and for her hatred of foreigners in general: as the *Daily Telegraph* put it, 'she disliked all foreigners equally'.[3] But above all she hated communism, and it was perhaps this – combined with the fact that her late husband had served in the International Red Cross – that made her send succour to the Royalists. Genuine gratitude certainly seemed to infuse a letter to Johnny. 'That we have succeeded even in such small measure to bring help to these suffering people is wonderful satisfaction,' she wrote in September 1963. 'What you yourself are doing is marvellous, and we are very grateful . . . One day I hope your courage and fine work will be recognised.'

When bureaucratic obstruction grounded her supplies in Aden, she herself flew out from England and, with Tony Boyle, and at some risk to themselves, broke into the store where the material had been impounded, so that the most valuable drugs could be sent up country by camel-train.

Under Lady Birdwood's auspices, a doctor, John Shepherd, made what was probably the first-ever medical tour of the Khowlan, taking with him eight camel-loads of equipment and supplies. He was on the mercenaries' payroll, at £300 a month; it was Jim Johnson who managed to extricate him from the Red Cross, and in a letter he warned Boyle to keep her ladyship in the dark as far as possible: 'She need not know too much about our set-up, so be discreet when you see her.'

Shepherd described his flight to Aden as 'uneventful, although I was unable to do any homework as I sat next to the Assistant Commissioner of police of Sarawak'. It took the doctor twenty-eight days to reach the Khowlan – seventeen of them waiting for a caravan. He had decided that he should take instruments 'for any reasonable operations', but that as no skilled help would be available, he would perform all surgery 'under local anaesthetic or nerve block'.

'It was interesting working among these people, most of whom had never seen a doctor before,' he wrote afterwards:

Nearly all are resigned to fate, and death holds no terrors for most adults. To the other members of a family [the] death of a relative is of only momentary significance. It is difficult, therefore, to persuade them that early calling of the doctor is sometimes a good thing.

The Khowlani is pleasant, hospitable, polite, cheerful, in some ways childlike. He likes guns and knives. The women are talkative. Although physically subject to their husbands, they do not appear to be mentally so. Although purdah is not strict in the mountains, and most women do not keep their veils up, it is difficult to examine any part of the trunk of a female, and impossible unless her husband is present and orders her to undress.

Travelling from village to village, Shepherd saw a total of 1,286 patients. Forty had wounds (only five of which were new and seen within three days; thirty-five were old); other patients were suffering from abscesses, hernias, and one from a large bowel obstruction ('refused operation – died'). There was also much conjunctivitis and trachoma, malaria, dysentery and a 'desire for aphrodisiacs – many'. Eye disease showed marked variation from village to village: in some places as many as 10 per cent of the people were blind in one or both eyes.

While the doctor was on his rounds, Johnny Cooper sent in an estimate of the military situation. 'Our build-up is still slow,' he reported:

In the seventy-four days I have been here we have received enough to skirmish with, but not to produce an all-out, supported attack on Sana'a and the Wog army concentrated there. My Int [Intelligence] has so far located fifty-eight tanks in Sana'a district. Therefore a stockpile of 75mm, 81mm and bazooka ammo is fast becoming the second priority after the small-arms position is settled.

Acknowledging that he would probably get no leave over Christmas, he said he did not regret it, 'as it is obvious to everybody that things should be humming round these dates, and I do not intend to miss the finale'.

Changes were taking place in the BFLF's small team. Because of his persistent migraines, Tony Boyle was about to be invalided out of the RAF, and needed a new job. Luckily he had impressed David Stirling during the Colonel's visit to Aden earlier in the year, and now Stirling and Jim Johnson decided to bring him into their London office, to act as Jim's second-in-command. Ostensibly, he would join Stirling's firm Television International Enterprises (TIE), a legitimate company distributing films and television programmes, but in fact he would be working with Jim. 'Some really good news,' Boyle wrote in a letter home:

I have the job with Television International Enterprises and start work as soon as I get back to England. The salary seems *fantastic*. I will be based in London and will travel extensively in the Middle East, all expenses paid. The attraction is that I am to be groomed as No. 2 in the set-up.

Clearly he was thrilled by the prospect of joining TIE and by the promised remuneration of £300 a month. He must have known that talk of films and television would be no more than a cover – but he prudently said nothing that might alarm his parents, and for the time being he remained in Aden, where he was able to train his unofficial successor. This was an exceptionally energetic and resourceful young officer, Peter de la Billière,[4] who had already, aged nineteen, fought in the Korean War, and distinguished himself as a member of the SAS in the Malayan jungle and in the assault on the 8,000-foot Jebel Akhdar plateau in Oman. Now, at twenty-six, he was on loan service, attached to the head-quarters of the Federal Regular Army as a junior Intelligence Officer – and it was a godsend to Jim Johnson, under whom he had served as Adjutant of 21 SAS, to find him stationed there.

Stretched though he was by his official duties, Peter was delighted to become an unpaid secret agent in his spare time, and he took over from Boyle the task of meeting the BFLF's emissaries as they came off the London Comet and posting them on to Beihan or directing them to hotel rooms booked in Aden itself. Newcomers were often surprised by the sight of a scruffy-looking young man in civilian clothes roaring up on a scooter and handing over a typewritten note, often concealed in a book, telling them what address to head for. These undercover arrivals sometimes led to ridiculous clashes: Peter's up country agents in the Federation would send back word that mysterious strangers had appeared in the rest-house at Beihan, and he would solemnly include these reports – of his own people's movements – in his regular intelligence summaries. He was in an excellent position to make sure that information about the mercenaries' activities went no further than his own desk.

In the middle of June 1963 the Royalists had gained an influential reinforcement in the form of Colonel David

Smiley,[5] a widely experienced soldier and an Arab-speaker, former commander of the Sultan of Muscat's army, but now, in his late forties, recently retired and working unhappily as an inspector for the *Good Food Guide*. When Billy McLean was about to set off for the Yemen yet again, he suggested that his old comrade-in-arms Smiley should drop his restaurant-hunting and go with him to write a report on the military situation for Prince Feisal.

The two started out together, but their trip had hardly begun, in Jeddah, when McLean was summoned back to London – ironically, to vote in a debate on Profumo – and Smiley carried on alone. He was not yet working for the BFLF, but for cover he carried a press card accrediting him to the *Daily Telegraph* (arranged for him by Julian Amery), and adopted the pseudonym 'Grin'.

He went in from the north, via Jizan, on the first of thirteen journeys on which he criss-crossed the Yemen during the next four years, all paid for by the Saudis, who valued his advice highly. A fearless traveller, impervious to heat, fleas, scorpions, snakes and barely edible food, and capable of endurance marches that would have finished most middle-aged men, he was frequently bombed and strafed as he went from one Royalist commander to another, trying to correlate their efforts and encouraging them to continue the fight. Living largely off *khubs*, tinned tuna and tinned pineapple, he grew a beard and tried chewing *qat*[6] but soon gave it up. During the summer he was sustained by his transistor radio broadcasting commentaries on the Test cricket series between England and the West Indies, and because he habitually photographed the tribesmen with his Leica, he was usually taken for a newspaper cameraman.

His first call, in July 1963, was on the Imam at El Qara,

7,000 feet up in the mountains. In his memoir, *Arabian Assignment*, he left a fine picture of the call to evening prayer among the ruler's followers:

> All around me, on cliff top, ledge and terrace, wherever there was a piece of level ground, hundreds of tribesmen were standing in silence. As the sun fell behind the western mountains, the priest raised his voice in the traditional chant: *Allah akbar, Allah akbar. Ashad an la ilah illallah we – Mohamed rasul Allah.* [God is greatest. I testify that there is no god save God and that Mohamed is the apostle of God.] The tribesmen, either singly or in small groups, turned to face north, towards Mecca, laid their rifles on the ground and prostrated themselves in prayer. It stirred me deeply to see these savage, bearded men, bathed in the crimson glow of sunset, bearing witness to their faith among the cliffs and crags of the High Yemen.[7]

Smiley found the Imam sitting on a carpet in the furthest of a labyrinth of caves, with only 3 feet of headroom, surrounded by piles of letters, a Thermos and a spittoon:

> He was taller and more heavily built than most of his countrymen, with a fleshy face, full lips and large, staring eyes; his moustache and beard were well trimmed, his hair long, thick and very curly. But although well groomed and carefully dressed, he had the puffy cheeks and sallow complexion of someone who has led for too long a confined and sedentary existence.[8]

That was the first of Smiley's numerous meetings with the Imam. In the course of his journeys he came to know many of the Yemeni princes, and his travels also brought him into ever-closer cooperation with the mercenaries, both British and French, until he himself became an ancillary member of their organisation and later was designated their Field Commander. From the start some members of the BFLF found his visits uncomfortable, as his rapid movements threatened to blow the organisation's cover. 'David came and went in a whirlwind,' Tony Boyle reported to Jim from Aden:

The situation here is becoming so well known that it is really likely that people who we do not want to know about it will soon start probing a little more deeply . . . It only needs one concrete piece of evidence, and the scheme is blown to the world, and the Government are going to be very hard pressed to explain it all away.

In a report to Prince Feisal, Smiley pinpointed the greatest weakness in the Royalist command structure:

There is no wireless/telegraphy contact between the Imam and his commanders; a message may take several days to reach them by courier. This results in the Imam having little control over his commanders; consequently he cannot coordinate his plans. From talking to the various commanders I gained the impression that each was fighting his own private war . . . though they would obey any instructions sent by the Imam.

His analysis confirmed that the Royalists were in control of the mountainous regions, 'where the warlike Zeidi tribes are strong supporters of the Imam' (the Zeidis had ruled the country for a thousand years). The Egyptians and Republicans were firmly established in the coastal area and the plains of the west, and in the southern part of the Yemen populated by the Shaffei tribes. The Egyptians also had garrisons in the main towns in the valleys between the Royalist-held mountains; but the troops there were frequently cut off by Royalist attacks, and generally dared not venture out from their encampments. The invaders were highly unpopular: if they withdrew their troops in accord with a recent agreement ('Grin' wrote), 'the Royalist forces would occupy Sana'a within a week'.

Grin also confirmed that the tactics already encouraged by Johnny – ambushes, mining and road-cutting – were the Royalists' best bet. He deplored 'the tendency, no doubt for prestige and propaganda purposes, for Royalist commanders to make frontal attacks with the object of capturing towns and villages', since such assaults almost always proved futile and wasted lives and ammunition. As for the Egyptians, on the plains they had the advantage of tanks, artillery and motor transport, but they were not trained to fight in the mountains, and were usually 'reluctant to do so'. Their greatest superiority was in the air, and their 'ability to bomb villages at will without any effective opposition has a marked effect on the morale of the villagers'.

On the night of 1–2 July 1963 McLean returned to the Yemen, going in from the north on a journey that took him to the Imam's headquarters at El Qara and then down the eastern side of the country, through the Jauf to the border of Beihan. At Mabta he was delighted to learn from the local commander that his tribesmen had perfected a novel way of disabling tanks: by stealing up on a stationary vehicle and ramming a mop or a rolled turban up its exhaust pipe, they could ensure that the engine would not start, so that sooner or later the crew would be flushed into the open, making excellent targets for the crack Royalist riflemen.

On 4 July a new element entered the arena, when the United Nations Yemen Observations Mission arrived in the country, with white vehicles, and its members wearing white armbands. It was charged with the task (according to its own report to the Security Council) of bringing about 'the disengagement of the two parties', Saudi Arabia and the UAR. In this it was conspicuously unsuccessful.

The mission was commanded by the sixty-year-old Swedish Major General Carl von Horn, who had alarmed UN officials with the extravagance of his demands: he would need (he said) not only 1,200 men, jeeps and helicopters, but also two fixed-wing aircraft. Once established in Sana'a, he cruised about the city in a palatial, chauffeur-driven Daimler, given to the late Imam Ahmed by King Saud. In the mornings he enjoyed cantering round the mud walls of the capital on the Imam's snow-white stallion, always slowing to a walk at the main gate to have a good look 'at the fresh heads which had been stuck up on spikes in niches, easily reached by milling crowds of vociferous urchins'.[9] If the number of heads was the same as on the previous day, he would conclude that 'local politics were reasonably stable'.

He spent much of his time flying on observation patrols above what he called the 'razor-edged mountains', and was not helped by the attachment to his mission of 122 Yugoslavs – described as a 'reconnaissance squadron' – whose every move was controlled by a political commissar receiving instructions through a secret radio in the Yugoslav Embassy. Yet what really prevented von Horn from achieving anything worthwhile was an order from U Thant, the UN Secretary

General: under no circumstances was he to make contact with the Royalist authorities, and he was specifically forbidden to speak to David Smiley.

Thus, from the start, and to the ever-increasing irritation of the British, the UN was firmly on the side of the Republicans. Von Horn's initial brief was to work for two months, but when no progress had been made in that time, his remit was extended for two months more. No wonder he became distressed 'by the complete lack of interest by the UN towards any Royalist complaints about the bombing and massacres in Royalist-held territory by the Egyptians'.[10] No wonder he concluded that 'in real terms, the whole story of the mission was one of calculated deceit'.[11] No wonder he resigned on 20 August. By the time his mission was officially wound up on 4 September, there were 50,000 Egyptian troops in the Yemen.

All the UN achieved was to station military observers in Jizan and Najran, with the aim of checking the vehicles and animal convoys that constantly went across the open border into the Yemen, 'to reduce the possibilities of this trade covering traffic in arms and military supplies'. Even on the border, where a little cluster of white tents stood out in the rocky wilderness, the mission was ineffective, for it did not have enough vehicles or other equipment to patrol the frontier properly. As for the interior, the Royalists claimed that whenever they were visited by a UN patrol, they would get some rather accurate bombing soon afterwards.

The mission's report parroted Egyptian claims that the Royalists' 'resistance and active hostility constitute a most serious obstacle to the withdrawal of UAR forces', and it had the nerve to maintain that 'the activities complained of [by the Royalists], especially bombing, are exclusively for the safeguarding of the security of UAR troops'. How bombing defenceless villagers with poison gas safeguarded the Egyptian garrisons, the report did not explain.

During July 1963 – in spite of the fact that the UN mission was moving around the country – the Egyptians launched an all-out offensive by land and air; but when they suffered heavy casualties and gained no ground, they pulled back. In August the fighting died away for the time being, and a ceasefire of a kind prevailed. Nasser was baffled by the fact that his huge army, of which he was very proud, could make little impression on the tribesmen, whom he dismissed as *shuyat qurood*, 'a bunch of monkeys'. For the time being he reduced his garrison from 32,000 troops to about 28,000, and many of his remaining soldiers withdrew to Sana'a. Yet in beating off the Egyptian attacks, the Royalists had expended much of their ammunition and urgently needed new supplies.

The French produced several schemes for flying plane-loads into Beihan or some other part of the Protectorate, whence they could be taken over the border by camel-train, and Peter de la Billière joined in the search for a suitably secluded LZ (landing zone). On 19 August, with his habitual optimism, he reported to Jim that he had found one, 'on a vast open plain of hard gravel . . . It is of course quite safe, and should be a roaring success.' But he was also irked by the lack of progress to date:

The French have been a lot of hot air so far and have not produced the goods as yet . . . It is more urgent than ever that Col. David [Stirling] or someone comes out here and we thrash the whole thing out and above all we get some hardware in here ASAP.

Two days later he wrote again, repeating his criticisms of the French effort and putting forward the local view of things:

As we see it, the aim of our organisation is to provide the Royalists with sufficient hardware to push the Egyptians out and to get themselves back into power. The French should be dropped, and we should set up our own organisation to deal with the whole supply.

In fact vital arms and ammunition had started coming in, and Peter's disparagement of the French was premature. By the end of October there were twenty-five French mercenaries in the Yemen, and four plane-loads of arms and ammunition from the French colony of Djibouti, on the African coast, had arrived in Aden for onward despatch to Beihan and beyond. Also, under the pretence of equipping a revolution in Africa, Jim Johnson, together with the French, had managed to bluff the Bulgarians into selling him a large quantity of weapons, and the problem of delivery was solved with the help of Jack Malloch, proprietor of Rhodesian Air Services, RAS, whose aircraft flew five plane-loads into Aden, the first on 11 August. The deal was organised by a former colleague of Stirling's, Bruce Mackenzie, the Finance Minister in Kenya and right-hand man of the President, Jomo Kenyatta. RAS's normal job was to ferry beef out of Rhodesia, but occasionally a plane would drop down under the radar, unload a cargo of weapons and then climb back on to its original flight-path. An assignment on 27 September included thirty bazookas, 150 bazooka rockets, twenty 81mm mortars, 200 boxes of mortar bombs, fifty MG34 machine guns and 15,000 rounds of 7.92mm ammunition. Jim was delighted to have diverted the communist weapons to the Royalist cause.

Reporting this latest delivery, Peter warned Johnny Cooper to watch out for a man called Abdurrahman Condé, 'a stinking rogue' who had just arrived and might 'quite possibly be working a double game'. The team in Aden were having nothing to do with him, for they felt sure he was reporting to the CIA – and their suspicions may well have been justified, for he was a man of many roles.

Born in Canada and christened Bruce, Condé spoke Arabic, and looked more like an Arab than a Canadian, being spare and wiry, with a long, thin face. He had served with the US 82nd Airborne Division in the Second World War, and in 1953 had settled in the Yemen, where he set up a business exporting postage stamps to collectors all over the world, now calling himself Abdurrahman. He then secured the job of postal adviser to the Government, becoming a Yemeni subject in 1958; but a year later he was expelled from the country, fleeing to the Lebanon and on to Sharjah, in the Gulf – only to return to the Yemen in 1962 and become the Imam's adviser on public relations. After the revolution, when the Imam took to his cave, Condé continued to represent him and carry out commissions in Jeddah. By then he was styling himself Brigadier General Abdurrahman Bruce Alphonso de Bourbon-Condé – a combination weird enough to make any British officer uneasy.

4

Beni Johnson

Tony Boyle did not yet know Jim Johnson, but when on 3 August 1963 the two met in a pub at Yarmouth on the Isle of Wight, they immediately hit it off. Then on 7 September, because the British Government still refused to take any action, and French attempts to import weapons and ammunition had proved a series of fiascos, a 'British plan of Assistance to Royalist Government in Yemen' was formulated. Entirely unofficial, in no way sanctioned by any authority, the scheme was sketched out at a private meeting in the Crescent Hotel, Aden, chaired by the Yemeni Foreign Minister, Ahmed al-Shami. Present were David Stirling, Peter de la Billière and Tony Boyle. According to the minutes, the aim was to set up a new organisation, 'formed on a military basis . . . to assist the legal government of the Yemen in every practical way to remove the invaders from their country'.

The most important task was 'to establish and maintain a regular supply of arms and ammunition to the Royalist forces in the field'. If possible, this was to be achieved by parachutage, or, failing that, by overland delivery from Saudi Arabia, the Yemen coast or Beihan. Another main aim was 'to deny the Hodeidah road to the Egyptians and assist the

Royalists in other acts of sabotage which may periodically seem desirable'.

Under Shami – a kind of non-playing captain – Jim Johnson was designated 'Force Commander and Treasurer', with Tony Boyle his staff officer (both to be based in London). Other members of the 'Strategic Planning Committee' were David Stirling and Brian Franks,[1] with Billy McLean designated 'Diplomatic and Political Adviser'. In Aden, Peter was to carry out 'liaison and operation of rat-line', providing a link between London and the field operators, and with the Sherif of Beihan. He was also to 'arrange reception and accommodation and onward movement for visitors'. In the Yemen, Johnny Cooper would be in command of the 'British Field Liaison Force', his remit being to arrange internal radio communications, receive supply drops and 'help the Royalists with skilled advice and practical assistance whenever it is requested, and in particular in the denial of the Hodeidah road to the Egyptians'.

The British operators would be mobile, with one lot based at Gara, in the Khowlan; one with the Imam at El Qara in the north-west; and others at Nihm (close to Sana'a), the Jauf (in the north-east) and Beihan in the south. Their chief functions would be to create a radio network between the various Royalist armies, to advise the Royalist leaders and to help train their fighters.

Requests for arms and equipment would be forwarded from the Yemen to Aden and on to London, where Boyle's formidable task would be 'to arrange to buy the arms and either collect them at a base within aircraft range of the DZ [dropping zone] or get them to a place . . . where the aircraft can collect them'. Plans for delivery were vague: if the cost of chartering aircraft became too great, and it appeared to be cheaper to buy an aircraft, 'this will be done'.

To maintain security, all radio and cable messages would be encoded, and cover names were assigned to principal players, places and objects. Some people retained their pseudonyms throughout their involvement in the operation: in letters and reports Jim Johnson was, and remained, Jay; David Smiley was always Grin, Johnny Cooper had already styled himself Abdullah bin Nasser, and Tony Boyle was Tea. But in cables, further obfuscations were used: Jay was known for a while as Elliott or Dundy, and Billy McLean became Whitney, Wagg or Turner. Dozens of simple transpositions camouflaged the names of weapons (*marrow* for 120mm mortar, *knife* for rifle, *dingbat* for rocket) and places (Britain became *Jutland*, Egypt *Coventry* and Cairo *Waterloo*) Furthermore, all these were changed from time to time.

When radio stations were established in Royalist areas, their call-signs were at first flowers or plants: Gara was *Bluebell*, Jauf *Rose* and Nuqub *Lilac,* while Aden was *Crocus* and the UK *Nettle*. Later these were changed to vegetables, and the UK turned into *Potato*, Aden into *Turnip* and Gara into *Sprout*.

And so *Beni* Johnson – Family Johnson – came into being. In London the organisation was greatly strengthened by the arrival of Fiona Fraser, the twenty-one-year-old daughter of Lord Lovat and niece of David Stirling, who joined Jim in a basement office in Sloane Street. She was recruited initially by a cousin, David McEwen, who rang her up and said that her Uncle David was looking for someone to work 'in Aden television'. She protested that she knew nothing whatsoever about Aden or television, but went along to the office nonetheless, and there was Jim, who told her what the job really was. Urged on by Uncle David, who said that it was the patriotic duty of the British to support the Royalists against the 'ghastly Egyptians', she agreed to join the firm, which had no name.

The office at 21 Sloane Street consisted of a single subterranean room, reached through a door and a passage that ran between Bally Shoes (known as 'Ballyhoo') and another shop. Up above, Stirling's film and television company, TIE, provided useful cover. The basement contained nothing except a couple of desks and chairs, and some filing cabinets, and the staff, at first, consisted solely of Jim and Fiona – until Tony Boyle joined them.

Although generous in the matter of pay for his soldiers, Jim was very careful (not to say mean) over office supplies. He prided himself on never needing to buy paperclips, having rescued a tin of them from the effects of his late Uncle Basil. These were used and reused over the years, and he saw no need to buy more, as incoming mail brought plenty of new ones. It was the same with carbon paper: if Fiona needed some, he would filch a sheet or two from his office in the City, where he said they had far too much. She herself was condemned to use a small portable typewriter, which she described as 'the bane of my life'.

Her work was largely administrative, and she ran things with great efficiency, arranging air tickets and visas for men going out to the Yemen via Aden or Saudi Arabia, and encoding and decoding radio messages. But sometimes she was despatched on unusual errands – as when Jim asked her to escort a suitcase full of plastic explosive round to his house in Sloane Avenue, or the occasion on which she took some Soviet detonators, brought back from the Yemen, to MI6, who were always asking for information from the interior. On that trip she travelled in a state of some anxiety, alarmed by her instructions to keep her two little packages well apart.

The procurement of visas for Saudi Arabia was no simple task, as the functionaries in the consular office always prevaricated and made difficulties when she went round with applications. She found she could get far better service from the establishment's butler, who, though Polish, was known as James. 'Leave those with me,' he would say when she appeared with a sheaf of forms and passports. 'I'll get them done for you' – and so he would. A different kind of hazard attended visits to Shami, who always tried to make Fiona sit down and listen to a recital of his own poems, first in Arabic, then in translation: rhapsodies about the moon, the starlit night, his visitor's eyes. Shami's own eyes (Fiona thought) were terribly sad, and she felt that all he really wanted was to go home. She was probably right, for the Foreign Minister was in an awkward position. He owed a deep debt of gratitude to Imam al-Badr, who had twice saved his life when he had offended the old Imam, al-Badr's father; but he had become unpopular with the Royalists inside the Yemen because he was not fighting with them, and at the same time had aroused the jealousy of fellow countrymen who saw how he had built up his position as an international negotiator. In spite of these pressures, he gave Jim a great deal of help.

A trip to Arabia evidently lifted Shami's spirits. 'He is in high good humour these days, and is a changed man,' Peter told Tony Boyle after the Foreign Minister had visited Aden:

Gone the benign old Foreign Minister without a mission; in, a rather ruthless and efficient organiser with a mountain of work and plenty of confidence. He had a continual stream of visitors when I was in his flat, and we had to do the KM [kini-mini, in SAS terms, any undercover activity] and disappear into the bedroom in a hurry.

Over the next eighteen months Fiona arranged the departures of numerous mercenaries, and sometimes she was amazed at the lack of experience shown by some of the recruits. One very small man had no idea how to travel from London to Heathrow: he did not even know how to use the Underground, and needed detailed instructions. And yet he could walk down a street and memorise the number-plate of every car he saw. To Fiona, this was 'an incredible thing to be able to do', but she saw that it was part of his training. She often felt that recruits were not given enough information about where they were going or what they would be required to do. 'They had no briefing about the politics of the situation in the Yemen, and most went out in ignorance.' Later, however, she realised that this deprivation was deliberate – a security measure to minimise the chance of information leaking out.

From time to time glamorous creatures blew into the office, among them the French mercenary and former Legionnaire Roger Faulques, who enjoyed talking to Fiona because she spoke French, and told wonderful stories of his time in Indochina. He smoked Gauloises continually, getting through sixty a day, until suddenly he stopped and revealed that his habit had been cured by a hypnotist in Paris.

A more frequent visitor was David Smiley, who always seemed to be on his way into the Yemen or out of it, and Fiona was fascinated by his tight-fistedness. Whenever he flew into Heathrow, she and Tony would have a bet about how long it would be before he asked for his taxi-fare from the airport. 'He'd haver about, and finally, just before leaving, he'd say: "By the way, I had to take a taxi from Heathrow, and I think the office ought to pay." Tony and I would catch each other's eyes, and usually I'd burst out laughing.'[2]

★　★　★

Many of the details in the 'British Plan' drafted in Aden merely confirmed what was already happening. Johnny, for one, was already at Gara. Supported by the two French mercenaries, he was rapidly increasing his score of enemy victims. By then his staff included one first lieutenant and one soldier from the Yemeni Army, 'plus a gang of criminals now nine strong who will do anything for money'.

An amnesty called by the Republicans in August 1963 had had little effect. The Egyptians had retreated from their FDLs (forward defence locations) towards Sana'a, but the Royalists had carried on attacking them regardless. A more sinister development was that Sheikh Nagi al-Ghadr – head of the Bakil federation of tribes, and one of the few Royalist commanders who did *not* belong to the Hamid ud Din family – had been approached by the Egyptians asking him to become President of the entire country: they bribed him with 800,000 MTDs and 2,000 rifles to switch his men to the Republican side. 'Nagi is brave and clever,' Johnny reported, 'but he can be dangerous to our cause.' The flirtation evidently did not last long, for a month later Ghadr was up to his usual tricks, ambushing two Egyptian convoys, with murderous results.

Johnny saw that the relationship between Ghadr and Prince Abdullah was a close one: that 'of an older man over a younger, keener perhaps, but still strong soldier'. Their personal friendship derived from fighting alongside each other, and their admiration was mutual. Johnny thought that Abdullah was slightly wary of Ghadr because of his dealings with the Egyptians; but since the Prince could not deal with the Egyptians himself, he relied on Ghadr for contact with the enemy.

Peter de la Billière was much cheered by a visit from David Stirling. 'It is the first time I have met him,' he told Johnny, 'and I must say he is a most exhilarating man and one would do anything for him.' Peter had been equally pleased to meet Tony Boyle, and praised his gift for diplomacy: 'He has a most enviable line of patter.' But Peter was nervous about the possibility that his own role might come into the open. 'It is vital that no-one finds out that I am out here,' he told Johnny, 'as there is a security leak, but it does not as yet involve me, so I am free to carry on operating.'

The last [Rhodesian] aircraft arrived on 10/9 had 600 Mausers and 100,000 rounds of ammo. Inevitably this aircraft was bubbled [noticed] by the highest authority, and they are not too pleased. However this may be a blessing in disguise as it will force the hand as far as parachuting goes. This bubble has not improved this end as you can well imagine – hence our concentration on security.

Other news was that the BFLF had recruited a friend of his, Jack Miller, in London – he was not only a skilled radio operator, but also a spare-time medic and a military parachutist.

Well Johnny [the letter concluded] we all feel very proud of 'our man on the spot', and I certainly am delighted to have the privilege of being part of your rear link. I only hope that we can get the support you deserve organised as soon as possible.

With or without support, Johnny was flourishing. On 12 September he told Tony that fighting had broken out near Jihannah, a town deep in the central mountains, garrisoned by the Egyptians and connected with Sana'a by a long, winding, single-track dirt road. 'Our mining has got the Wogs angry with the tribes south of the Jihannah–Sana'a road,' he wrote:

> I am pushing Abdullah to keep up these pinpricks. The mines and siasi [intelligence-gathering][9] work have been handed over to me, or should I say I have started it off, and Abdullah is only too happy to let me run the show, so all success down to Brits and French. I feel we are doing our share, it is full time, what with doctor work as well.

On 24 September he was even more ebullient. 'Our mining/sabotage efforts have now expanded to alarming proportions!' he told Jim:

> Confirmed NOW 32 [Egyptians] killed, 18 wounded, 4 vehicles destroyed, one road demolished . . . It takes [them] two days to clear the road Sana'a–Jihannah using two tanks with prong-type diggers out front.

A few days later he wrote again, to say: 'Mining has thrown both the Wogs and the Repubs into complete confusion. They simply have no idea what to do.'

On the same day, however, in another long missive he gave vent to various vexations: he had been sending out frequent reports, but in the past forty-seven days only one letter had reached him. He was so dissatisfied with the lack of information that he threatened to walk out to Beihan, 'to find out what the British position is'.

Not knowing that his own letters were failing to get through, Peter sought to encourage him:

How's yourself? No doubt well and causing chaos as usual. Your last letters were a tonic, especially the accounts of the mining . . . Your info is being used as ammunition to convince the right people that there should be more official help, and so you can see it may well be the key to final victory.

Even though such messages were designed mainly to keep up Johnny's morale, they did not exaggerate the importance of his information, for at that stage he was the only Briton in the whole of the Yemen with a front-line view of the war. GCHQ (Government Communications Headquarters, the listening station at Cheltenham), was able to glean some intelligence about Nasser's order of battle from intercepts of radio messages, because the Egyptians were still using technology based on the wartime German Enigma machine, which they believed to be perfectly secure. But MI6, the Secret Intelligence Service, though well established in Aden and the Protectorate, where its agents were officially 'Political Officers', had nobody inside the Yemen, and no source of intelligence from the interior except the sporadic reports of the itinerant McLean and Smiley.[3] Nor, when they did fortuitously acquire a valuable piece of kit, did they know what to do with it. When Johnny once sent a captured Soviet radio to the SIS in Aden for evaluation, he was dismayed to have it returned to him, months later, bearing a note: 'Hoping that this will be of great use to you.'[4]

At the end of March 1963 Sir Dick White, head of the SIS, had told Rab Butler, the new Foreign Secretary, that even if men of the right training and calibre became available, it would take six months before they could be effectively deployed up country, 'and even then they might not have the required talent for the operation'.[5] But White did at least allow the SIS officers in Aden to help the mercenaries by giving them information and the use of their facilities. The MI6 men were known to members of the BFLF as 'the Friends'.

Johnny eventually got his mail on 28 September, after 'a great hold-up' in Beihan. Some of the correspondence was six weeks old, but he responded with immense taped messages to Tony and Jim, ending one:

> All for now. But you have given me much to do. Not that I am idle: last day off seems months ago, but being alone one must work. I talk too much, Jim, but only because I speak Arabic all day long, bad Arabic at that! Yours aye, Johnny.

The arrival of outside news seemed to revive his spirits, and within a week he was reporting that, in accord with the amnesty agreement made in August, the Egyptians were withdrawing to Sana'a in trucks, helicopters and transport aircraft, and that El Argoub, their strongest outpost in the Khowlan, was 'heavily mined'; also that he had spent five days doing medical work. One morning he walked out to the nearest front line, only about one and a half hours' trek from the capital, and looked down on the only route by which Egyptian tanks might seek to approach and attack the Second National Army's forward defences. 'The wadi is now well mined, with large US anti-tank mines, twenty-four in number,' he reported, 'and I can't see the Wogs catching us napping. Also, the Sheikh here, Abdullah bin Ali, Paramount Sheikh of the Beni Balool tribe, is a fine chap, very anti-Wog!'

House of [Republican] Sheikh Ali bin Hassan al Hamza blown up by mine ploy . . . Sheikh in Sana'a but house demolished, plus all animals, camels etc. Details to follow, but fear wife killed, this unfortunate, but whole area against this fellow . . . The home front is throbbing with rumour and counter-rumour of Wogs leaving for good.

At 1200 on 9 September another mine went off close to Sana'a. Ten troop carriers fully loaded with Egyptians had just set off for Jihannah when the sixth vehicle in the convoy set the mine off under its rear wheels. Like all the Russian vehicles, the truck had a wooden floor, which gave no protection from the blast, and nine Egyptians were killed and at least nine more wounded.

In spite of such losses, Egyptian morale seems to have been moderately good at that stage of the campaign. Units of the Expeditionary Force came and went regularly, and the first troops, on returning home, were greeted as conquerors: articles in the Cairo newspapers described how the country's heroic soldiers were supporting the Yemeni revolution and winning the war – but imaginative propaganda was always high on Nasser's agenda.

Early in August 1963 Tony Boyle had returned to London for a medical board, at which he was downgraded to A2 G1, and so effectively invalided out of the services. Although he did not formally retire from the RAF for another three months, he began working with Jim in the Sloane Street office on 1 October and quickly became the indispensable second-in-command of the British Field Liaison Force, not only briefing the men who went out to the Yemen and arranging their journeys, but also working to establish radio communication with the mountain bases. Within a week of his joining, Stirling wrote to Johnny Cooper to say that 'We are camouflaging his 'kini mini' activities with a respectable front as a representative of TIE Ltd, and he is becoming quite a dab hand already on our television activities!' Over the next four years Tony travelled indefatigably, visiting Israel more than a dozen times, making numerous visits to Saudi Arabia and several to Aden, besides going into the Yemen on four occasions.

Peter de la Billière took over from him as the BFLF's man in Aden, and soon wrote to Boyle, 'Am finding that pressure has increased considerably since you left and am in danger of having to give up the army altogether as it gets in the way.'

By now Peter was getting so many letters from Fiona that people began to assume she was his girlfriend. Yet always on his mind was the risk that his involvement in the covert campaign would be discovered, and he told Boyle, 'I feel the less I know about what you are up to in London, unless it concerns me, the better.' Once Fiona spent a sleepless night, after she had somehow forgotten to encode a message and sent it to him in clear. When she confessed to Jim in the morning, he, with his usual urbanity, just said, 'Oh well – don't worry – it's one signal in a million, and the chances are no one will notice it.' Nevertheless, she wrote a letter of abject apology to Peter, saying, 'I can't get over the horror of sending you that cable ... Do please forgive me.' He forgave her – but the memory of her mistake, which could have brought Peter's army career to a premature end, still torments her almost fifty years later.

As London reported that recruitment was going well, and more mercenaries came through Aden, the pressure on Peter increased still further, and he asked if the office could find 'some form of relief'. 'By the way,' he added, 'my grand-mother is dying and it is possible I may come home for a week to see her in a month or so.'

Remembering the ruse by which they had extricated Johnny Cooper from Muscat, London suspected that this last statement was a joke. 'I'm so sorry to hear about your grand-mother,' Tony wrote. 'Is she really ill, or dying like John's mother was?' To which Peter replied indignantly: 'Is my grand-mother really dying, indeed? In fact, believe it or not, she is. I can see you have gone past the stage where you will ever be able to think straight and honest again!'

Such was the demand for weapons from the interior that he conceived the grandiose idea of bringing in a whole ship-load. 'I don't see why it should not work,' he wrote in a letter to London. 'We must watch that they do not put too much on the first load. I think 100 tons would be enough to start with.' He suggested that the vessel should be a dhow, which could be beached at high tide, unloaded and floated off at the next tide. The timing would have to coincide with a high tide at about 1800 hours, so that the ship could come in as dark was falling and be away before dawn. He reported that Whiskers, the Sherif, was quite happy about the security side, but he insisted that there must be a European on board the boat, and that the arrival and reception must be carefully planned 'to avoid a cock-up'. This ambitious plan came to fruition in November, when a French ship landed some 75 tons of military stores.

One curious feature of the civil war was that, for much of the Yemeni population, life went on as usual. In the narrow streets of Sana'a people walked around normally among the high tower-houses elegantly façaded with white-framed windows – of great fascination to architects and historians – and in the mountains the tribesmen continued to cultivate their crops and orchards. Newly arrived mercenaries were often astonished by the fertility of a land that appeared at first sight to consist of nothing but jagged rock mountains with precipitous flanks or, in the east, deserts of sand and gravel.

On the sides of the hills, over the centuries, people had laboured to build thousands of walled terraces, piling stone on stone to enclose strips of fertile ground, some only a foot or two wide, in which they were growing corn, vegetables and fruit. Wadis watered by streams were also productive, and there was an abundance of grapes: dried raisins and almonds were often on sale in the villages. The one major difference in the life of Royalist areas was that many people had forsaken their mountain villages, for fear of being bombed, and had taken to living in caves. Others cooked and slept in their houses at night, but before first light moved out with their animals and spent the day in caves or under rock overhangs, well away from their normal habitations.

In the Khowlan Johnny Cooper was, as usual, in pugnacious form, and when not plotting to kill or maim the opposition, he was working hard as an amateur doctor. In his diary he noted that during the period from 21 September to 21 October he saw 1,059 patients, administering 238 injections and treating nine cases of VD – which brought his total for the past two months to 1,859 patients and 388 injections.

On fine days, from his vantage-point 10,000 feet above sea-level, which he called 'a perfect grandstand', he could enjoy 'a complete panorama of the front line', with a view over Sana'a to the north-west and El Argoub to the east. But glorious landscapes were not everything. Looking ahead, he asked Peter de la Billière if he could somehow send 'six bottles of any good brandy, VO, not Martell, and any Christmas goodies you can pick up' – for even he was feeling the strain. 'I keep on having to borrow money,' he wrote, 'and it's not a nice thing, because they keep coming and asking, "Well, has your money arrived?"'

I do need it for paying these crooks, and you know what type they're like. They certainly demand the money before the event. In fact I don't pay them the full amount before: I give them about a third, jingle the remaining two-thirds in front of their eyes and say, 'Right – when your cookie goes off and you return, you get the balance.'

Mining – I am having difficulty now in getting mines on the Jihannah–Sana'a road because of the guarding. Every morning it is swept now by foot parties before any transport uses it. It is completely unused at night now, so we have slowed things down there. To change tactics, I am now going to lay anti-personnel mines on the road to have a crack at the people clearing the anti-tank mines.

In this he was so successful that soon Republican drivers refused to use the road at all, and the Egyptians were obliged to supply the large garrison in Jihannah with helicopters, which flew high in transit to avoid small-arms fire and then descended in rapid spirals as they reached their destination. The necessity for making four flights a day put a useful strain on the aircraft, their pilots and the fuel supply.

On 30 October 1963 another BFLF recruit arrived in

Aden to man the radio links, up into the interior and back to London. This was Rupert France, a large and ebullient bachelor known as 'Franco', who proved one of the organisation's most valuable and long-lasting members. After distinguished wartime service with the Special Boat Service and the Greek Sacred Squadron, he had become a signals officer with 21 SAS, and then a contract officer in the Muscat Regiment. Now he was middle-aged and portly, with a neatly trimmed moustache and receding hair, much liked, but mildly mocked for his fastidious habits. He was addicted to dietary supplements (black molasses being a favourite), and maintained a daily routine of physical jerks, during which he stood thrusting his stomach hard against the wall of a passage, in the belief that it kept his muscles in trim. One colleague described him as 'very soft-spoken and considerate – a textbook gentleman, always spotlessly turned out', and to another he was 'very like Jim, in that, when something went wrong, he wouldn't blame anyone. He'd just say, "OK. How do we get out of this?"[6] He was also an inveterate gambler, and taught another of the mercenaries, David Bailey, his allegedly infallible system for winning at roulette.

For a while Rupert stayed in Aden, reinforced by Major Stan Symons of the Royal Corps of Signals, a skilled radio ham who was on a regular posting to the colony, working in the Middle East Command headquarters. Soon, at de la Billière's invitation, Stan became a covert and much-valued member of the BFLF. The radios of those days were bulky and delicate, and long camel journeys often left them in need of repair, so there was always work to be done getting spare parts and replacements, and fitting them into place. One of Stan's first tasks was to visit Israel, to work out the signals procedures for the parachute-drops that Tony Boyle was planning – when (or if) they began. He quickly discovered that he needed two passports, one for Israel and one for the Arab countries, as the Arabs would not admit people with any stamp of Israel in their documents.[7]

Stan was already friends with another radio ham, David Harrington, who was living with his wife in a flat in Aden; but Harrington soon came to suspect that Stan was involved in more than amateur radio traffic: when he went into his room one day, he found him engrossed in deciphering a message with a one-time code pad. Then Harrington himself was drawn into the network, first allowing Rupert France to use his equipment, then taking him in as a lodger in the flat.

As always, MI6 agents were eager to glean information about what was happening upcountry in the Yemen, and James Nash, one of the Political Officers, maintained close liaison with Peter. On 1 November Peter wrote to Johnny:

As you know I have been passing tit-bits on to Radcliffe [code name for John de Silva, the MI6 Station Chief], who I gather has met you in your previous occupation. He has asked me to see if I can get him an ORBAT of gyppos and Republicans, if possible with complete establishments and unit numbers etc . . . Can you help? Keep up the bangs, from the outside the Egyptians sound most unhappy.

In England Jim had been busy recruiting. 'This letter is to introduce you to David Bailey and Cyril Weavers,' Tony Boyle told Johnny on 4 November 1963. Weavers, described as 'a communications expert', was indeed a technical wizard, but also (in the view of one colleague) 'a bit of a simple soul' and rather disorganised – an amiable fellow, but not a warrior.

Now thirty-five, and formerly a signals sergeant in the SAS, he took so much equipment with him on the aircraft to Aden that his extra baggage cost £165 – but in due course he proved invaluable at establishing a reliable radio network linking the Yemeni commanders with each other and with Aden.

Bailey, a former National Service officer with the Royal Sussex Regiment, who had had some grounding in demolition work, was, at that time, the only British mercenary *not* to have served with Special Forces, and over the next three years – most of which he spent living in caves – he conceived enormous admiration for the reticence of his companions, with whom he was often at very close quarters. Never once did any of them speak of their SAS background.

On the Comet he found himself placed next to Weavers, who told him that if it turned out he was not the person he claimed to be, he would be eliminated. This friendly greeting made Bailey nervous, and he realised belatedly that he should not have told his mother where he was going. He therefore went to the back of the plane, wrote a note to his parents asking them not to let anyone know what he was doing, and put it in an envelope which he gave to one of the air-hostesses. 'The organisation must have had someone on the plane watching us,' he recalled years later, 'because they took the envelope away – but luckily the girl had the gumption to pass the message anyway.'[8]

With him and Weavers came the dark and bespectacled Chris Sharma (from Birmingham, of Anglo-Indian descent), who had been hoping to win a place at Birmingham University, and who now called himself 'Mansoor'. He was accompanied by Liam McSweeney (always known as 'Mac'), a heavily moustached, forty-year-old bachelor, also from Birmingham, who had served for five years in 23 SAS and in civilian life had wrestled professionally under the name Milo the Greek.

For dealing with close encounters, Mac had a simple formula: 'Don't take out a gun unless you're going to use it, and if you do take it out, use it. Don't talk.'

Some of the volunteers objected to being called 'mercenaries'. A true mercenary, they said, was someone who was paid to fight. Their role was specifically *not* to fight, but to advise the Yemeni commanders on tactics and help train their men. All the same, they had to admit that they were being paid to take part in a war, and that they were doing it for the money. Besides, in the Yemen they went about armed, and it was clear that if – or when – they got into difficulties, they would fight as ferociously as anyone.

Some of them may have been fired by the patriotic sentiments that drove Jim to form his private army, and some just saw the experience as a big adventure. But money was also certainly a strong incentive. At the start of the operation Jim began making payments to individuals out of his own account at the Pont Street branch of the National Provincial Bank; but when the tempo increased, with the arrival of a Saudi cheque for £10,000 at the end of October 1963, he opened a No. 2 Account, still in his own name. In April 1965, to cover his involvement, he opened another new account in the name of Rally Films, and then at the start of January 1966 he changed the ficititious firm's title to Foster Productions, which, for cover, moved briskly from one address to another: from Sloane Street to Montpelier Street (opposite Harrods) to North Audley Street, to yet another basement in Earls Court.

To part-time soldiers the rates of pay seemed astronomical. At the outset Johnny Cooper received £400 a month, lesser operators £300 or £250 (worth about £5,000, £3,500 and £2,900 by the standards of 2011), with most of the money going straight into accounts that Jim had opened for them at the Guarantee Trust of Jersey, a merchant bank in the Channel Islands. Johnny was also getting £200 a month 'expenses', for paying what he called his *siasi*, his little gang of three or four tribesmen whom he trained to gather information about the *adoo* – the enemy. Some of the money went on 'kini-mini' – another SAS expression (pronounced 'keeny-meeny'), which could cover anything from bribery to rewards for underhand services rendered. As the mercenary operation expanded, the expense rapidly increased: by June 1966, with twenty-two men on the payroll, the monthly wage-bill came to nearly £8,000 (£100,000 in today's terms).

The source of funds was Saudi Arabia. While things were going well, a cheque for several thousand pounds from Jeddah arrived in London every month, whereupon the BFLF office allocated pay to the mercenaries' accounts; but whenever Saudi enthusiasm cooled, Jim had to lobby repeatedly for support to be continued or increased, and he flew to Jeddah or Riyadh time and again in his attempts to convince the Saudi rulers that they were getting value for money.

The Saudis were spending fortunes. Not only were they paying the British and French mercenaries' wages; they were also pouring gold sovereigns and Maria Theresa silver dollars into the Yemen, from north and south, so that the princes could pay their tribesmen and hand out bribes on a lavish scale. The silver dollars were handsome great coins, nearly 2 inches in diameter, and were used as everyday currency, the precise value of a particular coin being determined by how much or how little the bosom of the Empress had been worn down by use.[10] More highly prized were the sovereigns, bearing the date 1915 and the effigy of King George V, all struck at the mint in Beirut. They arrived in Beihan or Jizan packed in small, extremely heavy strong wooden boxes, for loading into camel saddlebags and onward distribution upcountry.[11] Whenever the money looked like drying up, and it seemed that whole tribes might defect to the opposition, the Royalist leaders appealed to the mercenaries, and the mercenaries sent frantic calls to Aden, for onward transmission to London, pleading for the flow to be restored.

Towards the end of November 1963 Franco (Rupert France) moved from Aden to a house at Nuqub that Whiskers had allocated for use by the mercenaries, and there he discreetly operated the hub of the new radio network. News of enemy casualties kept coming from deserters — as on 23 November, when Johnny reported that 200 Egyptians had been killed at Thilapa, that Colonel Mohamed Hartram, Commander of the 3rd Infantry Battalion, had died on the 10th, that on the 12th Colonel Mohamed Said, one of the Egyptian tank commanders, had been killed, and that on the 20th Captain Mohamed Alakwarth had been seriously injured near Sana'a.

In Aden, Peter de la Billière was in chirpy form. 'Well, you old rooster, how's your mud hut?' he enquired of Franco. 'Continue with your press-ups to avoid obesity.'

Franco himself was cheerful. 'Life seems to have settled not unreasonably here,' he told Jim:

My link to Stan [in Aden] has never failed yet (*inshallah*) . . . As we are not issued with arms until we leave here, there is a daily stream of MK5 rifle and revolver vendors, all locals and all terribly friendly (we hope) . . . but at least we don't have to rely on knives, forks and spoons to defend ourselves.

I have an absolutely gorgeous .25, brand-new STAR revolverette, my dear! In fact it's so fucking small everyone asks me whether it will fit in my handbag! Actually a most convenient house defence weapon . . . Like most of us I had my hair cropped, and I'm bloody certain I shall be bald for ever more.

I have decided to go into business after this: I intend manufacturing and placing on the market an aphrodisiac called Ever Hard. The advertising slogan will be, 'It takes the wrinkle out of your winkle'. Should make a fortune. How about getting some capital for it?

Tony Boyle, meanwhile, had returned from London to Aden, his old stamping ground, on a special mission. 'Tony has so far avoided arrest and is in good form,' Peter reported. The Royalist commanders had been demanding with increasing vehemence that arms and ammunition should be parachuted in to them, and Tony's practical experience of flying and aircraft management made him the man best qualified to plan any such operation. His particular task on this, his first journey into the Yemen, was to make his way into the Khowlan and check an area that Johnny Cooper had identified as a possible DZ.

Having flown to Beihan on 28 November, he was driven to Nuqub, where he found Rupert France, Cyril Weavers, Chris Sharma, David Bailey, 'Mac' McSweeney and David Walter, together with a Frenchman known as Freddy, 'all in good health and high morale', gathered in the mud house that the Sherif had lent the organisation.

'Rupert is well and has got this huge madhouse which is his headquarters into very good shape,' Tony reported to Aden:

Some of the messages he has sent have been a little odd, because J.C. [Johnny Cooper] tells his French operator to translate it into French, then it is encoded in a French code, then transmitted, decoded, translated, encoded, transmitted and finally decoded. The miracle is that we can understand it at all.

After a lunch of pancakes, meat and onions he allocated his companions tasks as follows:

Rupert and Chris Sharma to stay in Nuqub and man the base radio.
David Bailey and Cyril Weavers to join Johnny Cooper in the Khowlan.
David Walter to join Jack Miller in the Jauf.

So the first real wave of mercenaries set off for the hinterland. Because word had come in that the Egyptians were trying to ambush an arms caravan on its way to the interior, Tony and his party made one false start, driving far out into the desert to the east, and, after three days, returning to Nuqub, where they heard that a man had just tried to murder Johnny in return for a Republican bribe of 1,000 MTDs. Another message came up from Peter, confirming that cigarettes dropped by an Egyptian aircraft were booby-trapped, and that one had exploded in an ashtray.

As Tony's party was preparing to start again, a message came in from Johnny saying, 'Crisis rpt crisis. If Abdullah money/arms do not arrive in seven days at the Khowlan 3,000 men will desert from Royalists.' Galvanised by this *cri de coeur,* a large camel-caravan set off on what turned out to be a five-day trek. Considering that Tony had been working in a London office, and had never had any SAS-type training, he withstood the rigours of the march extraordinarily well, and in his diary left a vivid account of moving through enemy-held territory at night.

Set off at 10 a.m. in convoy of twenty camels. Ride across a sand desert, stop for 1½ hours at three, then ride and walk until sunset (5.30) for the Bedou to pray, a few miles from Egyptian-occupied Marib.[12] We have a quick meal, then set off to ride through the night.

We have to ride in silence, without cigarettes. Become tired, irritable, uncomfortable, every slip of the camel painful, going up and down over endless enormous sand-dunes. Camels plod slowly up each one, then slide down the steep descent from the crest.

Lights appear ahead. Then, looming even blacker than the black horizon, a camel moving fast towards us. We stop. The leader goes to meet the newcomer – one of the spies warning us of Egyptians right ahead, waiting for us in the wadi we are entering. We canter back, tension mounting. We try the next wadi at a trot – all clear.

The lights of Marib appear again ahead, not many and not clustered. Then we are among them. A shout close on the right, answered by others all round us. The glow of a cigarette. My neighbour whispers they are Egyptian guards, shouting to one another to stop themselves being frightened in the dark.

Caravan strings out. In front of me a camel falls and rolls descending a steep dune. Mine narrowly misses it in the dark. The Bedouin riders' laughs and curses crank up the tension, then quickly fade in the immensity of our universe, a myriad bright stars captured for eternity in an immeasurable dome of black velvet, in which we alone are moving.

We are through the lines now. I slip off my camel, preferring to run rather than endure the bone-shuddering jolts of the beast's trot. Angrily, the caravan leader tells me to mount again, as my big footprints in the sand will tell the Egyptians that a European has passed this way, and they may take reprisals on the local tribes. Mounted again I almost wish the Egyptians would capture me, to halt the pain of this ride.

Dozing sometimes, then jerking awake as I start slipping from the saddle. What slaves we are to sleep: reality becoming fantasy, camels appearing as prehistoric ships. The bowl of the horizon seems sometimes tiny and enclosing. We progress towards it, yet it never gets any nearer. Dunes become houses, mansions, castles, palaces. As we move into the hills west of Marib stunted trees look like monsters swaying in the cold night desert wind.

At last, as it must, night ends. At our back the sky lightens and the world around us starts to come back into normal focus. In the cold light my companions are grey and drawn, with cloths wrapped round their heads to keep out the wind. Then sharply the sun lunges above the foothills behind us and dispels the strange atmosphere of cold tension and hallucination. We smoke desultorily. One of the Bedouin starts to sing, a quavering falsetto of infinite poignancy. At last we find a wadi, off the main dried river-bed we followed until now, and lead our camels into shelter.

Pressing on into the mountains, they met some Bedouin who showed them two mines marked with Cyrillic lettering. Two others had exploded, one killing a camel, the other a hyena coming to eat its corpse. In the afternoon members of the local tribe, the Beni Dhabian, tried to charge them money for passing through their area. The argument raged for hours, and the party was virtually held hostage until the confrontation ended peaceably in the evening, when two families of the tribe arrived with two goats, which yielded dinner for them all.

Early on the morning of 9 December they were joined by Sheikh Nagi al-Ghadr – 'an impressive man, kind, firm, and strong', who was emphatic about the need for parachuting, but had obviously ceased hoping for it. 'Why did Johnny have to blab about it before we had finalised the arrangements?' Tony wondered:

I'm still uncertain of Nagi's loyalties. He is besieged by people wanting to join the Royalists and so receive rifles, ammunition and money he has not got. Abdullah bin Hassan finds he has been given only 50,000 rounds of rifle ammunition of the half-million he was promised by Feisal. It has no doubt been eaten away at every stage of the journey from Saudi Arabia.

That night they reached Musainah, where they spent the night in the Sheikh's house, in:

an absolutely bare room which was full of people squatting down watching our every move out of pure curiosity. Most had probably never seen Europeans before, and several pulled up my trouser leg to see if I was the same colour under the clothes.[13]

On the 10th[14] – 'after a feast: eggs for breakfast!' – they rode mules along a wadi with flowing water, then up a mountain into a fertile plain and to the village of Gara, many of whose houses had been smashed to rubble by bombs. Five minutes further on they came to Johnny's stone hut, and found the occupant 'fit, thin and slightly overwrought'. Not only had two people recently sworn to kill him, but his radio shack had been attacked by five men with rifle-fire; no one had been hurt, the radios were undamaged and four men had been caught, but one had escaped to Sana'a.

On the 11th Tony was up at 7 a.m. for a breakfast of eggs, after which he went to the radio hut to send messages, getting good reception. Then he climbed to the point that Johnny had christened 'Grandstand', from which there was a phenomenal view down to Jihannah in the south-east and, in the other direction, to a hill overlooking Sana'a. As for the DZ – the object of his visit – this, he thought, seemed 'absolutely ideal'. The land was ploughed, and there were 3 miles of open ground on either side, with 'any amount of undershoot and five kilometres of overshoot'. He returned to Gara in time to hear Johnny debrief his *mullaizim*, or lieutenant, who garnered the information from spies and passed it on.

After a long talk, he concluded that Johnny was doing a magnificent job. Information was flowing in all the time; mines were being issued for laying and exploding daily – Tony heard one go off in the distance with a dull thud at 11 p.m. one evening. Next day he set out on the return journey, and in three hours reached Abdullah bin Hassan's house at Musainah. When the Prince arrived, he had:

crowds of people around him trying to get his attention and give him little notes. Both his hands were stuffed with them and he was clenching an armful against his chest. We were all called to an upper room at about 4 p.m. and we talked for seven and a half hours.

Tony returned to London via Aden, where the influx of mercenaries was stretching Peter to the limit. Having just sent Johnny 200 pounds of explosives, Peter told him: 'I have been worked off my feet with all these operators passing through. Although they are old friends of mine, I have seldom been so glad to see the departure of them ... My god, I wish I had half your patience.'

The new operators were placed under Johnny's command, to be organised as he saw fit. The first priority (in Peter's view) was to establish radio links between the various armies, so that Johnny could advise the commanders and set up some coordination in the field. The second essential was to open a rear link to Jim in London, so that intelligence information and physical requirements could be passed back rapidly. The new men were assigned individual roles. David Bailey was to become Johnny's relief adviser, and Cyril Weavers the radio operator at his base area. Chris Sharma was designated Johnny's radio mechanic and personal operator, and Mac McSweeney was to go to the Imam as operator and adviser.[15]

At Gara, David and Cyril found Johnny in 'very lively' form, and their posting turned out to be a typical mercenary station: three or four Brits living in the most primitive conditions, housed in a cave alive with fleas and scorpions, with minimal cooking facilities – only a primus stove or a small wood fire – and nowhere to wash, no form of entertainment, under intermittent air attack and continuously pestered by the noisy arrival of tribesmen coming to call on the local commander.

To David Bailey these privations meant nothing. For him the whole campaign turned out to be 'enormous fun, and a tremendous adventure', which he enjoyed so much that, after going on leave every six months, he kept returning. He soon got used to the dirt, the boring food, the fleas and scorpions, and was not put off by the frequent bombing and strafing – although he did once find it a strain to sit out an air-raid with a lot of tribesmen perched on boxes of ammunition as the Egyptians targeted the entrance to their cave.

In particular, he found it an adventure to be led by Jim Johnson, for whom he conceived the highest regard. Even though Jim made only one short tour of the Yemen, the warmth of his personality and the strength of his moral support could be felt 4,000 miles from Sloane Street. David was also very pleased to have £200 a month going into his account in Jersey: the fact that he had £1,200 to spend every time he went home made him popular in London society – he once took Fiona Fraser out to the Saddle Room, Britain's first discotheque, in the King's Road, where (she remembered) he 'threw money about' and she cautioned him for being so spendthrift.

He came to love being with the Bedouin and riding their male camels. He quickly mastered the essential art of wiping his own backside with a stone held in his left hand, never offering his left hand to an Arab and never displaying the soles of his feet. He also learnt the ways of the tribesmen, who, if the local prince failed to hand out gold that had arrived from Saudi Arabia, tended to make their displeasure known. One evening a man appeared and said, 'Tonight we are going to shoot. Do not worry – we will not be shooting at you. Nor will we shoot *into* the Prince's cave: just over the top, to make sure he understands that we want to be paid.'

Among the tribesmen David always felt safe. Once, while he was on his travels with a guide, a Republican patrol came into the village, so his companions covered him with rugs and built a shelter of twigs over him. When the opposition appeared, his friends pointed to the bundle dimly visible on the floor in the corner and said, 'Don't go near him. He's dying.' 'They could have made 40,000 MTDs on the spot by handing me over,' he recalled, 'but they wouldn't give me away.'

Eight thousand feet up in the mountains, the extremes of climate were severe. During the day the sun was usually scorching, but at night the temperature plummeted. In summer, if the mercenaries were on the move, they generally wore some form of Arab dress; but if they were at home on their own station, a pair of shorts was all they needed. In hot weather the tribesmen wore *futas* and drab-coloured blouses; but in the winter they decked themselves out in a kaleidoscopic variety of garments, as the journalist Scott Gibbons reported:

The first man . . . wore a Royal Canadian Air Force officer's jacket, complete with wings and medals. He had bare feet. Another wore a relic of the Gay Twenties – a woman's thin black evening coat with a tattered fur collar. There were long Edwardian-style coats and double-breasted European businessmen's jackets. There were waistcoats of every description, plain, embroidered, silver-buttoned. Most of the men went barefoot, but some of them wore suede desert boots, carpet bedroom slippers, tennis plimsolls or plastic beach sandals.[16]

David Bailey's main regret was that the Sam 70 shoulder-held anti-aircraft weapon had not been invented, and the Royalists had no effective defence against the MiGs, Yaks and Ilyushins. 'If we'd had anything like that, we could have done some damage,' he recalled. 'We did fire at them with machine guns: as a Yak pulled out of an attack, we'd emerge from hiding and have a go – but it was incredibly difficult to score a hit.' An Il–28 was an even more unpleasant proposition, because it had a rear-gunner ensconced in the tail.[17]

5

Digging In

The main contingent of French mercenaries, together with some Belgians, designated the 'Groupe Expert Voluntaire', or GEV, had established itself at Khanjar, in the Jauf, a semi-desert region of gravel, sand and scrub dotted with colossal boulders, between the eastern foot of the central mountain massif and the edge of the great desert, the Rub' al-Khali – the Empty Quarter. The importance of the area lay in the fact that it controlled the eastern road from Najran and the Saudi frontier in the north to Marib, Hazm and Harib, in the south-east, and it had already been fiercely fought over.

At Khanjar seventeen French and Belgians had set up a training camp, and their number including an armourer capable of repairing captured Egyptian, Russian and Czech weapons: mortars, machine guns, tommy guns and bazookas. The instructors were living in caves, or tents tucked away among the colossal boulders that rose out of the sand and marked the beginning of the mountains. Across the mouths of the caves the mercenaries had built rock walls to protect themselves from blast – a very necessary precaution, as they were under daily air-attack.

The training unit was under the command of the

redoubtable, self-styled Colonel Bob Denard – a former *gendarme,* as rough and tough a mercenary as France ever produced[1] – whose headquarters and radio station were tucked away in a long cave running back from an entrance protected by sandbags and scarred by the impact of enemy rockets. His main aim was to train tribesmen in the use of heavy weapons – mortars, and particularly 57mm and 75mm recoilless rifles (the Royalists' best weapons, which were effective against the Egyptian tanks) – but every morning a semi-formal parade was held, with barefoot recruits marching up and down the sand in columns three abreast and going through the rudiments of arms-drill with their ancient rifles. In the opinion of David Smiley, who visited them, the French might have been better employed if attached individually to various Royalist units, as the British mercenaries were.[2]

At any one time there were some 450 men around the site, but they were either undisciplined old hands or recruits who came in for a day or two out of curiosity and then left, having learnt nothing. Denard's reports showed that his unit was having a difficult time, not least because the camp came under persistent air-attack and the trainees kept running away. On the last day of October 1963 an Ilyushin appeared at about nine o'clock and dropped sixteen bombs around the *jebel,* or mountain; the pilot seemed to be aiming for the nearby cave in which Prince Mohamed bin Hussein, Commander of the Royalist Jauf army, was then living. The raid caused little damage, but it made the tribesmen disinclined to emerge from their hideouts during daylight, and for the next four days no training took place.

On 3 November the Egyptian Air Force returned. An unidentified twin-engined transport plane flew over, followed by an Ilyushin 28, then two Yaks and again an Ilyushin. No bombs were dropped, but in the afternoon at about 1630 two Yaks made a pass, firing rockets and strafing. Again the Prince's cave appeared to be their main target. Next morning two MiGs rocketed some abandoned vehicles, and two Yaks scored a direct hit with a rocket on a tent belonging to a merchant. In the evening an Ilyushin came strafing and bombing; two men were wounded and treated on the spot. As dark fell, Denard directed his men to start digging a shelter that would offer better protection than their cave.

Such airborne harassment, irregular but frequent, made life tough for the mercenaries. During the day they kept having to abandon whatever tasks they were trying to accomplish – repairing weapons or servicing vehicles – and dash for cover, and at night they were constantly awoken by hordes of tribesmen arriving or leaving. They had no set mealtimes, but snatched something to eat whenever they could.

In the middle of November the camp suffered a major setback, when a bomb hit Mohamed bin Hussein's main ammunition store. The magazine exploded, killing fifteen men, wounding the Prince in the leg, arm and shoulder, and detonating a large proportion of the force's reserve ammunition. The news was quickly relayed to Aden, whence Peter de la Billière sent a cable to London: BLACKLEG PIGEON PUT LARGE DOG ON ROLLO STOP ROLLO BITTEN AND NOW IN AUSTRALIA STOP . . . ALL DUTCH RECENTLY SENT DESTROYED – which, being interpreted, meant 'Egyptian aircraft dropped large bomb on Mohamed bin Hussein. Hussein injured and now in Saudi. . . . All ammunition recently sent destroyed.'

The Prince was evacuated to Najran, and convalesced in Jeddah, but later returned to the front. Had he been killed, his death would have dealt the Royalist cause a heavy blow, for he had exceptional powers of leadership and was the most

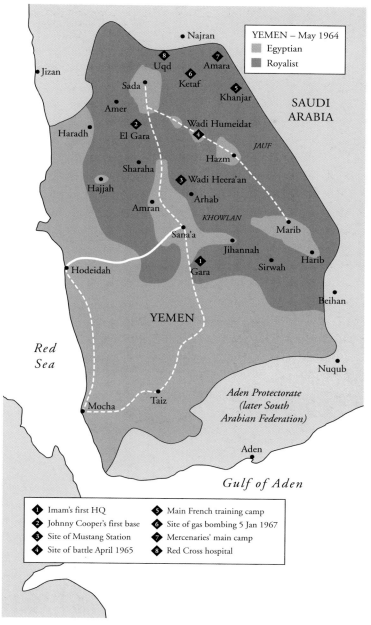

YEMEN – May 1964
Egyptian
Royalist

• Najran

◆8 Uqd
◆7 Amara
• Jizan
◆6 Ketaf
Sada •
◆5 Khanjar
Amer •
SAUDI
ARABIA
Haradh •
◆2 El Gara
Wadi Humeidat
◆4
JAUF
Hazm
Sharaha •
◆3 Wadi Heera'an
Hajjah
• Arhab
Amran •
KHOWLAN
Marib •
Sana'a •
Jihannah •
Harib •
Hodeidah •
◆1 Gara
Sirwah •

YEMEN
Beihan •

Red
Sea
Nuqub •

Mocha •
Taiz •
Aden Protectorate
(later South
Arabian Federation)

Aden •

Gulf of Aden

❶ Imam's first HQ   ❺ Main French training camp
❷ Johnny Cooper's first base   ❻ Site of gas bombing 5 Jan 1967
❸ Site of Mustang Station   ❼ Mercenaries' main camp
❹ Site of battle April 1965   ❽ Red Cross hospital

No detailed maps of the Yemen were available to the mercenaries, and
many named features existed only in the minds of the local inhabitants.

Johnny Cooper: 'a sinewy major with sun-blackened skin and the features of a Greek bandit.'

Jim Johnson, founder and commander of the mercenary force, on his one visit to the Yemen.

Tony Boyle (*left*) and Jim Johnson on a captured Jordanian tank, after the Six-Day War in June 1967.

Bernard Mills high in the Khowlan.

Liam McSweeney – 'Mac' – who had wrestled under the pseudonym 'Milo the Greek'.

Tony Boyle, Jim Johnson's second-in-command, organiser of the Israeli supply flights.

Jimmy Knox, radio operator and specialist cave-enlarger.

Rupert France – 'Franco' – lynch-pin of the mercenary organisation in Aden, Beihan and Jeddah.

Alastair Macmillan, recruited by Jim Johnson while walking through St James's Park.

Duncan Pearson (Gassim) about to inject his favourite patient, with her mother in close attendance.

Meals were always irregular: the mercenaries ate whenever they got the chance.

Chris Sharma – at the right, with spectacles – from Birmingham, styled himself 'Mansoor ibn Nasr al Beni Borhwa, Honory [sic] Emir of the Royal Kingdom of Yemen.'

John Woodhouse on his reconnaissance trip to the Yemen: he was eager to bombard the Sana'a airfield with 120mm mortars.

Envoy extraordinaire: Billy McLean on one of his innumerable missions to recruit political and financial support for the Yemeni Royalists.

Mercenaries give elementary instruction in the control and maintenance
of a captured Russian heavy machine gun.

Sundown in bandit country:
a lone sentinel keeps watch from
an outpost in the Khowlan.

Jim Johnson in city slicker mode.

popular of all the royal family among the tribesmen. At twenty-eight, he was the ablest of the Yemeni commanders, and the most flamboyant – given to wearing a turban of yellow cashmere. Born of a part-Persian mother, he had enormous charm and a good sense of humour, and (unusually in a Yemeni) was generally imperturbable. He had also seen a little of the world: he had been to secondary school in Cairo, but then, instead of going to university, as he hoped, had been sent by his uncle, the old Imam, to lead the Yemeni Legation in Germany, where he became the Minister in Bonn. In Smiley's view, he was by far the most capable, gifted and inspiring of the Yemeni princes. His ready smile 'created a misleading appearance of indolence,'[3] but behind that façade he was ambitious and determined, and had his eye firmly on the possibility of succeeding al-Badr as Imam.

During the war Hussein had frequently fought in skirmishes with the Egyptians and, in controlling the supply route through the Jauf to the whole of east Yemen, had (in McLean's view) 'gained enormous prestige and power and some wealth'. Unlike most of his fellow commanders, he tried to wean his tribesmen off their habit of decapitating prisoners, preferring to keep officers in custody until they could be exchanged, and to send other ranks away without their weapons. For the time being his role was purely that of an effective fighting commander, but his loyalty was to the Prime Minister, Hassan bin Yahya, rather than to al-Badr.

Mac McSweeney did not share McLean's enthusiasm: he found Hussein exasperating. Contrary to all the mercenaries' advice, the Prince began planning a major, setpiece attack on the Egyptians in Sa'ada. 'I fear that it is far too ambitious,' Mac told Jim, 'and if it fails it could result in disaster if the Egyptians react vigorously.' Mac had continually begged and suggested that Hussein's forces should launch small harassing raids, but the Prince was deterred by memory of the severe reprisals that had followed such actions in the past, and would not agree. He seemed determined to build an organised army, and had even bought uniforms and badges. 'I am sure he considers himself the next Imam,' Mac told Jim, 'and will have an army to influence the doubters.'

While Hussein dithered, a momentous event took place in the outside world. In a letter written during October, President Kennedy had told Nasser that he was confident the British were not backing the Royalists in the Yemen; but then, on Wednesday 20th November 1963, Kennedy called Sir Alec Douglas-Home (by now Prime Minister) on the transatlantic scrambler telephone to London and, in the course of a heated conversation, indirectly accused him of being a liar. The CIA, he said, had firm information that the British were officially helping the Royalists, and he demanded that the Prime Minister close the operation down. Douglas-Home, who knew the score perfectly well, parried Kennedy's accusations by saying that he needed to make enquiries and would call him back in a day or two. He kept his promise, and tried to ring back on 22 November, but on that fateful day Kennedy went to Dallas. News of his assassination reached the Yemen within hours, and the Royalist tribesmen, hearing it on their transistor radios, went wild with joy and excitement, firing prodigious volleys into the air with their ancient rifles – for they had regarded Kennedy, the supporter of Nasser, as an arch-enemy.

An unsigned intelligence report, which came into Aden on 24 November, gave a clear idea of the Egyptian build-up around Sana'a. By then there were thirty jet aircraft on the northern air-strip, guarded by ten tanks and seven field guns. A thousand Egyptian soldiers were deployed round the radio station, with ten field guns, eight anti-aircraft guns, fifteen heavy machine guns, seven tanks and seventy Republican troops. A 6-foot-high barbed-wire fence had been built round the north, south and east sides of the city, with one entrance only. There was a permanent guard of fifty on the gate, but only five actually on duty at any one time. The anonymous author of the report had obviously done his homework, for he added, 'The duty gentlemen prove to be fairly easily bribed.'

Another of Jim Johnson's recent recruits, Jack Miller, was moving around in Royalist areas, trying to establish a reliable radio network. Grin (David Smiley), who met him at Khanjar, saw that he was irritated by the 'persistent unreliability' of the Yemenis – and Miller did become exasperated by continual delays and failures: 'More or less a wasted day' . . . 'Absolutely nothing achieved' . . . Such phrases stud the admirably vivid diary that he kept during the six months of his tour;[4] but, in spite of multiple vexations, his journal gave a lively account of the life that a member of the BFLF could expect to lead when reconnoitring the Egyptian front lines:

16 Nov 63 Buy goats from Bedouin. Girls do the bargaining . . . Small child drinks milk direct from one goat . . . Arrive Sobrahin. Slit goat's throat and guzzle. Sobrahin would be a good position.

17/11. Arrive Agba area. Walk up hillside and overlook isolated hill in desert from East . . . Move south to another hill and look over onto plain. Egyptian camp about 3,000 yards away, right in middle of plain. B vehicle movement. What a target – but lack of action attributed to lack of munitions . . .

18/11. 1445. Travel 28 km to captured USA tank. Inspect vehicle and corpses of a number of enemy in what must have proved for them a Valley of Death some months ago . . .

19/11. It is obvious that allies are frustrated by the appalling disorganisation of the Arab Emirs, who have allegedly no idea of the problems of re-supply and even less of time . . .

This country favours the defender sitting back on a steep hill . . . Knowing that Egyptians tend to falter once they have to leave their MMGs [medium machine guns] and tanks to swarm up a hill, I feel that no efforts should be spared to sting them into attacking chosen Royalist positions and annihilating them.

24/11. 0945 Get up! Tea party on my bed with Sherif Ahmad and others. Much cash changes hands. Sherif spits accurately onto my track suit at foot of bed. Last night Nasr Ahmad pretended to put snake down the neck of one of the servants, who promptly stripped; I am not sure for whose benefit!

At the end of December David Walter (now known as Daoud bin Qassim), who had been with Miller at El Qara, got a note from the Prime Minister's secretary, Ibrahim al-Khibsi, to say that seven unexploded bombs needed dealing with in Sharaha, two days' walk away, and on 2 January 1964 he set off to sort them out. 'I was the first white man to ever set foot in this mountain-top city, which obviously dated from days of Arab greatness,' he noted when he reached his destination, 10,720 feet above sea-level, after a strenuous journey by donkey and on foot. Finding that four of the 150-pound bombs had buried themselves in the surrounding paddy fields of the wadi, he decided to leave them where they had fallen. Three others were lodged in houses, and the locals wanted to drag them out of the buildings with ropes, but, as he remarked, 'they would certainly have killed themselves doing so'. He therefore proceeded to detonate the three, using 4 pounds of plastic explosive and 3 feet of safety-fuse per bomb:

The large, impressive stone houses turned out to be not as strong as they appeared. The bangs, however, were most impressive. Total destruction was two houses and a row of small shops. Left for Coomah 1530 hours. I thought that this was best, since my host was the owner of one of the houses.

He concluded that he had probably saved half a dozen lives – and his conviction was strengthened when he returned to El Qara on the evening of 5 January, to find that there had been a raid the previous day, and two men had been killed and two wounded trying to move a bomb that had not gone off.

Lackadaisical as they might appear, some of the Royalists were doing their best to implement the mercenaries' instructions. On the night of 20 October 1963 Sheikh Ali Abdullah had tried to mine a convoy of twenty-five Egyptian trucks on their way from Jihannah, but his men were surprised by a foot-patrol coming to clear the road. Although the party was not hit, there was much firing, the mine was lost, and eighteen local sheikhs were put in gaol by the Republicans for implication in the offence.

Peter de la Billière, in Aden, was enthusiastic about the amount of intelligence that the mercenaries were sending back. 'Your map is excellent and so is the info,' he told Johnny:

> I can't tell you how important that we get as much info as possible even of irrelevant details like place locations and names. This factor could well have very far-reaching effects as the more the official boys get, the more they want and the more they commit themselves.

It is not clear how much of this intelligence was reaching Whitehall; but the Cabinet, meeting on 2 December 1963 to discuss the Yemen situation, at last came to the conclusion that Nasser could not be trusted, and that there was no realistic hope of him withdrawing his Expeditionary Force. It was agreed that HMG's policy of non-intervention should be retained; but at the same time it was hoped that the rulers in the Federation might become more amenable if 'we ceased trying to prevent them from supplying arms to the Royalists'.[5]

As always, Johnny was fizzing with energy and optimism. In a bulletin to Jim on 21 November he had reported that 'mining and kini mini go from strength to strength'. He had supervised the laying of fifteen 'effective' mines, and claimed sixty-five enemy deaths. Seven more mines were about to go in. The Egyptians had partially withdrawn, regrouping closer to Sana'a, but 'the WAR is due to start any day now . . . The tempo is quickening towards all-out attacks on the Wogs.' He himself had been due to pull out of the Yemen at the end of the year, but now felt that he was 'too committed' and must stay on. 'The snowball build-up of informers, mine-layers etc is alarming,' he wrote. 'My kini-mini set-up works to me only, and would take ages to hand over successfully,' he told Franco. 'No – I am *not* indispensable, but it has taken six months to build up, and the Arabs do not trust new faces on this tricky subject.'

Scraps of news kept coming in from all quarters. On 22 November it was reported that the Royalists were managing to steal weapons from the Egyptian post near Ghayman. On the night of the 26th fifteen Republicans deserted from Asnaf with four machine guns. On the 30th a mine placed in one of Sallal's houses exploded, but the extent of the damage was not known. Also on the 30th the Egyptians tried an offensive in the direction of the Jauf: they attacked with 300–400 men, but twenty of them were killed, two tanks were burnt and two armoured cars destroyed.

Coded radio reports were coming into Aden every night from Gara and El Qara, and intelligence was passed back to Jim in London. But Stan Symons, a professional communications expert, had strong views about the abilities of the radio operators: he advocated that they should all be withdrawn for the time being, so that they could be retrained in his way of doing things, or that new men should be found and trained from the start. He considered that there was too much radio chatter, and no control over the operators, who were all working in their individual ways.

During November the International Red Cross had established a field hospital in a cluster of white tents at Uqd, out in the north-eastern Yemeni desert. The site, in a horseshoe-shaped re-entrant among big boulders at the edge of a gravel plain, was by no means ideal, as it had no water (which had to be brought by lorry from a spring an hour's drive away), and it was too far removed from the fighting for wounds to be treated quickly; but this was the first medical facility that the people in that area had ever known, and its fifty beds were almost always occupied, largely by men wounded in the war.

The hospital was staffed by a team of six or eight Swiss doctors, backed up by twenty ancillary medical personnel, and its centrepiece was a German mobile operating theatre, known as the Clinobox, which had cost £50,000, with transport to the Yemen adding another £25,000 to the outlay. It was solidly built, with two side wings which could be folded down so that the whole became more compact for transport purposes, and included a conventional operating table and air-conditioning. The hospital also had an X-ray unit, operated by a Swiss girl, who obtained remarkable results in the unpromising surroundings of a tent, her darkroom being the packing case in which the X-ray equipment had arrived. Jack Miller, who visited the hospital towards the end of November, was impressed by the whole set-up and described it as 'very clean and full of bright, affable Swiss, mostly young, including four women'.

On the last day of November 1963 Jack and David Walter left Jizan in a truck at 2230 and travelled through the night, bound for the Imam's headquarters at El Qara. It took them four days of driving and walking to reach their destination, and once there David moved into a nearby cave at Qafl, in which an American doctor, Dr Bill Bartlett, and his English medical assistant, Arnold Plummer, a volunteer male nurse, had established a small outpost of the Red Cross hospital.

David proceeded to set up the radio, and to build doors and cupboards for the cave. Later he devised a plumbing system so that it became possible to wash and have showers.

On 4 December Jack met the Imam, who discussed the military situation in a two-hour interview, and asked his visitor to go on at once, to advise Prince Abdullah bin Hassan in his headquarters, then at El Medah.[6] So, on the 6th, Jack was on his way again, accompanied by one donkey, an escort of twenty-five soldiers and two followers:

1840, arr Shaib. Spend night. Meat, biscuits, tea. Cats under bed. Donkey within 6 ft all night. Camel nearby. Bints [girls] here wear trousers and seem from a distance quite fetching. But doctor's description of their habits discourages investigation, as does local aversion to Europeans . . .

9/12. 0425, Amir and staff leap out of bed to pray. 0700, eggs, bread and coffee. 0730–0750, grandstand view of two Ilyushins bombing El Jahali and El Jabr to west, above Shamsan (on map). Clockwise runs over targets and turn between us and Bait al Wali. One run over us flying straight and level. Could see bombs leaving aircraft. Several apparent hits, others wide . . . Lunch – two hens (that had been hanging upside-down from a donkey for some time), pineapple, Yemeni soup, bin and bread . . .

1815, arrive Bait Idhaqah (on map). Amir Abdullah is here by a stroke of luck. Have seen him briefly. His guards are the biggest apparent crowd of cut-throats I have yet seen!! Now installed in state on a sofa, with people continually calling to look at me . . .

10/12. Breakfast – eggs, bread and tea . . .Village is quite beautiful, with market and lovely trees like lilac in blossom. Have shaken hands briefly with Amir [Abdullah], who has not yet been polite enough to say what my programme will be or even when we will talk. He looks like a native of the Australian bush . . .

1300, Summoned suddenly to presence of Amir and talk before and during lunch . . . In spite of appearance, Amir Abdullah seems more businesslike than some of the younger princes, and we should get on all right. Has a great sense of humour. Seems very keen to have help such as I hope to give . . . Thinks guerrilla warfare plus isolation of enemy positions a good idea. We shall see . . . Says his spies go everywhere, right into Sana'a. He wants 'bombs' to put in houses. Says he has so much info that interrogation of POWs is not necessary!! Splendid chap. He 'knows all enemy most beforehand'.

On about the same date early in December a British journalist, John Osman of the London *Sunday Telegraph,* managed to reach both Abdullah bin Hassan and the Imam. Propaganda was being showered on Royalist areas in the form of leaflets dropped by Egyptian aircraft and headed 'In the name of God the Merciful'. One, seen by Osman, warned that the inhabitants of two villages would be 'extinguished completely' to make them an example for others, if their sheikhs and other leaders did not report to the nearest Republican headquarters within twenty-four hours.[7]

In London, Jim was continuously extending his search for weapons, and berating the French for not keeping up with promised arms deliveries. 'We have spent £50,000 on arms in Spain,' he told Peter on 6 December 1963:

> These will go to Amman next week, officially. We then decided the French were not getting anywhere, so I have got to go to Amman to collect them from there from the 21st onwards. This has not been paid for by Sammy [Shami] yet, so it is not firm. The *moment* he pays it is on, though . . . After that, subject to the cash keeping going, I will buy regular shipments along these lines once a week for as long as he wants. The Amman–Yemen a/c [aircraft] will fly regularly for me too.
>
> All this is I'm afraid behind the French backs, but they are impossible. However, it is Top Secret from everyone, and we must let everyone think it is still a 100 per cent Frog effort.

At the end of the year the weather in the mountains turned very cold. On 13 December 4–6 inches of snow fell, and, as Jack Miller put it, 'Amir Mohamed is delighted that it is cold, as it keeps his followers huddled in their blankets and he can be alone.'

> He says this snow is the worst in living memory. Asks to be photographed. He is twenty-seven, educated partly at Bonn University – has been in UK. Loves guns. Has built himself a house in Sana'a and wants to be in business when war is over, developing tourist trade and exports – good hotels in mountains would be wonderful.

In Aden, Peter de la Billière continued to amaze colleagues with his energy. Not only was he doing his legitimate job as Intelligence Officer to the Federal Regular Army and at the same time acting as the BFLF's covert link-man: he was also studying for the Staff College exam, which he sat at the start of December; and in spite of the overpowering heat he regularly ran up and down Jebel Shamsan, the extinct volcano towering 1,800 feet above the town. In May he had organised a race up the mountain, the Shamsan Scramble, which attracted forty-six entrants, including two women, and was won by a seventeen-year-old Arab schoolboy, Muhammed Deria, whom Peter described as being 'wiry as a spider and incredibly fit' (Peter himself came fourth). Further, he devised a combat survival course, out in the desert, which was so tough that, although it did not quite kill anybody, it left both participants and supervising authorities in a state of shock.

His time was running out, for early in the New Year he was due to return to the SAS; but before he left, the BFLF suffered an unpleasant jolt. Somehow a cable was sent in clear to Sana'a and New York, provoking Peter to protest to Jim:

> The cable office out here is fully staffed by people in the pay of both Egypt and the United States, and one must be fully prepared for all this text to have been leaked to these two countries. I have been very careful to guard my [personal] security and the security of this organisation. It must now be assumed that I am blown not only to MI6 but to Egypt and America. It is just as well that I am going.

Discontent was spreading among the mercenaries. From Nuqub, Franco reported that Cyril Weavers ('a bloody good man') was fed up and threatening to leave if he wasn't moved somewhere more interesting. Jack Miller, at El Qara, had become even more critical of the Yemenis' attitude and called for 'less talk, more action'. In particular, he complained of the tribesmen's wilful refusal to observe – or even pay lip-service to – Western ideas on working to schedule, or to look after any weapons except their own rifles. He was maddened by the almost total lack of discipline, and by the soldiers' tendency to attribute any failure to the will of Allah. 'I should like to know,' he wrote acidly, 'how many consider whether it is the will of Allah that the Egyptians remain in Yemen for twenty years.'

At the end of January 1964 a new doctor, twenty-eight-year-old Colin Wilson-Pepper of the British Red Cross, arrived, and on Sunday, 9 February, in Bait Idhaqah, Jack watched him stop the bleeding in the arm of a man hit by a hand-grenade fragment twelve days earlier. Another man had a Kalashnikov bullet in his leg muscle, but the doctor decided he could not operate until he was given a clean room. Yet another casualty, lying wounded in the *suq* (the bazaar), was not being fed, because he had been unable to draw his cash allowance. Jack wrote:

In the suq there is still talk of 'Egyptians' and 'djinns' (devils) when we appear. However when Ali [the interpreter] and I offered to fight a couple of chaps who called us Egyptians, they backed down . . . Colin estimates that the average villager here is living about the standard of peasants in the time of Alfred the Great (and he has done social anthropology).[8]

Chagrined though he was by the prevailing inefficiency and irresolution – he once twisted the arm of a donkey-driver who had insulted him – Jack occasionally came upon something much more agreeable:

In late afternoon Colin and I walked up to Turkish remains to west of village. Up there is a kind of utopia untouched by war that is very pleasant to see. Green terraces (at about 10,000 feet) and pretty little hamlets stretching away down towards a wadi far below.

In the Khowlan, Johnny Cooper had recently organised a major assault on the Egyptian garrison outside the town of Jihannah – a tented camp surrounded by barbed wire and mines. On 25 December 1963, in preparation, he and what he called his *gaish Abdullah bin Nasser* (his little army) of seven moved out to the village of Bishar to carry out a reconnaissance, but met with a mixed reception. Many of the villagers did not want them to attack the town, because they knew it would provoke reprisal air-assaults. Others wanted action, but not from the site Johnny had already selected. 'So,' he reported to Jim, we moved down on the night of the 26th and shivered to death under some fig trees.'[9] Next morning a reconnaissance of the proposed mortar site proved abortive, as it was too far from the target:

So we looked further and nearer to Jihannah and found an ideal site about 1,700 yards from the town. We returned, gathered our crew and man-handled from the camel road-head the mortar and 28 bombs. On arrival we checked for ambush signs, but our aiming posts had not been tampered with. We fixed the night aiming-lights and we parted, I to the OP [observation point] behind a fine jebel 300 yards forward of Philippe and Georges [another French mercenary] on the gun site.

We awaited the moon (full that night) and at 7.10 p.m. we opened fire on a convoy of five tanks entering the Ordnance Depot compound, their lights giving a fine target. After ten bombs the mortar jumped the base-plate and damaged the plate. The [enemy's] reaction was slow, but after ten minutes all hell broke loose – tanks, mortars, MMG and small arms. We sat this out and checked the mortar site, to find the damage not so bad.

We lined up again, and this time at 8.15 p.m. we took one correction, 200 up, and we put the remainder seven-teen bombs (one misfire) down in RAPID [fire]! Most spectacular display, and there was a negative reply this time.

When bombs started raining down out of the night, the defenders were terrified. In contrast with the Royalists, who could take refuge from air-attack in caves, all except the tank crews were caught in the open, and their tents gave them no protection. As Johnny remarked, 'Observed from the top, the panic was fantastic.' Unable to pinpoint the source of the initial bombardment, the Egyptians loosed off indiscrimi-nately in all directions; and then, when the second fusillade came in, they simply lay low. After two days of confusing reports, Johnny got confirmation that seventeen people had been killed, among them the second-in-command of the detachment, and that one medium machine gun and one mortar had been destroyed. 'No question of Royalist feel-ings,' he reported. 'They hate the Republicans, and even more so the Wogs – but you know Arabs: money, rifles and little all-out war is their cup of tea.'

As he expected, the attack did provoke a reaction, but a less violent one than he had feared. Although planes flew over Jihannah next day, there were no attacks on Royalist positions; but all Republican troops were evacuated to Sana'a and the north, and Egyptians took over the forward defence locations in the area. There is no doubt that the occupying soldiers lived in dread of sudden, opportunist attacks like this one: being unwilling or physically unable to climb into the rarefied environment from which the Royalists were operating, they must have felt like sitting ducks.

One hazard with which the mercenaries had to contend was the arrogance of some Yemeni commanders, all too well illustrated by the disaster that befell a caravan of 120 camels commanded by Sheikh Ali Hantash. In January this great armada set out for the Khowlan from the Beihan border, loaded with arms, ammunition, money and some radio equipment for which Johnny had been waiting for months. The caravan passed Harib unchallenged, but about 20 miles further west the sheikh decided to lay some anti-tank mines on the track behind them, to frustrate any attempt by Republicans or Egyptians to follow them up. The mines were laid without difficulty, but then Sheikh Ali ordered the caravan to march over them, to disguise the places where they had been buried. When the caravan was straddling the field, a heavily laden camel triggered one of the devices, causing a stampede, and in the ensuing chaos another six mines exploded. One man and seven camels were killed, and sixteen of the camel men refused to go on.

The sheikh disdainfully ordered the remaining ninety-seven camels to resume their journey, but they were stopped by men of the Beni Dhabian tribe, who demanded a levy for every animal. Hantash refused to pay anything, suggesting that he would fight rather than hand over money, and in the end he was allowed to continue unmolested. Johnny, however, reported that he received only eleven out of thirty-six packages despatched for Abdullah bin Hassan. As Peter de la Billière had remarked about one of the Rhodesian Air Services' deliveries, 'I'm afraid this air landing is a dead loss, as the loads do not find their way to the correct location and there is nothing we can do about it.'

At Boa, 20 miles south-west of Khanjar, chaotic scenes ensued when the local commander, Mohamed bin Nasser, was assassinated by a shot through the head from about 300 yards. Mac McSweeney, who was in Boa at the time, reported that for about an hour utter confusion reigned, with people shooting in all directions. He himself grabbed a machine gun and a few magazines and moved up onto a hill, waiting till things quietened down, alarmed by the realisation that he did not know at whom he should be shooting if a serious gun-battle broke out. Almost worse, the Arab radio operator refused to let him use the set to transmit news of the assassination – and not until the next day, when the man had gone away, was he able to send a message to Nuqub.

Frustrated at Boa, Mac moved to the French camp at Khanjar, where he could at least help with weapon training; but even there work slowed almost to a standstill because of constant Egyptian air-attacks, mostly by MiGs now flying in groups of six and firing machine guns, explosive cannon shells and rockets. The final blow came on Boxing Day, when in what Mac described as a 'very big bang' rocket-launchers, mortars and ammunition were all destroyed.

At much the same time Jack Miller went with an escort of four to reconnoitre Egyptian outposts near Amran, a few miles north-west of Sana'a, from the forward Royalist positions. Moving a mile to the west along the Souda ridge, he could look down on white enemy tents around Bait al-Wali, and more tents and troops beyond the road to the north. From the number of shell holes round Royalist positions, it was clear that the enemy had perfected the range for their artillery. When he said he wanted to get a closer look at the road, a general argument broke out: his guides told him that the villages ahead were Republican, and that there were enemy units close to the road. Jack proposed going forward, nevertheless; but two of the guides disappeared, so he carried on regardless with the other two, down a steep descent into the foothills. Then he met a man called Haji Ali who agreed to take the party to the road. At this a third guide disappeared, leaving Jack with Haji Ali and the last of Prince Abdullah's men.

At about 1730, after allegedly passing unseen enemy positions, they suddenly emerged onto a forward slope above the road. There Jack found 'plenty of corners, [a] steep hill and possible site to blow road into small ravine'. Armed with this intelligence, he could now advise on ambushes, mining, and demolition on the road and its Egyptian traffic – but had he not insisted on making a close approach, he would never have got the information.

The next few weeks amply confirmed the frustrations of the mercenaries' existence, recorded in David Walter's journal. On 14 January 1964 he was due to leave the Imam's headquarters on a mission to cut the road between Amran and Hajjah, an important road-junction north-west of the capital, notorious as a prison town, but also an important religious centre. Dr Bartlett was to go with him, to attend to battle casualties; but too few donkeys turned up, so David sent them away with instructions to return the following day.

On the morning of the 15th: no donkeys at all. Instead of leaving, David staged some training in mining and demolitions; but an accident occurred, 'resulting from the necessity to improvise', and he sustained injuries to his hand and face, which left him with a perforated left eardrum and fragments of metal embedded under the skin. This made him decide that his materials were too dangerous for the training of raw recruits, and he cancelled further instruction.

On the 16th the doctor passed him fit to travel, but still no animals were available. Five more donkey-less days passed, and only on 22 January did transport at last appear. For the next two days the party was on the move, but on the 24th their start was delayed by the number of patients who demanded treatment. Arriving at the village of Affar, they were invited to dine, but afterwards the donkey wallahs did not wish to proceed, and in the argument one of them pulled his *jambiya* knife on Bartlett.

Once it had been decided that the man was to be put in gaol, they proceeded with speed, passing through groves of banana trees said to belong to the Imam. They then went up a very steep ascent and in mid-afternoon came to Bait Adhaqah, where they were entertained by the local Amir for two hours, before proceeding to Mabda, which they reached at 2100 hours.

Meeting Abdullah bin Hassan in his 'very dirty cave', David discovered that the road he had come to destroy had already been dug away in several places, and its use denied to the enemy. Hassan made it clear, however, that his visitor would not have been allowed to do the job anyway, since this was a task for the Yemeni Royalist soldiers. David's role would be to train them.

Next day, having treated a case of toothache with a pair of engineer's pliers, Bartlett went off, and David remained behind to teach techniques of demolition. Although he had cancelled such instruction at El Qara, he decided that his visit should be justified somehow, so he taught some improvisations as if they were standard, 'the only trouble being one stampeded camel train'. On the way back to El Qara he found that the camel-load of mines which he had intended should supplement his supply of 852 plastic explosive had 'disappeared from the face of the earth', and that Bill Bartlett had treated only three battle casualties, all of whose wounds were more than two months old.

In the cave at El Qara, to his chagrin, there was still no sign of the battery acid for which he had been waiting. It was reported to have leaked and killed the donkey that was carrying it, but Bartlett said this was not possible, and David concluded that it had gone the same way as the camel-load of mines. 'The pace of this war is being dictated by the donkey wallahs,' he decided, 'and no one else seems to care. My temper is easily roused.'

Tony Boyle, meanwhile, had flown to Saudi Arabia to enquire about the possibility of using an abandoned airfield as a despatch-point for parachuting supplies into Yemen. First he was granted an audience with Prince Feisal, who seemed genuinely interested in the idea; but when he went on to see Prince Sultan, the Defence Minister rejected the proposal. The Saudis' reason for refusing was feeble in the extreme. 'Somebody might find out about it,' they said. Tony's trip proved not only disappointing, but dangerously divisive. The idea of using a Saudi airfield had come from David Stirling – but he had told Tony that Jim and Billy McLean must not know the true purpose of his journey. The abortive trip thus widened the split that was opening up between Jim and Tony on the one hand, and Stirling and McLean on the other.

Jim considered that Stirling had become so indiscreet as to be a danger to the whole mercenary operation. Ideas mentioned to him in confidence one day kept coming back from other people, and in the end Jim and Tony decided, for safety's sake, to cut him out of their loop. This annoyed Smiley, who began making critical remarks about them, and also began to undermine McLean's faith in the mercenary organisation. Serious differences arose also over attitudes to the Hamid ud Din family. McLean wanted it restored to full power, but Jim and Tony had no wish to see it reinstated. Although they came to like some younger members of the Imam's clan, they considered the regime unenlightened and cruel – and Tony, struggling to reconcile opposing views, briefed his own people by saying that the aim was to get the Egyptians out of the Yemen, and that the only way to do that was to back the Royalists.

Meanwhile, the pressure on HMG from America was increasing: In a cable Lord Harlech, the British Ambassador to Washington, asked that 'vigorous action be taken to stop the involvement of British mercenaries and British territory in the Yemeni war, in order to avoid feeding American suspicions of our motives.'[10]

HMG ignored this request. No pressure was put on Jim, then or later, to withdraw his teams; and in fact the mercenaries, beyond the reach of far-off arguments, were having small successes – as when, at the beginning of March, at Bait Adhaqah, Jack Miller 'nursed' a sick .50 Browning machine gun back to health, and people began calling him 'doctor'. But he was still exasperated by the task of goading idle tribesmen into action, and had composed a new 'peasant-driving song', to the tune of 'Colonel Bogey':

Yallah is what we say to you.
Yallah, the only thing to do.
Yallah, and then by Allah,
We'll get there somehow, on some day, it's true.
Lazy, you're on your backside still,
Lazy, you know your job is 'Kill!'
Lazy, you'll drive us crazy.
We're here to help you, and help you we will.

On 10 March he spent a long day supporting Amir Mohamed Ismael on an inspection of the front line west of Hajjah:

0725, depart cave. 0730, passing Mabian town. Caught by two Ilyushins diving low over town. Surprise complete. No bombs on this run; why not, I shall never know. Dash to overhang of rock on edge of houses and slightly below. Shell from Hajjah suddenly lands less than 100 yards away. Then bombing starts: too close for comfort, five bombs in area, two failing to explode. Showers of stones and debris. One plane attacks every seven to eight minutes; other cruises round high up, no doubt to observe and report to bombing aircraft.

0800. Depart and find Amir sheltering lower down hill below Mabian. 0930 Hot sun. Amir announces he can go no further. 0940 Halt at home of Sheikh in Beni Shaumi. 1030. Comb honey eaten off knife. 1100. Bomb explodes in Mabian. Lunch, hospitality terrific. This is more like a picnic than a tour of the front line. Qat. 1700. Dep[art] Beni Shaumi. 1800. Arrive village of El Adbar on low ground. Thus all day we have done about two hours' serious travel. Coffee, chatter and qat, crammed into a small house in great discomfort. Heat terrible . . . Notables arriving all the time to kiss the hand of the Amir – and add to the crush.

The worst thing is having no chairs. I cannot get used to the floor, and I have given up not pointing the soles of my feet at people. The best people don't seem to worry, anyway.

Amir says the peasants believe that unexploded bombs can move about over the ground. This is the best yet! The bonhomie of the soldiers is terrific and to some extent atones for the hostility encountered among the peasants in Bait Idhaqah.

Grin had also been on the move, touring the country on yet another visit, and in a cautiously optimistic report to Prince Feisal played up the mercenaries' role. The influence of the foreign specialists was beginning to make itself felt, he wrote, and without them the Royalists would be in a much weaker position. 'I consider their presence essential for the continued conduct of the war.'

He reiterated that most of the Royalist soldiers were no more than armed tribesmen, best suited to guerrilla warfare, and that they must be discouraged from trying to capture towns or take part in pitched battles against trained soldiers in defended positions. He also reported that money was playing an ever-larger role in the struggle: the Egyptians, having realised that they could not advance into the mountains against the Royalists, were making more and more attempts to buy the tribesmen with large-scale bribes of money and rifles.

Jack Miller, who was closer to the ground and had reduced

a pair of desert boots 'almost to ruin' in just over two weeks, was more cynical. 'I feel about ten years older in the last two months,' he wrote:

> Quite soon I shall reach breaking-point, as I do not think many people really care who wins this war. The Brit. Govt. obviously does not mean to do anything either. Therefore it could be better to leave these people to go their own sweet way.

Occasionally, however, he saw a happier side of Yemeni life – as on the day he and a French mercenary, François, made a 'triumphal entry' into the town of As Sudah. Accompanied by little boys carrying their weapons, they joined a procession and were installed in the large private house of the Emir, where they spent two days 'in the lap of luxury':

> Lunch was bread and milk, *bintasahr* (pastry and honey), *helva*, milk pudding, bread and honey, tomatoes, stacks of meat (only the best bits). It is such a relief to be able to eat as much as one can hold before the Arabs finish it all, as they eat faster than we do!

6

Manna from Heaven

Early in 1964 Royalist morale was greatly strengthened when weapons and ammunition began dropping into the Khowlan from the skies. The princes and tribesmen had no idea where this bounty was coming from – and they would have been astounded to learn that the source was that arch-enemy of Arab states, Israel.

To members of the BFLF and their Royalist allies, the advantages of air-drops were potentially enormous. Until then, whenever arms had been delivered in Beihan, there had been no proper control over how they were distributed, and the expense of sending the weapons on into the Yemen had been considerable. Since one camel could carry only 300 pounds, large caravans were needed to move each consignment upcountry, and every journey meant up to twenty-four hours' hard riding through territory occupied or patrolled by the enemy. Some of the tracks were mined, and caravans had to pass through avaricious tribes, who demanded money and a share of the arms to let the travellers go. In the words of one BFLF report, 'an inordinate amount of equipment is being siphoned off at the behest of the Sherif to bribe tribes on the Yemen side of the border'.

The hazards of an overland journey had been all too clearly illustrated by the disaster that overtook the Hantash caravan in January. Air-drops would bypass all such dangers and deliver munitions straight to the front line. 'The question of parachuting is very important,' said Cooper on a tape sent home from his redoubt in the Khowlan:

For over four months now we have been saying we are going to parachute. Everybody talks about parachute. If one plane arrives and drops something, it is going to clear up the great problem of re-supply. At the moment the camel men are pointing a pistol at the Emir and saying 'You *will* supply fifty, sixty, seventy Rials per trip' . . . but when the Emir can turn round and say 'Look – I have my aircraft, you can go fly your kite,' the position is going to be much better.

Jim's earlier schemes had proposed that containers of arms and ammunition should be flown into Beihan, unloaded, fitted with parachutes and placed in smaller aircraft for dropping into the mountains. The BFLF had also considered the more ambitious idea of buying its own aircraft: a second-hand Lockheed Constellation C 749 with freighter configuration (though capable of seating eighty-two passengers), two owners since new, at a price of £65,000, plus brokerage of £5,000. 'As you can imagine,' said a letter from the firm's contact:

the calculation of running costs is a very difficult problem. I have no idea for example what your crew-costs (one Captain, Second Pilot, Navigator and Engineer minimum) will be in the area in which you intend operating the

aircraft, [but] I have approached a Lockheed Captain with
a view to converting any pilots you have in mind.

Casting around for a simpler solution, Jim went to see the
Iranian Ambassador to London, Ardeshir Zahedi, the son-in-
law of Shah Reza Pahlavi. When Zahedi agreed to send
weapons in through Saudi Arabia, Jim flew to Teheran to
negotiate the deal with the Iranian Foreign Secretary – only
to find himself abandoned incommunicado for five days in
the Hilton Hotel. Eventually he established contact, and tried
to arrange for arms supplies to be parachuted in – to which
the Iranians agreed, but asked that, in return, he would arrange
training for a few of their Special Forces personnel, to give
them some experience of guerrilla warfare.

In due course four men arrived in London, regular officers of the Iranian Special Forces, one of them a sergeant of
astounding breadth; they had already been trained by the
Americans at Fort Bragg, but they turned out to have no
equipment of any kind and had to be comprehensively kitted
out. In cables and radio messages Jim described them as 'the
cubs', and in due course he sent them out to the Yemen; but
they proved perfectly useless (see page 217) and the Iranians
never parachuted any weapons.

Into the breach stepped the Israelis. It was very much in
their interest to give the Royalists extra fire-power, and so
keep as many Egyptian troops as possible in the Yemen,
draining Nasser's coffers and bleeding his forces closer to
home.

The missions had to be planned with elaborate secrecy, for
their implications were as explosive as the munitions that
they were designed to deliver. As Johnny Cooper remarked
afterwards, if the true origin of the drops had become known,

'the political repercussions would have defied description'. Nasser would have been incandescent with rage that his bitterest enemy was entering the fray, and the Saudis would almost certainly have withdrawn their support, for (as Prince Feisal told Billy McLean in a private interview) at that stage they believed that Israel was secretly supporting Nasser.[1]

The contacts with Israel were entirely private: HMG was neither consulted nor involved. It is no longer clear from whom the idea of collaboration came – but it was from the British side; and when Jim asked Shami about the feasibility of bringing Israel in, the Yemeni Foreign Minister said, 'Go ahead – but don't tell anyone, and be very careful.' The first feelers were put out by Billy McLean, who flew to Tel Aviv to meet General Moshe Dayan, the Israeli Minister of Defence, and Meir Amit, head of the intelligence service, Mossad. Then, after consultations in London with Brigadier Dan Hiram, the Israeli Defence Attaché (conducted, naturally, at the Hyde Park Hotel), Jim and David Smiley left for Tel Aviv on 20 February 1964 to negotiate details of the first flight, designated Operation Leopard. A basic plan was agreed, but then Jim went out again, this time with Tony, to settle the details.

On the way they stopped off in Geneva. There, acting on instructions, they booked into a hotel at a pre-arranged time and walked into an empty lift in the lobby. Just before the doors closed, a man followed them in, identified himself and, while the elevator was climbing to their floor, gave them passports made out in other names, in exchange for their real ones, for their onward flight to Israel.

In Tel Aviv they met Shimon Peres, Director General of the Ministry of Defence, and Major General Ezer Weizman, Commander-in-Chief of the Israeli Air Force,[2] who spoke good English and was described by Tony as 'sarcastic, clear-brained, good memory for faces and personal details'. The visitors were also introduced to other senior officers, as well as to Nahum Admoni, who had been appointed Mossad's 'case officer and liaison' for the operation. The Israelis had by no means decided whether or not they would take part: for two whole days the visitors sat round a table in one of Mossad's safe houses, conferring with up to twenty other people in an exhausting series of debates about what might happen under various circumstances. Because Jim and Tony were convinced that microphones had been planted in their hotel rooms, they conducted serious discussions sitting back-to-back on the lawn.

Tony had some difficulty convincing his hosts that the para-drops would be technically feasible, the main cause of concern being the exceedingly wild nature of the Khowlan terrain: flying low at night into 12,000-foot mountains, without navigational aids, was not a prospect that appealed to any pilot, however experienced. Another worry was the proximity of enemy forces: the main Egyptian base at Sana'a was barely 15 miles from the proposed DZ (dropping zone), and the approach would have to be almost over the capital.

In the end the Israelis agreed to go ahead – provided the mercenaries would guarantee three things: they would send an accurate description and photographs of the DZ; they would take two Israelis into the Yemen with them, and they would show them their safe house in Nuqub.

Plans developed slowly, and in the mountains Johnny Cooper became irritated by the delay. 'I accept the job of remaining here until the para is over and then must come out,' he wrote to Jim on 15 March. 'Today is number 226 since I returned to the Khowlan – seems ages too.' Himself a veteran organiser of para-drops in France during the

Second World War and later in Malaya, he had already recon-
noitred a possible DZ, but knew that it might have to be
changed to meet the Israelis' requirements. 'We are waiting
ready with eagerness the first drop,' he wrote on another
day. 'The morale value alone will be terrific, Jim, plus the
end of five months' wait for the Yemenis to see us keep our
word. *Inshallah!*'

Operation Leopard began in earnest on Friday, 20 March,
when Tony Boyle flew into Aden escorting two Israelis, travelling as Robert Lichtner from Austria and Alber Babayea
Pour from Persia. They brought with them their personal
gear for an expedition into the hills – sleeping bags, blankets, and so on – and also a radio and codes, for their mission
was to go up into the Yemen and make their own assessment
of the DZ that Johnny had selected. As they checked in at
the Hotel Metropole in Aden, they were met by a man who
greeted them with the identification passwords 'Do you know
Louis?', and one of them, known as 'David', replied, 'Yes –
do you know Tim?'

For their journey into the hinterland Tony furnished them
with personal weapons, ammunition, radios, Sarahs (Search,
Recognition and Homing devices), a Verey pistol (for firing
flares) and other equipment for the drop. He then flew with
them to Beihan. Thence they continued to Nuqub; David
stayed there, and his companion Louis went on.

To preserve security, the BFLF at first referred to Israel as
'Wales', and to the Israelis as 'the Welsh'. Later the dropping
scheme was known as 'Mango', and Israel became 'Mango
Land' or 'Scotland'. An 'Exercise Plan' drafted by the London
office issued a series of code names. The Israeli control-point
at Tel Nof Air Force Base, a dozen miles south of Tel Aviv,
became 'Headquarters'; the reception area in the Khowlan

'the harbour'; and the Egyptians 'birds'. There were also strict instructions for the men on the ground:

> The minimum number of people should know about the operation, and these should only be told the shortest possible time before the operation. Unusual activity in the harbour area should be kept to a minimum, and when unavoidable should be explained away with a cover story.

Tony returned to London via Aden; but when, on 25 March 1964, he went out to Israel again to join the first flight, taking details and photographs of the DZ, he found that there had been a difference of opinion between Weizman, who was in favour of the operation, and his second-in-command, Colonel Motti Hod, who was against it. Several senior officers shared Hod's opinion that the assignment was too risky; if an Israeli aircraft crashed in the Yemen, Nasser would have an almighty propaganda coup.

Nevertheless, it had been agreed that the drop would go ahead. The aircraft detailed to fly the mission was a Boeing Stratocruiser – the biggest, four-engined transport of the day – which had been modified for earlier operations by fitting clamshell doors at the back of the fuselage, and rails running the length of the cargo hold so that boxes attached to parachutes could be rolled out under the tail. The plane was painted white on its upper part, silver below, and carried no markings.

Johnny Cooper, meanwhile, had been reinforced by the arrival of Cyril Weavers and David Bailey; but their radio batteries had run down, and they were anxiously awaiting the arrival of a camel-caravan bringing new ones, together with the Sarah beacons. During the days before take-off, volleys of radio messages passed back and forth between Tel Aviv, Leopard (Rupert in Nuqub) and Johnny, many of them occasioned by a last-minute debate about whether or not to change the drop zone from the one known as 'Red' or 'Avocado' to another, designated 'Orange', some 12 miles away. Johnny had decided that Red was too dangerous, because there was a risk of an Egyptian attack; instead, he favoured Orange, at a place called Beit al-Ghadr, which had the advantage of being further from Sana'a. Tension rose all over the network as ideas flew back and forth. The supply caravan reached Orange on the 25th and Johnny sent the following:

Strongly advise operation Orange March 30 alternative 31 or first April. Extreme secure drop zone. Plateau not mountainous. No administrative difficulty defence and so on. Amir Abdullah bin Hassan receives benefit and credit.

He pointed out that if they used the Avocado drop zone, the supplies would not go directly to Abdullah. There was also the worry that Avocado was closer to Sana'a and Egyptian armour. At Orange, on the other hand, there was no enemy artillery close enough to shell the DZ after the drop, even if the Egyptians woke up to what was happening. Johnny therefore announced that he would go ahead at Orange.

The Israelis were inevitably nervous about venturing into uncharted, hostile terrain at night, to a DZ 7,000 feet up in ferociously steep mountains. They needed every scrap of information they could collect, and now were unhappy about the change of plan. Louis – their one man on the ground – had not seen the Orange site, and had had no chance to take photographs of it, so they were reliant on verbal descriptions.

On their behalf, Tony (by now in Tel Aviv) insisted that the drop take place at Red. At 0300 on the 26th he messaged Leopard: 'Imperative John accepts drop at Red. Inability to do this cancels whole plan.' Then at noon he added that four nations were standing to assist on the nights from 29 March to 1 April, and that if the British failed to organise a drop between those dates, the chances of the friendly countries cooperating in future would be negligible. Without them, no future drop would be possible. Tony therefore urgently requested Johnny to stick to the original plan.

Johnny, however, was emphatic that he had had to move the rendezvous for security reasons. He sent back a message saying that the Orange DZ was completely organised, and that it was safer and sounder than Red, where the security was dubious: 'Expect repeat expect and standing by for drop.'

In justifying the switch to Orange, he made a list of points:

1   Better DZ. No mountains near.
2   Not observed by Egyptians.
3   Can clear [stores from] DZ with transport.
4   Petrol [for signal fires and battery-charging] coming here now.
5   Sheikh Nagi al Ghadr as commander is great asset.
6   Position only 12 miles from Red.
7   Nearer by two days to its destination Amir Abdullah.
8   Security much better . . .

At the end of the message David Bailey added: 'John has received 100 drops before and wonders why you cannot rely on his judgment. Severe heartbreak here if job cannot be done.'

Sheikh Nagi al-Ghadr had 'obtained' – that is, captured – sixteen tins of paraffin (for fires) 'from enemy sources'. A large supply of wood was on hand, and sixty gallons of petrol were on their way. 'This [is a] great effort by Ghadr,' Johnny told Tony. 'If you fail us now to meet your obligations, our word, honour and reputation gone for ever.'

Bowing to Johnny's experience, Tony gave in and asked for details of Orange. Back came the answer:

Bearing of DZ centre line 260 degrees. Length 1,800 yards width 1,000 yards approx altitude 8,000 feet. Bearing from Sana'a 100 degrees distance 25 miles. Bearing from Jebel Lawz 118 degrees. High point above DZ 360 degrees 500 feet one mile. No problem circuit approach bearing 260 degrees.

The most critical task was to ensure reliable communication between the incoming aircraft, code-named Rhumba, and the ground. On the afternoon of 29 March Tony sent instructions to Leopard:

1   Direct contact Rhumba–Orange can be established on one of Orange's existing frequencies.
2   Rhumba will answer on Orange frequency.
3   Inform night frequency in use Orange–Lemon. Shall use same frequency for Rhumba–Orange.
4   Fix call-sign for Orange.
5   All stations calling own call-sign only.
6   Contact Rhumba–Orange will start two hours before Rhumba arrival to Orange.
7   Inform Orange will use BRM rpt BRM call-sign.
8   This to enable Rhumba to be in direct contact with

Orange in order to transmit if all OK. Emergency msgs [messages] will be transmitted plain language.

Next morning – 30 March – Tony told Johnny and David:

1 Glad inform you as result yr info Louis accepts Orange.
2 Stand by from now.
3 Date and ETA [estimated time of arrival] rpt ETA to be notified on day of Op. Code name for night of operation is Moonlight rpt Moonlight. When received Moonlight means op. tonight.

The countdown started at 0900 on 31 March, when Tony messaged Leopard: 'As from 1600 we shall listen to you permanently . . . You must contact us once an hour.' Starting at 2100 GMT, Orange was to contact Rhumba for five minutes every fifteen minutes – but in all the calls no messages were to be sent: the contact itself would mean that all was well. Only in an emergency would plain language be used for warnings.

During the day Johnny sent out weather reports, including atmospheric pressure, and at 1440 back came the code word 'Moonlight'. The operation was on.

In Israel a huge security operation had surrounded preparations for the flight, designated Operation Rotev. Because the Stratocruiser would be vulnerable to the Jordanian Air Force over Jordan and to the Egyptian Air Force over the Red Sea, and then again over the Yemen, some 200 people were involved: the air crew, a marine rescue crew, several helicopter crews (for sea and land rescue) and an army insertion unit all attended the briefing, together with the Mossad chief,

Meir Amit. The primary alternative – the first airfield to which the mission could divert in case of emergency – was set as Asmara, some 30 miles inland in Eritrea, and the second was Djibouti, further down the African coast.

Captain of the aircraft was Major Arieh Oz, an experienced transport pilot of the Israeli Air Force, who knew the limitations of the Stratocruiser all too well. Its four Pratt & Whitney engines, each with four rows of seven cylinders, tended to run hot, particularly in the last row, and when this happened the pilots had to open big cowl flaps on the engine casings, which caused a lot of drag and upset the aircraft's trim. Another common problem was dual magneto failure, which meant that an engine had to be shut down. As Oz recalled later, 'you had to be very careful and fly by attitude more than by airspeed, as the hull was not too aerodynamic.'[3]

With a crew of co-pilot, navigator, radio operator, flight engineer and loadmaster, five paratroopers to provide manpower in the cargo-bay, and an intensely interested passenger in the form of Tony Boyle, Oz took off at dusk on 31 March 1964. His instructions were to radio his estimated time of arrival ahead to the reception party in the mountains, and if his signal was not acknowledged within three hours, he was to return to base.

At first he flew due south, over a corner of the Jordanian desert, keeping very low to stay under the radar, and on over Saudi Arabia, heading for the coast between Al-Wajh and Yanbu, then over the Daedalus reef and on down the Red Sea for more than 800 miles. On the flight deck tension gradually built up, for the acknowledgement from Orange did not come through until fifteen minutes before the deadline. Thereafter all was well. Over the Red Sea, with Egypt on its right and Saudi Arabia on its left, the Stratocruiser climbed to a cruise height of 15,000 feet; then, before reaching Hodeidah, it turned left (east) towards the Yemen coast.

Tony, perched on a small extra seat installed at the captain's left shoulder, between him and the side window, later described the approach:

We turned in on schedule, with the lights of the harbour shining bright forty miles to our right (the south). Then a ten-minute haul over the sand-plain and up the incredibly steep mountains . . . then over several valleys and peaks until the lights of the capital appeared very bright – like Piccadilly – to our left. Then the flash of a car headlight to the south-east of the capital. Then, with a sigh of relief, we picked up the homing beacon (radio) and used it for the final six minutes. Then, when the beacon indicated we were nearly overhead, the lights blazed.

Oz later described the atmosphere on the flight deck as 'tense, but very professional, with minimum conversation'. His big aircraft was heading for jagged 12,000-foot peaks in a country none of the crew had ever seen, and for a rendezvous lacking all the navigational aids to which they were accustomed, with the possibility of a hostile reception from Egyptian anti-aircraft gunners on the ground. Peering ahead at the dim outlines of mountains, he could not discern natural features clearly, so he let down very gradually, making sure he had clear air ahead. Then at last he spotted a tiny, faint yellow cross twinkling from the black massif, and increased his rate of descent.

On the ground Johnny and his little team had been waiting anxiously. The only electric lights he had been able to muster were a pair of car headlamps running off old batteries, so he had also prepared a number of petrol and diesel fires. To minimise the chances of betrayal or ambush, the smallest possible number of Arabs, picked for their reliability, had been chosen to help on the DZ: they were told that an aircraft would be coming over, but had no idea of its nationality or departure-point.

The Stratocruiser was a relatively quiet aeroplane, and as he came in Oz tried to avoid any change of engine speed, which would have created extra noise.[4] After one preliminary reconnaissance circuit round the lights and fires, he made a low pass over the markers, with the clamshell doors open, running in at 130 knots on steady engine power with the rpm set at 2,350 and steady manifold pressure for the climb-out. Only 300 feet above the rock-strewn plateau, he switched the light in the cargo bay from red to green and pulled up the nose – whereupon the loadmaster whipped out the pins holding the boxes in place, and a shove from the paratroopers sent all twelve containers sliding out from under the tail. The moment his air-speed was down to 110 knots (the minimum he dared risk), Oz put on full power and started to climb out, aiming for the only gap in the ridge ahead. 'Last para-chute for you,' Tony radioed. 'Report.'

'Drop excellent,' came the answer. 'Bull's-eye. Only one candle.'

'Everybody on the ground went wild,' Johnny reported later. The Arabs who brought out bullock carts to collect the containers, and get them away under cover, found themselves the owners of 180 rifles, 34,000 rounds of Mauser ammunition and 17,000 rounds of .303, besides seventy-two 6-pounder, armour-piercing shells and 150 pounds of plastic explosive.

As the aircraft made for home, Tel Nof reported that the base was shrouded in fog; so, passing Jeddah, Oz decided to loiter, to give the sun time to rise and burn off the mist. He arrived over Israel to find a huge blanket of fog still lying, and only one side of the runway clear, but he touched down and completed the landing blind, on instruments, shutting down the engines with fifteen minutes' fuel remaining in the tanks, after a fourteen-hour fifteen-minute flight.

At 0050 on 1 April Mango radioed Leopard: 'Rhumba confirmed successful drop. Our best wishes.' To which Leopard replied at 0650: 'Congratulations and many thanks for your wonderful performance.' At 0900 a final word came in from Mangoland: 'Rhumba landed safely at 0630 GMT.'[5]

That morning the Egyptians put a reconnaissance aircraft up over the Khowlan, but not in the right place. They had evidently heard or seen something in the night, and had been alerted to the presence of an intruder, but where it had come from, what it had done and where it had gone remained a mystery. Confirmation of their suspicion came when they tried to bribe people to kill the DZ party and then heavily attacked the area from the air – as usual, causing few casualties.

The source of the weapons and ammunition had been efficiently concealed. Every serial number had been brazed out; the parachutes were of Italian origin, and even the wood shavings used in the packing had been imported from Cyprus. But the last container would have been a give-away, had it fallen into enemy hands, since it contained personal mail for the reception party, English newspapers and a bottle of Scotch, thoughtfully packed with a lavatory roll round its neck to cushion the shock landing. Johnny, who had not touched alcohol for more than a year, found that the whisky tasted 'absolutely vile'; but he, David and Cyril lost no time in finishing the bottle.

In a report for Jim dictated onto tape immediately after the operation, Johnny made a number of points. The drop would have been a 'fantastic morale boost' even if the chutes had been empty. There had been only fourteen Arabs on the DZ, and they had not known what was happening until one hour before the plane arrived. The security had been 'very good', but the parachutes had been too small and overloaded, and there had been no packing between the rifles, with the result that some of them had been smashed.

In the middle of May, Tony went out to the Yemen again to perfect arrangements for the second drop. After meetings in Jeddah he flew not to Aden, but to Jizan, in the north, where he arrived on the 19th. Next day he travelled on southwards across the Yemeni border by truck, then at the base of the mountains took to his feet, walking for a total of seven hours to reach the Imam's eyrie at El Qara at 2.30 a.m. There he found Chris Sharma looking 'thin and ill', and he had hardly taken his first sip of tea when he was summoned, and found himself surprised by the ruler's 'considerable presence, charm and sense of humour', and by the fact that (at thirty-seven) his hair was turning grey.

In the morning he inspected the area proposed for the second DZ, which he thought 'about as unpromising as possible', as it was 'perched on an eyrie, and in places only 500 yards wide, with sheer sides falling away; but he assured the Imam that the operation would go ahead, and got him to agree that on the evening of the drop he would invite all the local sheikhs for a *qat* session, at which he would explain to them part, at least, of what was happening.

Next day Tony set out alone to build stone cones, to mark the positions for lights on the DZ. Two Bedouin who passed by carrying wood told him, 'Go away', but he riposted, 'No – you go away!', which they did. There was just room for the lights in the pattern that he wanted, and that evening he sent a message to Headquarters confirming, 'We ready'. The Israelis, however, were still nervous, and asked for further clarification of Egyptian positions, which Tony gave them. A day later he went out again, only to find that his carefully placed stones had been removed by Bedouin, who had surmised that they were markers showing the Egyptians where to bomb.

With the DZ relaid, everything looked good. During the afternoons storms tended to brew up, but in the evenings they died down, leaving the sky clear at night. As always, special code words had been set to confuse any eavesdroppers: 'Wolf' for Headquarters, 'Tiger' for DZ, 'Lion' for aircraft, 'Bear' for 'Operation within twelve hours', 'Birds' for Egyptians, 'Baboon' for successful completion of the drop. Radio communications with Tel Aviv were variable: sometimes reasonable, sometimes impossible. One night, when contact was good, Tony sent a message saying, 'Security difficult to hold. Please help by Bear as soon as possible.' That evening 'the radio came alive with numbers of boxes, lists of contents and instructions to burn cardboard containers and dispose of damaged mines'.

Next morning, 26 May 1964, with the first contact at 1100 GMT, in came 'Bear, rpt Bear'. On the DZ Tony found Chris Sharma bandaging a man with a 4-inch cut to the bone in his shin. When Chris injected a local anaesthetic so that he could start stitching, the man got up to leave: the pain had gone, so he thought he was cured. As the day went on, the weather deteriorated until cloud covered the mountain and fog was rolling in wet billows up the gorge outside the radio cave. The spirits of the reception party fell steadily as thunder crashed overhead, and they prepared to send a message asking for the drop to be delayed. Then the clouds began to clear, and in came a message 'Dollars 2100' – the aircraft's ETA – which showed that it had already taken off.

At 1800 they briefed the fire-lighters. At 1815 another radio message warned that the aircraft might be half an hour early. The Imam had duly summoned the local sheikhs to his cave, and sent messengers out to surrounding villages and gun positions, telling them not to open fire on aircraft they might hear during the night. Tony's assistants went off to their allocated stations. One man, detailed to sit on top of the wall of a derelict house, lost his nerve, until Abdullah [al-Khibsi] said *he* would do it – which shamed the man into doing it himself.

Once again radio messages from the Khowlan, relayed through Nuqub, gave Tel Nof all possible information about their distant, dangerously placed target:

Johnny: No. 1: DZ is as briefed, except following. One: drop direction now 224 rpt 224 degrees. Two: max length three-quarters mile. Prefer over to undershoot. If poss make four dropping runs . . . DZ on plateau at 6,000 feet. Highest point on plateau 238 degrees, five miles, as briefed. Nothing higher within 30 miles. DZ plateau descends sheer to 2,000 feet, then slopes to sea level at Jizan. Can see Jizan from here. Nearest birds 35 miles south at Qafl.

Tel Nof: *Received yr No. 1. Please state exact map reference or distance and direction from nearest known town to DZ.*

No. 3. Your No 1. Jizan bears 296 degrees, 97 kms. DZ position sixteen degrees thirty-one minutes north forty-three degrees twenty-two minutes east. Correct my No. 2: Birds at Haradh 31 kms east . . .

No. 5: Due surface obstructions, 'T' laid out as follows. Lights four, six, two and one comprise cross-piece indicating commence drop. Lights three, five, six and seven comprise tail with lights three and five on DZ. New light nr. eight marks other end DZ . . .

No. 5: Reconfirm birds' distance at all directions from DZ. Do you know if birds have AA guns? Is Jizan lighted at midnight?

No. 8: Yr No. 5. Nearest birds at Haradh thirty-one kms west rpt west with no AA guns. At Qafl thirty-five miles south birds have 40mm AA guns. Jizan has electricity. Maybe lighted midnight . . .

No. 13: Have you any radar in area? If yes, details.

Yr. 13: None this area.

Tony left a vivid account of the final hour:

At 1935 we turned on the Sarahs, Chris one by the radio cave, and I one in the centre of the T. At 2000 there was no sign of the aircraft, nor at 2030. Abdullah could not sit still, but had to walk up and down. Fire-lighters were beginning to look suspiciously at us.

I decided to light the fires at nine, whether the aircraft

was in sight or not. With Abdullah protesting strongly, I fired the green Verey to signal the fires to be lit. All sparked quickly, and the T looked impressive. A long five minutes, then a drone from the West, getting louder. Another green Verey. Then the aircraft was overhead, flashed its lights to signal to speak on the Sarah. Thinking it must be Egyptian, Abdullah disappeared, to hide under a rock.

Tried to tell the aircraft to drop slightly to the left of the T. Luckily they could not understand me. The aircraft disappeared to the east in a wide, descending circuit, then roared in overhead – still too high – almost exactly over the T. Another wide circuit, then in again, with doors open, but nothing dropped. A third circuit, roaring in again exactly over the T.

Then they came. Three or four boxes fell, kicked to the left, a gap, then more, all kicking left. Would they drift back? No – the wind was dead calm. Then *crunch, crunch,* and they were landing, fifty yards left of the centre line and 100 yards down the DZ. Then the aircraft circled left and swept in low over the T in a final pass on its way home.

One man had been so close to a box when it landed that a rope from one of the chutes had tangled round his leg. One box fell in a mosque a yard from a deep-water reservoir. Another landed in a house and fell down through two stories to the ground floor. Arabs appeared out of nowhere to guard the boxes (under the Imam's orders) and would not allow even Abdullah to open them without considerable argument. We folded the chutes and sent them to the HQ, and left a guard on each box. Bedouin squatted on the chutes, hoping we would not notice them. An old sheikh exulted, 'By God, we are so strong that not only will we take Sana'a, but Aden as well!' This – as the stuff was supposed to have come from the British – was pretty rich.

Back in Jizan, Tony went to see the Governor, Prince Mohamed Sudairi, who congratulated him on the mercenaries' efforts and told him that, according to Cairo radio, there were 500 of them in the Yemen. It turned out that the people of Jizan had had two unpleasant frights. By chance the drop came in a year to the day since they had first been bombed by the Egyptians – so, when they heard a big aircraft passing overhead in the night, they immediately switched off the electricity supply and waited, blacked-out, in trepidation, which increased when then they heard the plane again, forty-five minutes later, flying low and fast without lights on its homeward run. Of course they wanted to know where it had come from, but nobody enlightened them.

News of the operation spread slowly, the Arabs reacting first with amazement, then with gratitude. A week later they were saying that tanks had come out of the sky and asking, 'When is the next one?'

The success of the first two drops made the Israelis enthusiastic about mounting further operations: at the end of September 1964, Tony, back in London, told Johnny: 'They are very keen to keep going,' and the code word for a drop became 'Repairs'. It was agreed that Repairs should be carried out once a month. One constant hazard was the danger that radio messages might be intercepted. On the one hand, the Israelis wanted the fullest possible information about the terrain around each DZ, and frequently asked for checks to be repeated. This created problems, because the men on the ground had no theodolites or sextants – not even any good maps – so they had to rely on marching compasses, which could produce discrepancies when coordinates were retaken. On the other hand, the reception parties were anxious to keep radio traffic to a minimum. Even in a static location, a sudden start-up of routine exchanges through day and night could mean only one thing to eavesdroppers, and moving a station to an isolated spot four days before a drop would be even more significant.

Over the next two years the Israelis mounted twelve more Repairs sorties, never using the same DZ on two successive occasions, and very considerable quantities of weapons and ammunition were delivered into the mountains. 'Special Consignment No. 8', for instance, dropped in May 1965, included 250 rifles of .303 calibre, 50,000 rounds of .303 ammunition, four Bren guns, twenty-four Bren magazines, twenty anti-tank mines, 200 kilograms of plastic explosive, 1,200 metres of fuse, 1,000 rounds of .38 pistol ammunition and two boxes of medical equipment – besides tins of beer, beef, baked beans, carrots, peas and sardines, and bottles of whisky and brandy. Other drops brought bazookas, anti-tank rockets, short-delay time-bomb fuses, gold sovereigns, and two Hispano-Suiza 20mm mobile anti-aircraft guns that Jim had specially ordered.

As Messrs Cooper and Bailey walked away from one of the drops in the dark, a single rifle bullet cracked past their heads. Both dropped to the ground, but a second later Johnny typically stood up and shouted out his cover-name, 'Abdullah bin Nasser!', and strode forward, confident that the shot had only come from some nervous guard.

Jim flew on one of the missions; Tony was on board for all but two, and during the long-haul flights he learnt to play backgammon, 'taught by masters'.[6] He also enjoyed the ritual, repeated twice at exactly the same stage of each sortie, of being encouraged to move to the side of the aircraft furthest from Israel's nuclear facility, whose existence the crew always hotly denied. He did once set eyes on the installation: early in the morning, in the final stages of a flight, he was sitting in the cockpit behind the pilots' seats, and as they came past the huge building, Arieh Oz turned round and grinned at him.

That tiny leak in security was a small price to pay for what the Israelis gained. Not only did they help detain and weaken the Egyptian forces in the Yemen; over the years they had also gained valuable intelligence about the capability and limitations of the air force, the size of Nasser's expeditionary army, the way it operated, the weapons and ammunition it was using, and the tendency of its soldiers, when pressed, to throw down their Kalashnikovs and run away.

On all his many visits to Tel Aviv, arranging the Mango drops, Tony was treated as a VIP – met at the airport and whisked out through a side door. Then, in the middle of one of his trips, he received an unpleasant shock. He had undertaken to act as courier for a consignment of sovereigns destined for the Royalists, and he had bought the gold in the *suq* in Jeddah (where it was cheapest). Because there were no flights between the Arab countries and Israel, he had been obliged to bring the money to London so that he could smuggle it out to Tel Aviv for loading onto the Stratocruiser.

To his dismay he heard that the new Labour Government had tried to forestall a run on sterling by banning the export of gold, and that customs were making spot-checks on travellers' luggage as they flew out of the country – but he learnt this only at the last minute, so that he had no option except to trust his luck. His locked suitcase was so heavy that he could scarcely carry it; nevertheless, the night before his flight he booked it in at the West London air terminal in Cromwell Road, hoping not to see it again until he reached Tel Aviv, and explaining its fearful weight to the girl behind the desk by saying that it contained legal documents for a big court case in Israel.

Next morning at Heathrow, travelling on a new passport made out in the name of Shlomo, he was horrified to find a currency search in progress, with passengers required to identify their baggage and open it for inspection. At a long counter suitcases were being disembowelled, wallets emptied, pockets turned out. His only hope, he thought, was to hang back, present himself last in the queue and pretend that he was in danger of missing his flight. With his case and brief-case open, he waited in mounting trepidation – but the customs officer merely fumbled among the clothes packed on top of the gold, closed the lid of the suitcase, chalked it, apologised for the delay and let him stagger through.

In Tel Aviv Tony had another fright. He had agreed to meet his contact in a certain hotel, and obediently sat waiting in the foyer. After a considerable time a rather irritated-looking man came up and said pointedly, 'MR SHLOMO, I believe?' You don't seem to be responding very well to our calls for you on the tannoy.'

7

Shortage of Gold

The mercenary effort was loose-knit, to say the least. Billy McLean, operating on his own, travelled to Saudi Arabia and the Yemen whenever he could spare the time; he kept Jim informed of his movements, but was not under his control. Similarly, David Smiley went wherever he felt like, without detailed instructions from the London office. Individual operators were sent to the mountain stations, but, once there, moved around their particular areas on their own initiative, or at the behest of their local prince or sheikh. It was never possible for Jim to coordinate the campaign from London, because the Yemeni leaders would not have responded to directives from somebody so far away – and somebody whom, in any case, they did not know.

All the same, in March 1964, after yet another tour of the country, Billy had summed up the situation in an optimistic memorandum, saying that HMG's decision not to recognise Sallal's Republican Government had proved to be 'both correct and wise'. It had become clear to all that the puppet regime had no popular support within the Yemen, and would have collapsed long ago but for the Egyptian military intervention. Nasser, he thought, had found the conquest of the

Yemen a much tougher proposition than he expected: already at least 8,000 Egyptian soldiers had been killed, and the war was costing Egypt not less than 500,000 US dollars a day.

McLean went on to make some alarming prophecies. If the war continued for any length of time, it might provoke Egypt to launch air-attacks on Saudi Arabia. The Soviet Union, which was already giving Nasser very substantial support, might infiltrate the Yemen in greater force. McLean therefore felt that the war should be brought swiftly to an end by forcing the Egyptian army to leave the country, and he thought this would not be difficult, 'if HMG were prepared to take certain steps now'.

What these steps were, he did not specify; but Grin (David Smiley), on his third visit to the Yemen, found the Royalists obstinately pursuing tactics that he and others had tried hard to discourage. By then the Imam had moved a couple of miles from his previous hideout at El Qara into two large caves, one of which had electricity supplied by a generator – yet his ideas had not changed. Far from accepting Grin's advice, he invited him to go and observe the all-out attack that his troops were about to launch on the Egyptian garrison in the town of Hajjah. When Grin asked why he had ordered the attack, the Imam replied that the place had been encircled for weeks (not true), and that its capture would raise morale, encouraging many Republicans to change sides.

Hajjah is a town on the southern slopes of a mountain rising to 8,000 feet, surrounded by valleys. Nine typical Yemeni villages, of solid, stone, fort-like houses, clung to the slopes at nine different heights, all now occupied by Egyptians or Republicans, who had turned them into defensive positions. The one motorable road, from Hodeidah, approached along a wadi from the west and climbed the south-west flank of the mountain in zigzags.

The Royalists held the sides of the valleys facing the town, and their plan was to open up a bombardment with their heavy weapons – 81mm mortars, 75mm and 57mm recoilless rifles – at dusk on the evening of Friday, 20 March 1964, while tribesmen moved forward to positions from which they could attack during the night. The forces to the north, under the command of Prince Mohamed bin Ismail, were to storm seven of the villages on the mountain, while the southern army, under Abdullah bin Hassan, was to capture three other villages, including Hajjah itself, and to cut the Hodeidah road in four places.

Preparations for the assault were so chaotic that on 20 March Jack Miller wrote in his journal: 'Progress there has got to be, or I will waste my time NO LONGER' – and he was further exasperated by the fiasco that followed.

The attack failed for several reasons. First, because it was expected: the Egyptians knew it was coming – not necessarily from any spy, but because every tribesman within miles had heard the date and time of the assault days in advance. The second reason was that the preliminary bombardment proved ineffective: weapons were fired at extreme range, and many had no sights, so that shells and bombs fell short of their targets. Besides, the gunners loosed off indiscriminately into Hajjah, rather than at the Egyptian positions.

'No attempt was made to go for Egyptian positions,' wrote Grin in a letter to Jack:

Oh for a trained British mortar team! They could have knocked out twenty trucks, the guns and a good deal more. As it was, I imagine the shells merely soured the local population. I saw a few parties of Royalist tribesmen moving forward in the evening but heard no firing. In truth I believe they never attacked at all.

Each tribe had been allocated a target, but several made no attempt to move forward any distance, and some did not even start. Nor did they cut or mine the road. The result, Grin reported, was disastrous:

> By next day not a single objective was in Royal hands, and the Royal tribesmen had returned to their usual occupations of drinking coffee and chewing qat. Though [they were] singing songs of their prowess, I did not see one with a bandolier with empty places, to indicate that a shot had been fired.

Far from pulling out, the Egyptians brought in more troops from the east, and forced the Royalists to withdraw and abandon seven of their precious heavy weapons. In a sharp, sarcastic report to Jim, Jack Miller savagely criticised Abdullah bin Hassan, who, he said, had completely ignored the advice given to him – principally to cut all approach roads and surround the city:

> His constant refusal to take advice, and his ability to waste whole days messing about, lead me to suggest that he should be put under close supervision or relieved. Yet, in view of the childlike belief of the peasants in the godliness of Amirs, it may be that a second-string Amir, however devoid of intelligence, could be used to support Abdullah and the cause by flag-wagging trips round the area . . .

The majority of the peasants, including soldiery, are very idle, extremely stupid and not unduly patriotic. Their reliance on Allah is almost total. If the enemy remained in Yemen for ten years, they would have to take comfort from knowing that this was no more than his will.

At the end of three days Grin returned, 'somewhat disgusted', to report to the Imam, and decided it was time for some straight talking. He began by saying that he knew it was customary for the ruler's men to tell him only things that he liked to hear. He, however, proposed to tell the truth, 'and be brutally frank in so doing'. Did the Imam wish him to proceed? 'Yes,' came the answer. 'Please go on.'

Grin said that he discerned four fundamental weaknesses in the Royalists' character: Ignorance, Incompetence, Inefficiency and Indolence. It was not for him (he said) to criticise the Arab way of life, but unless the Imam's men changed their ways, they would have little hope of winning the war. Time meant absolutely nothing to them, and three words typified their attitude: *ba-den* (later), *bokra* (tomorrow) and *inshallah* (if God wills it).

He also lectured the Imam on the care of weapons, and reminded him that the tribesmen were not professional soldiers, but peasant farmers carrying rifles. They should be used, he said, as guerrillas, attacking Egyptian lines of communication, mining roads and ambushing convoys, rather than in set-piece assaults against large targets.

Still more contentious was the subject of the young amirs, or princes, the Imam's commanders. Although in Grin's view they were keen and intelligent, and popular among the tribes, far too much of their time was taken up with petty detail, and in particular with the writing of letters. Grin amused the Imam by saying, 'Wars cannot be won by writing letters' – and the ruler took all his criticisms 'in extremely good humour', often laughing and saying that he quite agreed.

The Imam was also thinking about his own future, and commissioned Johnny Cooper and David Bailey to furnish a house that he had bought in Jeddah. Reaching under his bed, he brought out a great box full of sovereigns: armed with some of them, the mercenaries went off on leave and bought furniture, cushions, carpets, television sets and pictures, thereby earning themselves useful extra money.

On 23 April 1964 Nasser paid a surprise visit to Sana'a; he was welcomed by a twenty-one-gun salute as he descended from his aircraft at the new airfield north of the city, and presented with a golden key to the capital. His routine propaganda speeches were countered by a cable addressed to him and 'the World Press' by Abdullah bin Hassan:

> I, Emir Abdullah bin Hassan, invite you to negotiate with the free people of Yemen. I am only sixteen kilometres from you, an hour's drive, and I will give you a safe conduct if you have time to accept this offer, as it would be to your advantage. It is useless to deal with the so-called Republicans, as the free people of the Yemen will not repeat not submit to their orders.

Down south, in the Protectorate, the British position was steadily deteriorating. On 5 May at a press conference in Aden, Major General J.H. Cubbon (General Officer Commanding, Land Forces, Middle East) announced the death of two SAS soldiers, Captain Robin Edwards and Trooper Nick Warburton, in the Radfan, to the north of the colony.

They had been killed five days earlier, in the first stages of an SAS operation against insurgents, when a long-range reconnaissance patrol had been cut off in the open by tribesmen. It had not been possible to retrieve their bodies, and their heads were reported to have been exhibited on stakes in the square at the south-Yemen town of Taiz (occupied by the Egyptians).

Another patrol did recover the decapitated bodies, which were buried with full military honours, and in due course the tribesmen returned the heads; but there was widespread anger, inside and outside the SAS, that the General had unnecessarily blown the gaffe on a secret operation. The public-relations battle over the future of Aden and the Protectorate was proving every bit as difficult as the military campaign: the United Nations, the Communist Bloc and Third World opinion were all lining up behind the nationalists, and Britain was being cast as a colonial oppressor.

The despatch of 'Radforce', which suppressed the insurgents in Radfan (although at huge cost), was only one of countless exchanges along the Federation's northern border, where sporadic warfare was the order of the day. One of the Political Officers, John Harding, wrote a vivid account of a visit to Dhala, some seventy miles north of Aden, where his colleague James Nash was running a vigorous counter-terrorist operation. Nash's house (Harding found) was a fortress, surrounded by a rocketproof stone sangar two yards high and one thick, with another barricade inside it. The walls were pocked with bullet-marks, and bigger holes had been blasted by bazookas. Nash explained that the rough-looking characters hanging about the establishment were members of his bodyguard, whose main task was to carry out raids across the border against the Egyptian-trained opposition based in Qataba.

One evening, after dinner of pâté, ratatouille and cheese, Nash's party adjourned to the roof to watch what he called 'the nightly fireworks display':

> The British and Federal armies would loose off Bren-Gun tracer, mortars and a particularly noisy anti-armour weapon, on fixed lines of fire in the general direction of Qataba, with James blazing away with his own Bren Gun. The enemy replied in kind. After an hour or so everyone got bored and went to bed.[1]

Nash was (and is) a man of many talents: an aggressive combatant, a chartered surveyor, a celebrated cook and an accomplished poet, he later rode the Crusader route to Jerusalem, to raise money for the Knights of St John eye hospital. But in 1964 even he found life in Dhala 'quite rough'. His house was being shot up three times a week, and in the course of one particularly tiresome night he was attacked by three different groups: the enemy (as usual), 'a rather badly-commanded company of [Royal] Marines, who ignored instructions', and his own protection squad:

> I found I had shells from a Saladin (armoured car) going through the side of my house, and, what was worse, through the fort of the gendarmerie, who were supposed to be looking after me. Having had eight of their people wounded, they mutinied, and started firing at me. So that night there were three lots shooting: the baddies, the Brits, and my own guards.[2]

While organising what he called his 'own gang of terrorists', Nash was struck by a notion for bringing the war in the Yemen to a swift conclusion. It would (he thought) be quite easy to get hold of an old Greek tanker, and have it catch fire and blow up in the narrow channel, only 200 yards wide and 10 miles long, that approaches Hodeidah harbour. Months would pass before the Egyptians could organise lifting gear to take it out; during that time the only route in for fuel for their army would be blocked, and the war would be stopped quite quickly and cheaply, without hurting anybody. Nash suggested the idea to HMG, but unfortunately they did not approve of it.[3]

Although he was meant to be acting as a Political Officer, his real role was to disrupt the Egyptians and Republicans on the other side of the frontier – and he did this so effectively that he was three times denounced on Cairo radio. As he considered a mention on that station rather like winning an Olympic medal, he concluded, 'Obviously we were upsetting them.' In general he followed the Sherif of Beihan's policy of 'two for one' – that is, blowing up two of the opposition's houses for every one of his own that was destroyed. On the ground, intermittent counter-punching was thus the order of the day; but at the same time streams of telegrams poured back and forth between the Foreign Office in London and the military and civilian authorities in Aden, endlessly discussing what was or was not permissible in the way of cross-border retaliation by RAF aircraft. At one stage the Hunters were allowed to indulge in 'hot pursuit' of enemy intruders, but in April 1964 this permission was withdrawn.

HMG did, however, privily sanction defensive measures along the border. A paper drawn up by the Chiefs of Staff, and discussed at a meeting of the Defence and Overseas Policy Committee on 23 April 1964, recommended a 'Range of Possible Courses of Action open to us'. Under the heading

'Retaliatory actions along the border with Yemen', it proposed '*Operation Eggshell* – Mine laying; *Operation Stirrup* – Issuing of arms and ammunition to tribesmen in the frontier area; and *Operation Bangle*, Sabotage and subversion in the frontier area'. All these activities were already well under way, whether or not they had been officially approved. And so were further possible actions listed by the Chiefs of Staff:

Aid Royalists by allowing them to use wireless stations in Beihan and Nequib [Nuqub].
Aid Royalists by allowing arms convoys to be received from Saudi Arabia.
Aid Royalists ourselves with a supply of money.
Aid Royalists with small arms, ammunition, mines, explosives, heavy machine guns and bazookas.[4]

Ironically enough, with the exception of supplying money, which was coming from the Saudis, these activities were exactly what Jim Johnson's men were carrying out: they were aiding the Royalists in all the ways suggested – and yet, while the Chiefs of Staff called for action, the Foreign Office continued to demand that the mercenaries be suppressed. One letter from Peter de la Billière in Aden reported 'a big rupsha' (row) over a signal from London saying that 'the Foreign Office did not know what the Colonial Office were up to'.

Definitely *not* sanctioned was yet another suggestion, for 'the assassination or other action against key personnel directing subversion against the Federation of South Arabia, especially Egyptian intelligence officers'. This idea was promptly rejected by the Committee, on the grounds that any help given should remain as covert as possible.[5]

In the Yemen the Royalists were squandering chances, and precious ammunition, as fecklessly as ever. Grin's strictures to the Imam on the subject of weapons were backed up by Jack Miller, who noticed that heavy weapons were being sited in positions from which rounds could only be uselessly expended in the general direction of the enemy. In vain he explained to the Royalist gunners that the best answer to random shooting by the enemy was to keep quiet and lie low, unless a worthwhile target presented itself. As an alternative strategy, he recommended more ambushes and aggressive guerrilla attacks, as well as the construction of dummy gun positions to confuse aircraft, and decoy movements whereby the enemy 'could be skilfully led deeper and deeper into the desolate country north-east of Sa'ada on futile and exhausting forays'.

Jack was nothing if not practical. When one of the Amirs complained that he had recently been attacked by MiGs whose pilots noticed his white donkey, Miller told him to paint it black and green – and during the next few days he was maddened, again and again, by the half-baked manner in which the war was being conducted. One evening early in May, in the front-line gun positions above the village of Ibn Tawa, south-west of Sa'ada, the Amir announced a bombardment of the enemy before the sun went down:

1800. We arrive at a 2-pounder gun position (what an achievement to get it up here, largely carried by peasants from El Meschef). Crowd of warriors all squeezed into narrow space. Amir will observe and correct fire from a flank. Range said to be one mile.

1830. Amir fires starting signal. Engage with APCBC, range 2,000 yards (max) . . . After three unobserved shots someone says, 'Drop a bit'. Fire one more shot at 1,600 yards. Chatter, much excitement. No word from Amir, who must be too far away to be heard. Am waiting at each moment for retaliation from enemy guns. Sheikh Abdullah of Ibn Tawa dashes in and fires one more shot (probably not aimed).

Then shell lands on rock behind which everyone is hiding. Gun dragged back behind cover. Second shell very close indeed and party is over.

Over the next two nights and days, as Jack travelled south with the Amir, he was frequently under fire. Although enemy shells poured over the party's heads on the march, they were not (he judged) in much danger. But then at 0700 one morning, when they reached a Royalist gun position on a ridge and the Amir decided to have a go with a .50 machine gun, an enemy machine gun promptly replied, and the aim was too good for comfort. Then at 0815 Russian aircraft began to appear: he was watching one approach from the west when bullets suddenly began to spatter the crest under which he was hiding, and another – unseen until the last moment – screamed over from the south.

Descending slightly into Jarf, the party came into an attractive little clearing, with green grass and water. There they had breakfast, to the accompaniment of further MiG attacks, and Jack concluded that the Amir did whatever came into his head, planning only for a very short time in advance: 'It is all like a comic opera.' By midday the Amir was under human assault from his own side, besieged by a bevy of tribesmen all yelling at him and waving *warraqas*, and at 1420, as they moved out and crossed an open space, they were almost caught by a shell:

Drag white donkey under cover. They were probably waiting for us to break cover. Abdul Hamid said later he was praying when he heard it coming. Being a man of some consequence he had to consider whether to risk 'having his head sent far away from his body' or being thought irreverent if he took cover!

1500. Two MiGs shoot up position just in front of ridge. Can see pilots as they circle . . . Abdul Hamid gets off his donkey en route and leaves it to follow him. When it fails to do so, he is in a flat spin as it is carrying MTD. Eventually it strolls in much later.

Thinking over the last two days – what a difference a few Europeans, heavy weapons teams, would make. Not only from the efficiency aspect, but also from the general behaviour one. Few teams putting down an accurate and disciplined curtain of fire on an area, instead of the shouting, disjointed mobs I have seen, would do so much to help these people.

Intermittent hostilities kept flaring up. On the night of 22 May 1964 there was an attempted *coup d'état* when the son of Sheikh bin Taji, fuelled by an Egyptian bribe, combined with some of the bodyguard to attack the camp of Prince Hassan (the Prime Minister) at Al-Gharir. The two soldiers who were supposed to capture the Prince warned him, and thus enabled him to escape; but his treasury was looted, all his possessions were stolen and the ammunition depot was blown up. The ringleaders of the coup were caught, and the tribesmen cut off the Sheikh of Al-Gharir's ears.

There was no doubt that the Royalist Yemenis detested the Egyptians, as did many of the Republicans, for bringing such destruction on their country. Yet some of the mercenaries felt almost sorry for Nasser's soldiers, fighting for a cause they did not understand. Many of the men came from the low-lying Nile delta, and the sheer physical effort of moving around at high altitudes was in itself debilitating. 'They had expected to be fighting in desert, not mountains,' wrote the author Victoria Clark (who was herself born in the Yemen):

A chronic lack of maps meant that, like the Turks before them, they were forced to rely on untrustworthy locals. Without suitable kit, Yemen's climate, which could veer between 130 degrees Fahrenheit on the coast to 18 degrees Fahrenheit in the mountains, was a horrible handicap.[6]

Stuck in tented camps in the valleys among forbidding mountain ranges, vulnerable to mines in the dust roads, they were scared stiff by the threat of ambushes in steep-sided wadis and the sudden, deadly arrival of mortar bombs in the night. It was not them, but their arrogant and duplicitous leader, President Nasser, whom everybody loathed.

In London, Billy McLean continued to lobby energetically for official action by HMG. Writing to Nigel Fisher, the Parliamentary Undersecretary of State for Commonwealth Relations and for the Colonies, he enclosed two letters and an ambitious shopping list[7] from Mohamed bin Hussein. 'I know that you and Duncan [Sandys] have convinced the

Government of the need for action,' Billy wrote, 'but I feel it my duty to tell you that, unless your political decisions are translated adequately into suitable action now . . . the whole anti-Nasser position in Arabia may suddenly collapse.'

Billy also wrote to the Prime Minister, Sir Alec Douglas-Home, saying that he believed Hussein's extravagant demand was not 'a bargaining list' but a 'genuine request', and could not be much reduced 'without prejudicing the scale of the effort'. Tony Boyle echoed McLean by confiding to Jack Miller that the point had come at which:

> we have to decide whether to drop the whole venture
> or carry on . . . One must consider whether the whole
> business of getting the Royalists motivated fast enough
> is not too big a task for us to tackle — not because of
> our lack of good will, but because of their apathy and
> indifference to what is happening five miles away.'

Although Peter de la Billière had returned to 22 SAS at Hereford, he had by no means lost interest in the doings of the BFLF, and on 3 June he wrote to inform John Wood-house (his former Commanding Officer) that M16 were now much more closely in touch with the BFLF, and had given it money and considerable moral support. The two air-drops during the last month had impressed not only the Arabs, but also the SIS, 'who now consider the set-up to be most professional'.

The Royalist armies might lack cohesion, but they were far from ineffective, and they had inflicted grievous losses on the enemy. Official Egyptian Army figures claimed that between October 1962 and June 1964 the Expeditionary Force had lost 15,194 men killed, including 456 officers and 1,029 NCOs

— twenty-four fatalities every day. Maybe four times as many men had been wounded or captured. Bonuses were paid to Egyptian soldiers in the Yemen — £2 to £3 a month for privates, £20 to £30 for officers — but these were hardly enough to compensate for the danger and discomfort of the campaign. The bodies of officers were taken home for burial, but those of other ranks were often left to rot where they fell.

Within the BFLF every effort was still being made to preserve the security of the operation. No word of the Israeli involvement had got out, but rumours were flying, and on 14 May in the House of Commons the Prime Minister had to skate across thin ice when, in reply to a question from the Labour MP Michael Foot, he replied:

Our policy towards the Yemen is one of non-intervention in the affairs of that country. It is not therefore our policy to supply arms to the Royalists in the Yemen, and the Yemen Government have not requested these or other forms of aid.[8]

When pressed to confirm that this policy would not change in the future, Sir Alec agreed, but sought to divert the enquiry by saying, 'It must be remembered that the Yemen is filtering people into the Arabian Federation, and this is becoming a very dangerous state of affairs.' Then, in response to a question from George Wigg, another provocative Labour MP, he confirmed that 'at no time in the last eighteen months have British arms been supplied to the Imam's Government'.[9] This may have been strictly true; but had Wigg pursued his enquiries, he might have discovered that a great many weapons of non-British provenance had been spirited into the Yemen through Jim Johnson's machinations.

8

Breach of Security

Once again the BFLF had escaped exposure; but in fact a dangerous hole had already been punched in the organisation's cover, when five letters written to Johnny Cooper the previous November had fallen into enemy hands. The Egyptians claimed that a helicopter crew, on a reconnaissance flight, had spotted a man moving near the Beihan border, and because he had been scrambling across rocky terrain, not on any known track, they had landed, arrested him and taken possession of his rifle and dagger – only to find that he was carrying messages from London, Aden and Beihan to people living in caves in the area of the Khowlan tribes. Because of the long delay before the content of the letters came to light, Johnny himself suspected that they must have been bartered through many hands before they reached the *Al-Ahram* newspaper in Cairo and were broadcast on Cairo radio on 1 May 1964.

The author of the article (and editor of the newspaper), Mohamed Heikal, a close associate of Nasser, concluded that:

There is undoubtedly a military and political set-up operating, directed from Britain and most probably under the command of British Intelligence. The set-up includes a number of British volunteer officers and soldiers, a number of Frenchmen, mainly pilots, who are obviously remnants of the Katanga army and the OAS [*Organisation Armée Secrète*], and a number of Germans who used to be in the French Foreign Legion. Many of the foreign sources in Sana'a, who are doubtless well informed, estimate the number of all these at over 300 officers.

Heikal added that the set-up had 'unlimited funds at its disposal' and 'a well-designed plan for propaganda', and claimed that its presence had 'almost become notorious in all South Arabia'. He doubted that the United Nations mission could be unaware of its existence, and suggested that the mercenaries had tried to get UN observers to 'turn a blind eye to the passage of certain caravans'.

In England, on 5 July 1964, after intensive research, *The Sunday Times*'s Insight team published a full-page article, reproducing the letters in facsimile. One – a communication to Johnny from Barclays Bank in Ongar, about personal matters – was almost innocuous, except that it mentioned that a sum of £400 was being sent monthly to his wife. Also harmless was a handwritten note from Lady Birdwood, which thanked Johnny for a letter he had written about medical supplies and sympathised with him for suffering such hardships:

You must be having a *very* tough time of it, and I hope the Yemenis will at least offer you a seat in any future cabinet! Seriously, they must be tremendously grateful to you and I look forward one day to meeting you and hearing a full account of your work.

The third letter baffled the Insight team. It began with 'Dear' and a squiggle – and even if they had deciphered this as 'Abdullah', they could not have known that it was Johnny's alias; the place of origin was given as NORMAL, and the signature was such an illegible scrawl that they failed to realise that the author was Peter de la Billière. Nevertheless, one unfortunate phrase – 'congrats on the mineing' (*sic*) – made the document suspect. The two remaining letters were from Tony Boyle and gave away dangerous secrets: they mentioned parachutes and dropping zones, showed that the writer was sending soldiers out to the Yemen, and revealed that he was involved in some covert operation, working from 21 Sloane Street.

The journalists were onto a red-hot story. In an introduction to the article they wrote that their investigations had produced a picture 'of a small – but apparently most effective – group of Britons combating Egyptian tanks among the rugged Yemeni mountains'. But they had also stumbled on:

a startling link between these Buchanesque freebooters and a man who, until January 29 this year, was a serving officer of the RAF: Flt Lt Anthony Alexander Boyle, a son of Marshal of the RAF Sir Dermot Boyle. Until October 1, 1963, Boyle was serving in Aden as ADC to the British High Commissioner – the official charged with implementing Britain's policy in the area.

British policy, the introduction went on, had always been 'not to get involved in this business', and the Foreign Office, in response to enquiries, had assured the newspaper that 'any activity by individuals in the Yemen is entirely unauthorised'. The article gave a detailed outline of Johnny's military career, and linked him with David Stirling, but did not follow up a mention of 'Jim' in one of the Boyle letters. Having failed to discern Jim's identity or involvement, the Insight team concluded that it was Cooper who had 'decided to organise his own military-aid programme for the Royalists' and had 'built up' the mercenary organisation, with 'some advice, at least, about recruiting from his old CO, David Stirling'. Stirling, for his part, seems to have been decidedly economical with the truth, and told the newspaper, 'Any suggestion that this was organised by an ex-SAS caucus would be completely wrong.'

Other newspapers seized on the story. AIR FORCE OFFICER IS ACCUSED OF ARAB ARMS DEAL, bellowed the front-page headline in the *Sunday Mirror,* which reported that Richard Marsh, the Member of Parliament for Greenwich, had tabled a question for the Prime Minister and demanded an immediate inquiry about 'shock allegations' that an RAF officer had been involved in deals to supply men and arms to the Royalists. GUN RUNNING STORM, cried the *Daily Express* on Monday morning. Reporters called at 21 Sloane Street, only to be told that Boyle 'had been there but wasn't now', and that Stirling was in Hong Kong. Tony's brother, Patrick, was quoted as saying, 'We have lost touch with him. We haven't seen him for some time.' The press also drew a blank at the home of Boyle's parents in Hampshire, and Lady Birdwood, run to earth in Kensington, staunchly maintained that she knew of 'no arms smuggling or secret army'.

By the time the first article appeared, Cooper happened to be on leave, at home in Essex, having just returned from the Yemen, and when he awoke that Sunday morning he did not see a newspaper until he went to his local pub, the White Hart, opposite his house, which was easily identified by its colours – white with yellow shutters – and in any case gave itself away by being named Cooper's Court. By mid-morning a swarm of journalists had begun to gather, setting up tele-photo lenses outside his home, so he decided his best option was to stay put in the bar, shielded by a crowd of friends, who told reporters that he was 'still away on holiday'. As he himself recorded:

Some of the stories that appeared in the Monday papers were like comic strips and were certainly written under the influence of too much drink. One or two stated that Major Cooper's country headquarters was manned by strong-arm men from the SAS . . . Lady Birdwood even stood accused of gun-running![1]

It was Jim who got Cooper out: over the telephone he told him to stay in the pub for the time being, and said he would send Fiona Fraser to collect him. Early on Tuesday morning a little red Mini drove into the car park at the back and he slipped into it. At the same time his brother-in-law took his own car out from his house and drove off in the opposite direction, pursued by a press convoy. Fiona took him to the nearby village of Fyfield, where clothes and other kit that he needed for his return to the Yemen had been deposited, and from there she drove him straight to Sloane Avenue, and then to Heathrow to board the BOAC flight to Aden.

Another brief panic ensued when she and Jim heard a man, or possibly two, chattering excitedly in what they took to be Arabic, in the passage outside their Sloane Street office. Unable to stand it any longer, she opened the door – and there was Colin Campbell, a brilliant mimic, who worked for TIE in the office above, winding them up by pretending to be two Egyptians, but in fact talking to himself.

Tony Boyle also had to take evasive action. One of *The Sunday Times* reporters had sent him a draft of the article two days before publication, asking for his comments; but the envelope had been addressed to him at the Royal Air Force Club in Piccadilly, and he had not received it. As he landed back at Heathrow after one of the Israeli parachute-drops, he found an anonymous message awaiting him: 'Don't go home. The Press are camped outside your house.' He therefore stayed overnight with his uncle in London, then drove down to hide with friends at Porlock Weir in north Devon, and made no contact with anyone save family and office; but, knowing that questions would be asked of the Prime Minister and the Colonial Secretary in the House, he waited nervously, close to a telephone.

At last it rang. Laurie Hobson, a friend from Aden days, now working in Duncan Sandys's office, had broken through his protective wall. He explained that the Secretary of State had to make a statement in the House of Commons. What was Tony going to say to the press?

'Nothing.'

'But you can't avoid them.'

'I have and I will.'

'Does Charles Johnston know what was going on?'

'You'll have to ask him.'

'He's on a plane that doesn't land until after parliamentary question time.'

'Well, I'm sorry – I can't answer for him.'

Boyle soon came to the conclusion that his 'head was on the block' – but he resolved that he would not 'be crushed by this steam roller'. He had met Sandys several times, and found him arrogant and overbearing; but he knew that, as Defence Secretary, he had tacitly authorised the Yemen operation in the first place. He also knew that Sandys knew that he knew, as Sandys had been present on one occasion when he went to brief Julian Amery in the House of Commons, and now Boyle determined to use that knowledge to stop Sandys throwing all the blame on him. So he called the Colonial Office back and told Laurie that his undertaking to avoid the press would be conditional upon the answers given by the Prime Minister and Mr Sandys. A chuckle at the end of the line affirmed his tactics. The questions were duly asked, and answered impeccably. The newsmen moved out of Boyle's garden, and he went home.

In the House of Commons on 21 July the Prime Minister was at his most equivocal. When asked about Tony's activities, he said: 'Both the present High Commissioner [Trevaskis] and his predecessor [Johnston] have assured us that they were not aware that the person in question was involved in any way.'[2] When Richard Marsh suggested that even if Johnston had not known exactly what was going on, 'he had a pretty good idea', Sir Alec replied:

No. The Hon. Gentleman has no right to make that kind of insinuation. Both Sir Charles Johnston and the High Commissioner have assured me that they had no idea at all that Mr Boyle was engaged in these activities – and I must take their word for it, and I do . . . Our policy is one of non-involvement in the civil war in the Yemen.[3]

The left-wing Sidney Silverman, MP for Nelson and Colne, referring to 'these very extensive, very dangerous and very mischievous activities', asked the Prime Minister if he did not consider that Johnston and Trevaskis – if they had been unaware of what was going on – had committed 'a gross dereliction of duty in not knowing what was completely obvious'. Sir Alec, however, was not to be shifted: 'I cannot say whether they should have noticed this. The fact is that they did not.'[4]

The furore soon died down – and might have been a great deal more damaging. But, as Johnny remarked, it 'gave Nasser a valuable propaganda victory and even soured relations between the Americans and the British Government – who naturally denied all knowledge of our activities.'[5] The sudden exposure gave everyone in the BFLF a jolt, and showed how fragile their security arrangements were. But the article did no mortal damage: Jim merely kept his head down, and carried on as before. Luckily, he had never had any direct contact with the Prime Minister, or with his predecessor, Macmillan.

As for Lady Birdwood: no matter how much she knew or did not know about the activities of the BFLF, she rose majestically to the occasion in a letter to the *Daily Telegraph* that extolled Johnny's virtues to an embarrassing degree. Major Cooper, she wrote, had gratefully acknowledged receipt of the medical supplies sent out by the Yemen Relief Committee, telling her of the 'long, weary hours in terribly difficult terrain' that he spent moving from one village to another:

> The enormous amount of Major Cooper's medical work in Yemen can have left little time for other activities . . . Major Cooper has performed miracles of treatment, and long ago he wrote to me: 'I only wish you could see the relief on the sufferers' faces and the great joy we

both get from curing these people . . . I would like to take this opportunity personally and publicly to thank him.

In the Khowlan, meanwhile, Jack Miller and his colleagues had been doing their best to bolster the morale of the Imam, who had sent out an alarmist message to the Aden Government, saying that many Royalist positions had been lost, that El Qara was surrounded, and that the whole of the north-west was in grave danger, all due to the lack of money, rifles, artillery and ammunition. 'Can you please send any help or supply as soon as possible, before all lost?' the ruler pleaded. 'Can you deliver us?'

At the same time, high-level diplomatic meetings were taking place, as the Saudis put pressure on Britain to send the Royalists official aid. When Sir Colin Crowe, the British Ambassador to Jeddah, had an interview with Feisal at Taif on 28 July, the Saudi Crown Prince told him sharply that the Yemenis were 'crying out for help' from the United Kingdom, and 'mocked the apparent weakness of such a 'strong nation' in supporting its position in South Arabia'.

In Crowe's despatch to London, he noted Feisal's attempt to invoke the spectre of a wider geo-political threat. Nasser's agents were everywhere undermining the area, the Saudi Prince had told him. The Egyptians were a spearhead for the Russians, who were putting in help secretly. Surely the British could likewise help the Royalists?[6]

In fact official British policy was veering in the opposite direction. In London the exposure of the letters had made HMG even less inclined to support the mercenaries openly – although Billy McLean and Nigel Fisher continued to press hard for money, weapons and food to be sent to the Royalist armies. The wrangling between Foreign Office, Colonial Office and Ministry of Defence reached such a pitch that on 22 July, in a memorandum to Rab Butler, the Foreign Secretary, Sir Alec decreed that the United Kingdom should 'make life intolerable' for Nasser, 'with money and arms', and that this 'should be deniable if possible'.[7] This led to the creation of a Joint Action Committee (JAC), charged with the task of coordinating policy towards the Yemen.

9

Business as Usual

At the office on Sloane Street, or at haunts such as White's and the Hyde Park Hotel, Jim was receiving a continuous stream of visitors: Ahmed al-Shami, Billy McLean, Dan Hiram, Rupert France – and occasionally a member of Mossad, disguised in his diary by the cryptic entry 'The boy'. Paul Paulson (of MI6) was another frequent caller. In the early days of the operation Jim had been required to deliver copies of his regular reports to an anonymous address in Paddington; but as the SIS gained confidence in him, Paulson disclosed his real name and job, and started coming in twice a week for a drink and to pick up the latest news.

In the running of the BFLF it was generally Jim who had the ideas and made the diplomatic or political contacts, but it was Tony Boyle who kept the engine of the organisation going. Nahum Admoni, who was posted to Paris in 1966 as Mossad's representative in western Europe, developed a great admiration for the courage and professionalism of both. Jim he saw as a natural leader of men, who could be tough and demanding, but at the same time was outgoing and had a strong sense of humour; whereas he found Tony 'more of a loner, very straight and proper'. Their personalities, he thought, were reflected in their military experience: Jim was a field commander, Tony a fighter-pilot.

Jim did a good deal of entertaining – and none of it was skimped: lunch at Scott's or L'Escargot, dinner at the Savoy. Whenever he and Tony were in London they helped with the day-to-day administration, but a great deal of intricate secretarial work was carried out by the excellent Fiona Fraser – as one typical letter (to Chris Sharma, on leave, and about to return to the Imam's headquarters at El Qara) will show:

Dear Chris,
    Enclosed with this note you will find:

    Your ticket to Jeddah
    Your passport and visa
    Your cheque for August
    £50 expenses for your journey etc
    A letter for David – to be delivered personally, and a parcel.

    During your stay in London today will you do the following:
    a. Buy 4 field telephones and take them out with you.
    b. Go to see Shami at 41 South Street at 11.30. He would much like to talk to you and has some letters for you to take out.

We were unable to book you a hotel room as the reservations office only takes bookings for the same day, so ring WEL 2555, tell them how much you want to spend and they will book you in f.o.c. [free of charge].

Khibsi has been informed what plane you are arriving on and should meet you, but you know the form if he doesn't.

Mac wants 10 miles of assault cable – buy it in Jeddah and get Khibsi to pay. Mac has been ordered to go via Jauf to take the next operation (parachuting).[2]

David will remain i/c at El Qara. You must work very closely together, remember he is in charge, and do all you can to co-operate –

I'm sure you will.

Tony.

In the Yemen the usual bloody exchanges were continuing. On 26 June 1964 Royalist commandos had attacked an Egyptian outpost close to Jihannah, killing five men. That night the commandos attacked another outpost at El Misharakah. 'Egyptian casualties are not known,' said a report, 'but dead bodies were seen coming on a lorry from the post in the morning.' On the morning of the 28th the Egyptians shelled the town of Bashar in retaliation: fire was directed by a spotter helicopter and maintained throughout the morning, but there were no casualties.

Sporadic skirmishes continued relentlessly. On the night of 30 June–1 July Royalist artillery shelled the Egyptians outside Sana'a, maintaining their bombardment until dawn. In the early hours of 1 July the Egyptian/Republican headquarters at Jihannah was blown up by a bomb, and the explosion, seen and heard by Royalist outposts above the town, was described as 'tremendous'. Egyptian vehicles converged from all around, and one set off a mine 100 yards from the walls of the town.

The vehicle, a lorry, disintegrated. Later, the Royalists learnt that it had contained four Egyptian officers, who were coming to investigate. In retaliation, the Egyptians cut down all the fruit trees and grape vines outside Jihannah and offered a big reward for information about those responsible.

For the time being, the Egyptians were on a losing streak. On the morning of 3 July one of their patrol officers discovered a bomb outside the house of Abdul Wahab al-Gabri, but before the device could be tackled, it exploded, killing him and seven soldiers. On the morning of 7 July a message from Johnny to all stations reported that, after a dispute in the headquarters at Sana'a, an Egyptian officer had shot and killed four Egyptian and three Yemeni officers while resisting arrest, before he himself was gunned down.

The fragmented nature of the war, and its viciousness, were graphically illustrated by a single report from the mercenary front, relayed through Bosom, the mother radio station in Jeddah, and sent home on 31 July 1964:

1 In the Khowlan the following Egyptian casualties are reported: three killed in Sharasah gap by rifle-fire. Eight killed, four wounded at Bait Thubaht. One killed, three wounded at Bait al Hamshmii.

2 There is still no increase in air activity in Khowlan area. Only one daily Ilyushin transport plane to Harib.

3 Two mines exploded in Wadi Assir, destroying one staff car and one armoured car — no indication of casualties.

4 The Governor's house in Bait Assaid was bombed, killing a Republican officer and wounding two soldiers.

5 A mine exploded in Wadi Maswar, destroying an armoured car.

6 Nine Egyptians were killed by a guerrilla group in Jihannah.

7 Three Egyptians were killed and a tank destroyed in Sayyan village by a guerrilla group.

8 In retaliation for the Egyptians raping a woman in the village of Al Jardah, the villagers killed four Egyptians and threw two of them down a well. They all refuse to work for the Egyptians.

9 An Egyptian was killed in a village three kilometres from Sana'a, and a Royalist while being interrogated had his eyes, ears, nose and mouth cut off (*sic*).

10 Ten Royalists ambushed an Egyptian staff car killing three passengers and the driver.

11 In Bait Assaid, near Sana'a, a tank was destroyed and four Egyptians killed.

12 There has been heavy fighting in the Hajjah area, with the following casualties reported: 150 Egyptians and Republicans killed, 250 wounded, forty prisoners. Some artillery and heavy machine guns and rifles captured.

In August the Egyptians launched an attempt to capture or kill the Imam. Had they managed to catch him, the Royalists would have suffered a catastrophic loss of morale and their whole effort might well have collapsed, leaving the Egyptian Army victorious.

For once the ruler was in acute danger. On 15 and 16 August the Egyptians made a determined effort to sever the motorable route from Jizan to the foot of the mountains at El Qara; fearing that he would be isolated and surrounded, the Imam slipped down out of his eyrie during the night of 16/17, leaving Mansoor (Sharma) to hold the fort, and went north to the area of Meschaf, almost on the Saudi border. There he made exceptional efforts to rally his troops, constantly moving on at night, never staying in one place for long. For day after day Republican and Royalist troops faced each other, holding the heights on either side of the road to the west, and expending prodigious amounts of small-arms ammunition. Jack Miller, with the Imam, feared that his party might be surrounded by Egyptian tanks sweeping round through the flat desert north of Meschaf. He thought they might even cross the border into Saudi Arabia. 'They are not frightened of SA,' he wrote in a report. 'They bomb it now, and nothing will stop them in this open country.' Trying to predict what might happen, he thought it unlikely that the Imam could return to his former hiding place 'for a long time, if at all':

What the political situation is, I don't know. All I know is that at the present time HM thinks Her Majesty's Government is a pack of liars who have stabbed him in the back by not keeping their promises of aid from the south — money, arms etc.

Another Egyptian push elicited an unusually agitated message from Johnny in Aden:

Imam position very bad indeed. Sharma [at El Qara] has my instructions to blow up all equipment and codes prior to getting out if necessary. Bailey is in Jeddah and is planning to return to Imam, but road is cut by Egyptians. Sharma will join me here if he has to evacuate.

Just as the situation was becoming desperate, the pressure eased. After taking heavy casualties, the Egyptians drew back – possibly (it was thought) in a deliberate move to lure the Imam into returning to El Qara, where he could be isolated. The Royalists issued a triumphant communiqué, claiming that 'near-disaster' faced the retreating Egyptian and Republican troops. A counter-attack, personally led by the ruler, had driven Nasser's troops into a trap, and 1,200 of them had been killed. The fighting had evidently been confused: 'Ill-defined battle lines in rugged mountain terrain with armour channelled in sandy wadi bottoms at right angles to the front.' Two tanks and five armoured cars had been destroyed, and twenty-five more Republican soldiers had been accidentally killed in attacks by Egyptian aircraft.

Even allowing for the characteristic exaggeration of such announcements, it was clear that the Egyptians had suffered a serious reverse, when their advance became bogged down by mud and rain. Two more ambushes in ravines sent the raiding parties back to Haradh in confusion, losing half their armoured cars and ten tanks. A week later the Egyptians did nothing to increase their popularity by machine-gunning fleeing remnants of the Republican assault force and killing another 200 of them. The Royalists claimed that in all the enemy had lost 2,000 men.

In spite of these victories, the autumn of 1964 was a time of acute anxiety for the BFLF. For various reasons the flow of money from Saudi Arabia dried up: the Sherif of Beihan was owed £500, and the Royalist princes were appealing urgently for new funds. With the Imam's sudden departure from El Qara, contradictory messages, back and forth between Aden and the UK, had left everyone confused as to who was in command. A cable from Johnny told London that the

Imam had left the country, but a message from London said that he was still in the Yemen. A letter from a Frenchman in EL Qara claimed that the ruler was in a small village close to the Saudi border, and 'was not seeing anyone'. Next he was said to be inside Saudi, hiding by day and coming secretly by night to a village in the Yemen for talks with his principal commanders, Abdullah bin Hassan and Mohamed bin Hussein.

Further uncertainty was engendered by reports that Prince Feisal and Nasser had struck a deal to end hostilities, when the Saudi Prime Minister visited Cairo. The British were immediately sceptical about a most unlikely-sounding statement that Feisal was alleged to have put out: 'I leave Egypt with my heart brimming with love for Nasser and the people of Egypt.' As Tony pointed out, the remark had obviously been made 'for the benefit of the UAR'. All the same, the future of the BFLF looked extremely uncertain.

Even though Johnny was in Aden for the time being, his mind was still very much in the Khowlan. From the unaccustomed comfort of an office, he eagerly passed on news from various fronts:

Two mine-layers placing plastic (Wog) mines caught at Bait Baruat (Sana'a). Wogs cut right arm and left leg off both prisoners! . . . Guerrilla group commanded by Col. Gassim Monassir attacked Wog forward defence location in Wadi Shaub, four minutes by vehicle from Sana'a, killing all eighteen Wogs (asleep). One armoured car set on fire. All Sana'a alerted, and Wogs still pooping off three hours after all Royalists miles away. Road to north closed all next day.

For all such successes, he was chagrined by the lack of adequate financial support. 'It really is a bloody waste of all our time, this continued living on a shoe-string,' he wrote to Tony on 13 September. Another of his *bêtes noires* was the Foreign Office. 'About time the ostriches got their heads out of the bloody sand . . . The UK really are the END, Tony. Agree?'

Johnny felt that the war was not being pursued 'correctly or eagerly', and suggested that Jim should visit Prince Feisal so that he could explain the mercenaries' predicament, the reluctance of the princes and their open lack of cooperation. If Jim went to Jeddah, he wrote, he might be able to obtain control of the money and supplies, 'so that they are directed to the areas that justify them, instead of people stock-piling for after the war'. To have a grip of the money supply would be 'wonderful' for the advisers.

Johnny's frustration was shared by Jim, and on 25 September he sent out a doom-laden cable:

In view reported deal between Burns [Feisal] and Christie [Nasser] over Dickens' [the Imam's] impending departure and total lack of knitting [money] your end stand by all to return next week stop your contracts cancelled 31/10 . . . Regret short of miracle this is the end jay.

Four days later, however, the warning order was overtaken by a more cheerful message: 'miracle now possible meanwhile one thousand knitting pins sent airmail Monday your contracts reinstated stop letter follows.'

The miracle was being wrought by Johnny, who went to Saudi Arabia – no doubt at Jim's request – and proved such a persuasive advocate that substantial funds immediately became available. His mission was almost aborted when, arriving in Jeddah, he found that his visa was out of date, and the authorities told him he must carry on to Beirut. But, as he reported, he 'turned on the charm and although pass-port-less was allowed into here' – and quickly obtained results. 'So far things are going OK,' he told Jim on the day after he arrived:

> I see Shami again tomorrow and perhaps Feisal also, as he has asked to see me. I have had a promise of five thousand to take back on Sunday 25th. [Then, a day later] Well, it's worked out fine and I have collected three months' money for inside from Feisal . . . I feel very happy about this trip.

Later he told Jim that although he had secured £5,000, some of the Saudi authorities thought he had asked for too little. 'The Imam does not want us or French,' he added. 'To quote: "I want men to fire the cannons, not advisers, radio operators etc.!"'

In the Khowlan, Johnny's place had been taken by Bernard Mills, the powerfully built, Arabic-speaking officer now in his early thirties, formerly of the Royal Anglian Regiment and the SAS, who had been obliged to decline Jim's orig-inal invitation to take part, and had recommended Johnny in the first place. Now, in May 1964, having completed his tour in Muscat, and propelled (like Jim) by patriotic fervour, Bernard flew to Aden and on to Beihan, where he collected a consignment of medical supplies from the Sherif's house. Then, in company with a couple of Belgians and Philippe

Camus – the Frenchman who had been blinded by gas during Johnny Cooper's first foray, but had recovered his sight after treatment in France – he joined a long camel train carrying weapons.[3] On their way in they were detained by a tribe demanding money – but when somebody paid off the aggressors, both sides settled down to what Bernard described as 'a kind of team tea, as after a cricket match. We sat on one side, they on the other. Goats were killed and we all tucked in.'[4] Thereafter the caravan proceeded to Gara, and Bernard soon established a good relationship with Prince Abdullah bin Hassan.

He also settled quickly into his strange new life. His first quarters were in a two-roomed house made of stone, but he preferred to sleep outside in the vineyard. Three of his bodyguard were stationed at the little post set up to stop people stealing the grapes, and one of them was supposed to be awake all the time – but Bernard could never be sure, so he moved around to a different spot every night to minimise the chance of being assassinated. His normal alarm call was the scream of a MiG overhead, for the Egyptian jets usually began their sorties at dawn, because the air was coolest then, and the airfield at Sana'a was 6,000 feet above sea-level – an altitude that made take-off difficult in very high temperatures.

He trusted his men absolutely, because they were his travelling companions – and Yemenis traditionally did *not* betray the people with whom they journeyed. Some of them he inherited from Johnny, and some he got from another tribe, always trying to have different tribes represented. Because he spoke some Arabic, and could communicate, he got on well with them – even though his Arabic was Omani, and quite different from theirs. Hearing his strange accent and archaic expressions, and seeing how tall he was, people often took him for an Egyptian, and in particular for an Egyptian Intelligence Officer, which came in very useful whenever he had to pass through Egyptian lines or spend a night in a Republican village.

Bernard's people were grateful to him for giving them employment, and for being the nearest thing they knew to a doctor – although, hating the sight of blood, he was reluctant to stitch up the wounds caused by *jambiya* fights. The villagers were desperately poor, and (apart from their transistor radios) were living in the sixteenth century. Driven from their houses by the Egyptian bombing, many had taken refuge in caves; but as he moved around the mountain country, on foot or by donkey, Bernard was struck by the beauty of the landscape, and by the amount of fruit growing in the valleys: going through villages, he used to fill his pockets with dried almonds and raisins bought from stalls at the side of the track. He soon became exceedingly fit, often covering 20 miles and climbing or descending 8,000 feet in a day – and his endurance was much better than that of his bodyguards, who liked to stop for a rest at frequent intervals and were not used to sustained walking.

He established an easy relationship with Abdullah bin Hassan, but realised that his own powers were limited: although he could advise and try to help, he could not give orders or tell the Prince what to do. His tact and good sense were evidently much appreciated, and Hassan was eager for him to stay on. But his first tour in the Khowlan was short, for he was given the urgent task of taking photographs of a new DZ and the surrounding mountains, and conveying them, together with plans of the ground, to Israel.

Having trekked back to Aden, he flew to London and thence to Athens, where he changed to an El Al flight for Israel. In Tel Aviv he briefed senior air officers – and when they asked what would happen if the aircraft came down in the Yemen, Bernard replied that he would do exactly the same as if the plane was one of the RAF's: he would make every possible effort to extract the crew safely from the country.

Returning to the Yemen in September 1964, he again walked out to the Khowlan, to a new station some forty minutes' walk west of Abdullah bin Hassan's own base. There was a clear advantage in being separated from the royal encampment, for it meant that the British team was not beset by the hundreds of tribesmen who constantly milled around outside the Prince's cave.

On 3 October the mercenaries' financial crisis was eased by the arrival in Aden of 5,000 gold sovereigns destined for Hassan; but the confidence of the BFLF team had been shaken, and on 8 October Johnny Cooper, David Bailey and Mac McSweeney held a meeting in Room 41 of the Rock Hotel in Aden. They agreed that their field organisation was running 'on a shoe-string', and that they were not giving of their best. One operator, Roy, had just been sacked for a variety of failings ('mental instability, "Walter Mitty" outlook, very bad physical condition, security risk appalling – talks too much'), which left only six men on the ground: Abdullah bin Nasser [Johnny] Bernard, David Bailey, Mac, Mansoor [Sharma] and Cyril Weavers, with Franco (Rupert France) as their base controller. They reckoned that if the organisation was to function effectively, they needed to recruit two new teams of three. 'It is apparent to all of us,' said the minutes of their meeting, 'that at the moment field work is nil, and local leaders (Arab) are becoming increasingly angry at our continual trips in and out and lack of continuity.'

After the fiasco with Roy, the impromptu committee directed some sharp remarks at the London office. 'All recruits must be thoroughly vetted on their self appraisal by going to root sources,' said the minutes:

> It *must* be realised in UK that moves in and out of any areas in the Yemen are not streamlined like VIP visits . . . Delays by tribal, political, absent princes, enemy activity, ransom and tolls all combine to delay our moves, therefore maximum warning of any UK-ordered moves must be given from now on.

Writing to Johnny from London in self-defence, Tony stressed that 'our main problem has been money for running the show':

> Sammy [Shami] is presently (we hope) renegotiating our contract with Seymour [Prince Sultan] . . . [but] it would be quite improper for us, and would put Sammy into an intolerable position, if we at this stage were to propose the plan of six outstations and two bases.

Jim and Tony were also worried about Chris Sharma, who was now styling himself 'Mansoor ibn Nasr al Beni Borhwa, Honory [sic] Emir of the Royal Kingdom of Yemen', and whom they thought had already 'become too Arab'. Earlier, Rupert France had described him going off to the Jauf 'with guns hanging from every crook and cranny, hand grenades and a bayonet. Sleeps with a loaded revolver and the safety catch off'. Now Tony wrote, 'The longer he remains, the more Arab he is going to become and hence the less effective. We all agree people must not be forced to operate alone for too long.' Sharma, for his part, was well aware of how much he annoyed Jack Miller, and apologised to Tony for the fact that he appeared 'to rub him up the wrong way'. 'I have always maintained that my primary concern is to establish and maintain communications,' he wrote stiffly, 'which appears contrary to Jack's policy.'

Now Sharma, unaware of the latest financial crisis, had rejoined the Imam at a temporary headquarters in a cave about half an hour's climb from the road-head at Shida, just inside the Yemen–Saudi frontier. There he found Shami, who reassured him that there was money in London; but when, in the morning Sharma asked the Imam's secretary, Yahya al-Hirsi, to arrange an interview with the ruler, he found himself caught in the usual thicket of delay, tersely described in his diary:

30/9 Request to see HM. Emir Yahya replies, 'Later'.

1/10 Request to see HM. Yahya replies 'Later'. Write to HM in Arabic. Answer: 'Please wait'. Ask Yahya for order to use radio in Jizan. He says, 'Must see HM first.'

2/10 Request to see HM. Yahya replies, 'Later'. Ask for order to go to Jizan to work radio. He says, 'Must see HM first.' Ask to see him at once. As always, told, 'Later'. Ask for truck to front to help Amir Abdullah al Hussein by tank hunting. Told by Yahya, 'Must see HM' . . .

Bloody cold at night, since Yahya said there were no blankets free. Yahya and HM slept on portable sprung-mattress beds!

Sharma did eventually gain regular access to the Presence, and enforced idleness over many days gave him a chance to write at length to Boyle, outlining his view of the situation:

As I now see HM every day I have had a chance to get to know him and vice versa. We get on very well, and he was quite worried when I said I would like a month's leave and that I was only here temporarily anyway. He told me today that he has written to Shami to ask you that I may stay here . . . Personally, I would like to stay, and I feel that I have his confidence and he will abide (to some extent) by my advice on weapons etc.

The guiding principle is at present that the Egyptians must leave sooner or later. HM also realises that the troops in this sector are not soldiers by anybody's standards, except for about 200 of the royal guard. It appears that as long as we can maintain the status quo territorially, we will win, as the Egyptians cannot afford the expenditure indefinitely. On the other hand, gold must flow into the Royalist hands, or the Royalists have had it . . .

It must be understood that the *gebile*, or peasants, like anywhere, only wish to live in peace and quiet.[5] Thus whether the territory is ours or theirs, the *gebile* are happy if there is peace. Thus the primary objective *now* of the sector commanders in the south is not to provoke an Egyptian attack. The *gebile*, who bear the brunt of the bombs on their homes and lands, justifiably get annoyed when they see their life savings go up in smoke.

As is generally admitted, the Royalists can only hold their own mountains, and since practically all mountains are Royalist, one just tries to stop the Egyptians increasing their territory. HM fully admits that the only real fighting has been done by John Cooper with Abdullah bin Hassan, where there were mountains to be gained. For the record, he thinks John C is great, and that the Khowlan would have been lost to the Egyptians long ago but for him. The locals here regard him as some sort of super-Emir, of infinite wisdom and strength, and are quite awed by what he has done, as well as hero-worshipping Abdullah bin Hassan.

Mansoor/Sharma was so busy talking to the Imam that he neglected his day-to-day duties – to the great annoyance of Lord Kilbracken, on assignment for his newspapers, the London *Daily Express* and the *Evening Standard*. Provoked beyond endurance by various delays, Kilbracken took out a blunt pencil and scribbled a furious note:

> The camel arrived *five hours* late. Of course there was no mule. So I have only just arrived here and God knows when the camel will turn up . . . You said at 4 p.m. yesterday that you would send down provisions to the hospital 'immediately'. Of course none arrived, so I had no supper. This meant that I had to walk today on an empty stomach – as well as in the full heat of the day.
>
> I regard these as typical final examples of your total inability to arrange *anything*. You presume to refer to yourself as 'Military Adviser to His Majesty', but in fact you couldn't give advice to a lance corporal in Fred Karno's army. At least it will all make good copy, which will NOT be subject to censorship.
>
> Kilbracken[6]

Sharma was worrying members of his own team, as well. 'Really Mansoor will have to consider himself less indispensable or we shall have a mutiny on our hands,' wrote Jack Miller, after the two of them had interviewed the Imam:

He was becoming almost condescending to the Imam and talking so much that I had to get rid of him half way through our interview in order to finish our agenda by daybreak. He wants to be sent here as resident operator, but I do not consider he is safe to be given authority to do more than operate and repair sets in case he makes a fool of himself by trying to run the whole country on his own!!

Mansoor seemed to attract trouble wherever he was. On one occasion all his kit was stolen by Mohamed bin Hussein's soldiers – but Jim, in Jeddah, managed to recover £70 from the Prince, and told him in a letter: 'I think we can all congratulate ourselves having got it from him.' Another time, at El Qara, Sharma had an argument with Mac and drew his .38 Webley – but the former wrestler had no difficulty getting the weapon off him.

In London, Jim's anxieties were sharply increased by the advent of a Labour Government on 16 October 1964, when Harold Wilson won the general election and became Prime Minister. His majority was so small – only four votes – that he could not immediately introduce sweeping reforms; but his party's traditional dislike of colonialism inevitably raised fears about the future of Aden and the whole of South Arabia.

For the time being the BFLF carried on as before, encouraged by the fact that in November King Saud finally succumbed to Feisal's pressure and abdicated, going into exile in Greece, whereupon Feisal – always a strong supporter of the British effort – succeeded to the throne of Saudi Arabia.

Bernard Mills had by then returned to a new station near

Gara in the Khowlan, where he spent two months on his own. In the middle of December fighting broke out for three days between the Republicans and the Ben Haridh tribe, whose Sheikh had been summoned to Sana'a to settle a dispute, but had refused to go. In an attempt to stamp out the squabble, a combined force of Republicans and Egyptians was assembled under the command of the Yemen Chief of Police, Abdullah Barakat, but when he found how strong the resistance was, he suggested a meeting, and in the end the Egyptian forces were obliged to pay 40,000 MTDs and four oxen, to obtain a precarious ceasefire. Republican casualties were mounting rapidly, and Royalist mining had become so effective that the Egyptians were obliged to sweep roads with 20mm cannons mounted on trucks, backed by tanks, in an attempt to detonate mines laid during the night.

Allegiances constantly shifted; treachery was ubiquitous. One ruler near Jebel Raza (where the Imam was in hiding) had been a noted Republican since the revolution; but in December 1964 he declared for the Imam, sending his son as a hostage, to show his good faith. The Imam returned the son, together with some money, saying he had never doubted the Sheikh's good faith, and quite understood the difficulties under which he had been labouring. Soon afterwards the Egyptians wanted to pass through the Sheikh's territory and were granted free passage – until they came to a narrow wadi, where the whole group was exterminated by men concealed among the rocks on the surrounding hillsides. Even if the figure of 400 dead, which the Sheikh claimed, was an exaggeration, he had dealt the invaders a nasty blow.

At about that time Bernard began to feel ill, with severe pains in his lower back. After radio consultations with Aden he thought the trouble must be kidney stones – and it was a measure of Abdullah bin Hassan's esteem that he proposed sending a party down to Sana'a to raid the military hospital, capture a couple of doctors and bring them up into the mountains by force to treat him. Towards the end of December Bernard was too ill to take the next planned para-drop, even though the Israelis were pressing for it, and from Aden Johnny told him to take no unnecessary risks over his health. Rather than risk letting his condition deteriorate by waiting, he should lock up everything in the camp and come out whichever way he thought best.

On the 16th Bernard was feeling slightly better, having followed radioed medical instructions and injected himself, but he was clearly very sick and decided to go out via the Jauf, east of the central massif. Leaving his station 'well booby-trapped', he set off on Christmas Eve, riding Prince Abdullah's own mule, which wore a chaplet of silver bells around its neck to announce that a Person of Importance was on the move. He spent that night in one of the highest villages in the Yemen, and as he listened to a Forces' broadcast from Aden on his radio, he felt rather low; but on Christmas Day, with frost on the ground and his bodyguards running beside him, his spirits lifted. Continuing to the north, he went through the Egyptian lines after dark on New Year's Day 1965, and made his way to the Red Cross hospital at Uqd, near the Saudi border. The doctors there decided that his problem was not kidney stones, but something else – so he carried on through the frontier to Najran, caught a plane to Jeddah, flew down to Aden and thence to London, where he arrived on 10 January 1965.

Meanwhile the BFLF office had suffered a serious loss with the departure of Fiona Fraser, who had decided to go travelling, on one of the long journeys that she favoured.

Luckily for Jim, she found an excellent replacement in the form of another Scot, Hannah Stirling.[7]

At the end of February 1965, cured of his illness, Bernard duly returned to the Yemen, with instructions from Jim to proceed to the Jauf , where he could ginger up Mohamed bin Hussein and 'get them fighting'. Another reason for his posting to the eastern sector was that, from there, should medical problems recur, he could be evacuated to hospital by the rough road that skirted the mountains and ran up around the edge of the desert to Najran. That way, he would not have to pass through the Egyptian lines, whereas – he knew only too well – there was no road to or from the mercenary stations in the Khowlan. A third reason was that Johnny Cooper was already back in the Khowlan, and there seemed little point in having the organisation's two best Arabic-speakers (him and Bernard) together in one place.

Johnny, however, was furious about Bernard's posting. He himself had been privately planning to take over from Rupert France (Franco) as anchor man in Aden, and now complained bitterly to Jim:

I am led to believe that Bernard is returning on his own account and not under my command to an area he wants. This I cannot accept. If he is in the Org he must come into line, or all order/discipline will cease. I want Bernard if and when he returns to go to Zone 3 in Arhab [the rocky plateau north of Sana'a] . . . His short stints have not made him very popular with the others, as they maintain the rules are for all to follow.

This is completely contrary to my planning. Consider your/Bernard intentions should have been sent me Field

Boss before implementation. Your policy all personnel
[re]moves my responsibility – if you lack confidence my
judgement please clarify.

In spite of this outburst, Bernard duly went up into the
Jauf, where in due course he masterminded the planning for
the most resounding Royalist success of the entire war, the
battle in Wadi Humeidat.

Apart from that problem, Johnny was in ebullient form.
'We are at the top of the popularity pole [sic] in all people's
eyes,' he told Jim. In the past twenty-three days three parachute-drops had come in; all the radio stations were operating; there had been a lot of medical activity; weapons
were being repaired. The worst problem was a shortage of
operators:

The French have lost their commander[8] and George [a
mortar expert] is filling the seat at Rose until a new
one arrives . . . They are down to twelve all told! Amiral
wants to stay with us and is first class in all respects.
George would like to join too so if their contracts do
expire we have the best here! The man under training
I want ASAP. We are too few chasing too many, and
when I leave for Aden it will leave my three on the
ground.[9]

So please what is the situation re recruits? We must
build up to about ten to allow leave . . . and to avoid
this problem of all due their leave at the same time . . .
Jim, can I recruit?!! If so how many and at what rank?!

Meanwhile there was a good deal of activity in the east,
where some of the tribes had begun to take action against

the enemy forces based around Harib, Juba and Marib. This pleased the Saudis, since their supply route to the Royalist forces in the southern Jauf ran through the area, and they accordingly increased their flow of weapons and money to Sherif Hussein of Beihan, who passed them on to the tribes. These people were not Royalist, being Shaffei (Sunni) rather than Zeidi (Shia), but they detested the Egyptians, and in early 1965 they stepped up their attacks on the occupying forces.

Under this increased harassment, the Egyptians withdrew their garrison that had been holding the vital Al Hagla pass above Harib, close to the Yemen border, and left a Republican force in its place. Spurred on by one of the British Field Intelligence Officers in the Protectorate, across the frontier to the south, the Murad and Abida tribes seized their chance and went on the attack. The assault began badly, when one lot of tribesmen bumped into another and started shooting, setting off an instant blood-feud and killing half a dozen men. But after a ritual shouting match the British officer managed to bring the leaders together – whereupon they got on with the war, recaptured the pass, held it, and on 14 March occupied Harib.

The Egyptians could ill afford to abandon outposts of such importance and, after once being beaten off, brought a whole brigade to recapture the pass. This they managed, losing their brigade commander in the process, but they were not strong enough to retake Harib. For the next two months their line of communication between Harib and Marib was so severely harried that they withdrew, first to Juba, then to Marib, and finally *from* Marib, so that the Royalists' southern flank was secured as far afield as Sirwah and Jihannah on the road to Sana'a.

By then, from Jim's point of view, the international political
outlook had taken a turn for the better, when the Americans at last admitted that in backing Nasser's assault on the
Yemen they had made a mistake. Belatedly they realised that
he would never win the war, and that he had been 'blinded
by his mission to promote revolutionary reform in the Arab
world'.[10] In talks with Parker T. Hart, the US Ambassador in
Riyadh, Feisal (now King) emphasised the extent to which
Nasser had become dependent on the Soviet Union for the
supply of weapons, and said that the Egyptian leader could
not easily extricate himself from the Yemen, even if he wanted
to.[11] In January 1965 the same point was taken up by the
Saudi Defence Minister, Prince Sultan, who told Billy McLean
that Hart had compared Nasser's position to that of a fly
stuck on fly-paper – he was caught in the Yemen, could not
escape from it and would slowly die there, like the fly.

Like its predecessor, the new government in Whitehall had
not publicly acknowledged the existence of Jim Johnson's
private army. But now the Foreign Secretary, Patrick Gordon-
Walker, began to argue that the mercenaries should no longer
be allowed to move through Aden and the Federation with
the freedom they had enjoyed until then. In particular, he
asked that McLean and Amery, who were planning another
trip, should not be granted RAF transport. 'I told you I
thought the time had come when these facilities should be
denied to them,' he wrote to the Colonial Secretary, Anthony
Greenwood, 'and that they should be told to move off British
territory':

Their presence there is inconsistent with our position
that we are not interfering in the internal conflict inside
Yemen: it complicates our efforts to get on better terms

with the UAR government, and it is liable to encourage
the Egyptians to increase their efforts to make difficulties for us in the Federation.[12]

Whatever might be said or thought in Whitehall, no pressure was put on Jim to call off his operation. As far as he
was concerned, business carried on as usual, and the only
constraints were financial: he was haunted by the continual
possibility that the Saudis might stop sending out gold to
the Yemeni princes, and cut off the flow of money with
which he was paying his own operators. This anxiety made
the frequent Israeli air-drops all the more welcome, for
although the volume of weapons and ammunition that the
Stratocruiser could deliver on each flight was relatively small,
the psychological value of the Repairs operations was beyond
calculation.

After a lull in the fighting, in February 1965 the Egyptians
went back onto the offensive, both politically and militarily,
dropping high-explosive bombs to destroy whole villages and
terrorising the inhabitants with poison gas. Rival commanders
threatened each other with rhetoric – as when Colonel Adal
Abas, Commander of the Egyptian garrison at El Argoub,
wrote to his 'dear friend', the Royalist Sheikh Nagi al-Ghadr:

Peace to my Arab brother. Why do you fight and kill
your brother Muslims? You know in the past our reprisals
have destroyed your homes and families when you have
fought us. We must now make an arrangement for peace.
I have received an order from the Vice-President, the
Commander of all Egyptian forces, General Amer, that
unless all fighting ceases, I must destroy you and your
people.

To which al-Ghadr replied:

Before, at the beginning, when we were weak, you killed many of us. Now we are in command of the situation, you whine like a woman and beg for a peace we shall never agree to. We shall never cease fighting until all Egyptians have left the Yemen ... I shall never stop fighting until I die. Tell Amer that in reality all Yemenis are Royalist at heart, and when the time comes even the Republicans will turn upon you. Beware, Colonel Abas: they shall join us when the time comes that the only Egyptians in the Yemen are those left on the roads and jebels.

The renewal of hostilities provoked Tony Boyle to draft a 'Proposal for Further Action against the Egyptians in the Yemen', which suggested that a successful attack on the aircraft at Sana'a and Hodeidah would deal a severe blow to Nasser's prestige, not merely in the Yemen, but throughout the Middle East. The document, though couched in veiled terms, in essence recommended that the Israelis should carry out an air-strike, but that the Royalists should take credit for it 'in a pre-planned, world-wide Press statement'. As he had recently returned from one of his many visits to Tel Aviv, it seems likely that the Israelis had shown interest in the idea, or even suggested it:

Experience has shown that very deep air penetration into the Yemen can be achieved with minimal risk, and the load carried on this operation [i.e. bombs] could be arranged so that it appeared to have been unprofessionally prepared, and so mislead the Egyptians into genuinely attributing the attack to a charter aircraft hired, modified and loaded by paid agents of the Royalists.

The proposal went on to claim that if the attack came off, and a number of Egyptian aircraft were destroyed on the ground, the other Arab countries bordering Israel would be 'less inclined to accept Nasser's assurances of effective and decisive help', and thus 'Israel's interests would have been well served, and the Royalists would go to their conferences in a stronger position than ever before'. Tony, however, added a caveat:

I would also like to establish that we can take no part . . . if any of the deception plans suggest that the operation was performed by the RAF or emanated from the United Kingdom. If your discussions continue on the lines of those we have already had, this aspect should not arise.

That last sentence alone suggests that he had talked over the idea with the Israelis; but for reasons that are no longer clear, the plan never came to fruition. Yet to a former fighter-pilot like Tony, the planes on the airfield at Sana'a remained an irresistible target, and in his neat italic handwriting, on lined paper, he sketched out a 'Proposal for Surprise Attack on Egyptian Aircraft in Yemen'. He suggested that a single Hunter fighter-bomber, flying from the Khamis Mushayt air-base in the south of Saudi Arabia, only 150 miles north of the border, could make 'two or three successful attacks . . . and so destroy the entire Egyptian concept of air superiority in Yemen'. The pilot of the Hunter would be 'standing by for immediate take off, with complete authority to select or reject offered targets', and the British volunteers in the mountains would try to ensure that he had a clear run by reporting enemy aircraft movements.

The Hunter should be fitted with two 230-gallon overload fuel tanks, to give it extra endurance. The Egyptians 'would not be expecting such action and would not have time to react against the attack', but 'the Saudi Arabian Government would obviously have to weigh the merits of the operation against the possibility of Egyptian countermeasures'. Tony used his own expertise to calculate, in some detail, the amounts of fuel that would be needed for various stages of the sortie, and he had no doubt that an attack would be feasible; but his ambitious project never came to fruition.

10

A High and a Low

In March 1965 a new political initiative briefly raised hopes that the confrontation in the Yemen might be resolved peacefully. Meeting in Jeddah, Royalists, Republicans and Saudis discussed the possibility of forming a Third Party, with the aim of producing a United Front that would rule the country and be capable of removing Sallal and the Egyptians. The Saudis appeared to favour the idea, but it foundered on the refusal of the Republicans to accept any member of the Hamid ud Din family in a new government. Another dissenter was Whiskers − Sherif Hussein of Beihan. Billy McLean, on yet another reconnaissance trip, found him highly critical of the Hamid ud Dins, but urged him to continue his support for them, since the tribes would not accept the leadership of any other family.

By then David Smiley was back in the Yemen on one of his freelance tours, still calling himself Grin, and on 18 March Jim Johnson himself went out, partly to get a taste of the prevailing atmosphere, but with the more important purpose of instilling some sense of urgency into the native commanders. On his way through Jeddah he received an ultimatum from King Feisal: Saudi Arabia (the monarch told him) had already supplied very large quantities of weapons and money, and yet the Royalist Yemenis had made no serious attempt to drive the Egyptians out. Unless they soon launched a major attack, he would cut off his assistance.

Once again Jim availed himself of the linguistic skills of Philip Horniblow, who was then living and working in Riyadh as technical director of a new hospital. Having seen the King, and stayed a night chez Horniblow, Jim flew with the doctor to Najran, where he himself lodged in comfort with the Governor, Prince Khaled Sudairi, while Philip was obliged to rough it in the clinic. Next day they drove across the frontier in a Land Rover and, after a stiff approach climb, reached the Imam's redoubt at El Qara, where, to Jim's distaste, they had to camp in a cave.

From there they proceeded to the Royalist headquarters at Amara, on the edge of the Rub' al-Khali. The camp was established in a sandy valley among the foothills, tucked away in a labyrinth of caves, tents and bivouacs hidden from the air among huge boulders and interconnected with tunnels. Here the troglodytes lived in some style. Many of the caves had had their floors levelled and their walls smoothed out and lined with concrete; some even had wooden doors and carpets, and there were primitive wash-places and lavatories, with electric light from a generator. But still the place was in a chaotic state, with piles of rubbish and weapons lying in the open, and hundreds of empty fruit tins scattered about outside, offering a useful aiming mark for hostile aircraft.

At Amara the travellers found David Smiley suffering from a persistent sore throat and cough, for which Philip gave him some medicine. They joined forces also with Bernard Mills and his signaller, the small, dark and excellent Jimmy Knox,[1] who in civilian life had been a miner, and was incredibly skilful at enlarging any cave in which the mercenaries proposed to take up residence. Armed with pick and shovel, he could excavate rock and earth three times faster than anybody else: as a colleague remarked, he was like a mole, and could burrow his way through anything.

The Royalists had been demoralised by recent gas attacks, and one of the princes appealed to Jim to send out gas-masks. When told that they were too expensive, the Yemeni announced that he had a much better and cheaper way of solving the problem. Having gathered his followers round him, he sat on a rock, took a large plastic bag, pulled it over his head and tied it round his neck. The onlookers watched in amazement as his head gradually disappeared in a haze of mist, until he toppled over unconscious and men rushed to release him.

One afternoon Jim and his party set out for the French training camp at Khanjar, normally some four hours' drive to the south, where they had arranged a rendezvous with Mohamed bin Hussein. They left Amara at 3.30 p.m., but their truck became stuck in the sand-dunes so often that they did not reach their destination until 10 p.m. Grin recalled:

From midnight until three in the morning Johnson, Mills and I harangued and brow-beat the unfortunate Mohamed Hussein, urging him to make an attack soon and justify the support King Feisal had given him over the last two years. Otherwise, Johnson warned him, all Saudi help would cease.[2]

Reporting the conversation to Mac in Aden, Tony Boyle said that when Jim waded into Hussein for not having taken the offensive, the Prince produced the usual excuses: that he would attack when money and weapons came through from Feisal, and so on. But Jim knew perfectly well that enough had already been sent for several attacks, and said that unless Hussein started something before he (Jim) left the country, he would report to Feisal that the Prince had no intention of doing anything, and the King would cut off his supplies.

After a couple of days Jim and Philip went further into the Jauf. One night they witnessed the latest Israeli air-drop – 'Special Consignment No. 7' – which included 24,000 rounds of .303 ammunition, 200 rifles and 148 mines, besides cans of corned beef, baked beans, pineapple and beer. They then headed north for the frontier, returned to the UK, and were back in London on 4 April, having been away for just over a fortnight. The image that Philip Horniblow retained from the trip was of the Boss, clad in a short-sleeved sports shirt and a futa, strolling about the camps with a sub-machine gun cradled in his right arm, smiling genially to one and all. Yet if his visit seemed brief and casual, it had a salutary effect, in that it galvanised Mohamed bin Hussein into action.

Soon after Jim had departed, he began moving up equipment for a major ambush on the main route from Marib to the north, at a point where the track ran through a gorge known as the Wadi Humeidat, overlooked by two massifs, the Jebel Aswad (Black Mountain) and the Jebel Ahmar (Red Mountain). The site of the ambush had been selected by Bernard and Louis, the French field commander of the GEV, after a reconnaissance two weeks earlier. Preparations for the attack were formidable, for weapons and ammunition had to be carried up steep slopes, and the Egyptians – who may have got wind of the plan – put in occasional air-raids during the days before the battle. These, however, did little damage, and as Grin recorded:

Our only casualties occurred when the European mercenaries, rushing out of the caves to shoot at the aircraft, would collide in the entrances with the tribesmen running inside to get away from them.[3]

Other foreigners on the scene included Billy McLean and the four Persian tiger cubs – the hapless Special Forces men sent from Iran to gain experience. Billy recalled how he and Mohamed bin Hussein took them up to the edge of the Jebel Ahmar escarpment, whence they had a grandstand view of the Egyptian positions. As they sat on the skyline, shells started whistling over their heads and exploding near them: although no one was hit, they all ran for cover, 'the Persians running even faster than the Yemenis'. One of them dropped his field glasses and passport, but these were found by a tribesman, who handed them back with a smirk.

Then, during lunch, another of the cubs started boasting to Mohamed bin Hussein about his expert knowledge of explosives gained on a course in America. Billy was surprised to see the Prince listening intently, apparently impressed – but soon the real reason for his interest became obvious:

He said to the Persians that he was sure that with such expert knowledge they could easily mine the road below Jebel Ahmar, and that he would give them guides to take them down that very afternoon. The Persian officers were very taken aback and muttered that they were really part of a liaison mission sent to observe the war in the Yemen and not to take part in it.

They were further disquieted when they mentioned to the French volunteers that Prince Mohamed had asked them to go down to the road to lay the land-mines, and the French had replied: 'You'll be mad if you go down to the road, because the Dahm tribes will sell you to the Egyptians.' Soon after this the Persians came to Prince Mohamed and informed him that they would be very willing to train any Yemenis to lay mines on the road, but they themselves would not be able . . . to do so because they had the strictest instructions from His Imperial Majesty the Shah that they were on no account to engage themselves directly in the fighting.[4]

Although Smiley gave Hussein advice on mounting the ambush, he had to leave more than a week before it took place – and when he departed, preparations had gone so far that it would hardly have been possible for Hussein to stop them. And yet, oddly enough, Grin's absence from the scene did not prevent him contributing an eye-witness account of the battle to the London *Sunday Telegraph*, in which he described how he had observed the action from the head-quarters of the Royalist forces on Red Mountain: 'I watched . . . as Nasser's Russian-built MiG jets and Ilyushin bombers counter-attacked with rockets and cannon fire to cover the retreat.' [5] This article did nothing to improve his standing with those mercenaries who heard about it.

Fortunately the Prince did still have an experienced European adviser on hand, in the form of Bernard Mills, who planned the battle with him, siting heavy machine guns and 75mm recoilless rifles on high points, so that the Yemeni forces could use the flat plateau at the top of the escarpment as a killing ground. Useful allies were men of the notoriously fickle Dahm tribe, described by Billy McLean as 'a lawless bunch of frontiersmen and freebooters whose main preoccupation was loot'. Normally the Dahm's habit was to rob the convoys and caravans of either side; now, though, when Mohamed bin Hussein promised them whatever loot might be captured from the enemy, they managed to trick the Egyptians into believing that they had no need to station troops on the high ground, since they, the Dahm, would make sure it was clear.[6]

When preparing for the attack, Bernard had foreseen that one of the most difficult tasks would be to provide enough water for several thousand men; but, providentially, heavy rain began to fall, and storm after storm filled all the rockpools, removing a major worry. After carrying out several recces, he made a sand model of the area so that he could brief the local teams manning the heavy weapons – but it turned out that he was in for a long wait. Day after day it was announced that Hussein was about to arrive, and day after day he failed to show. When eventually he did appear, he asked why the mercenaries had not come to him. 'Refrained from row,' Bernard wrote in his diary. 'We discussed operation.'

Planning was not easy, for the Prince habitually stayed up all night and slept through most of the day, and during a temporary stop at Matara tribesmen began to gather in droves, all clamouring for his attention. Bernard noted:

Thousands of people now living all around defecating, pissing, sleeping all day, and singing and talking and playing radios all night ... Spent forty-five minutes stitching one of the Prince's soldiers wounded in an argument ... First day of Eid [the period of celebration after the end of Ramadan]. Morale bloody. Thousands of rounds fired in air ... Roger [Faulques] arrives, on flying visit. Long talk with him ... Big go at Mohamed about responsibilities etc ...

14 April. Arrived Rahaba 0200 hours . . . Mohamed wants to stay another night here . . . alarming tales of thousands of Egyptians . . . Woke after sleeping well on three rocks suspended. New cave built. Two MiGs over this morning but no attack . . . Mohamed left recce too late – i.e. sun in his eyes. All sheikhs laying down law about where artillery [should be]. Got very angry . . . Bed 0500. Trained more mine-layers in the morning. Slept. Went to Mohamed 1530 but he still asleep. Woke him at 1600 . . . When I told him we were leaving he suddenly took notice.

At last, on the afternoon of 21 April 1965, the battle began with an artillery bombardment. Next day well-coordinated diversionary attacks distracted some of the Egyptians, as intended, and the main assault into the wadi, launched before first light, proved a resounding success. MiGs made many low passes overhead, but held their fire because the Egyptian and Royalist positions were too close to each other for aerial gunnery to be safe. Caught in a bottleneck half a mile wide and a mile long, some of the enemy surrendered, while others fled, and the all-important road to the south was cut. More than 100 Egyptian soldiers were killed, and more than fifty were captured. The Egyptian press, needless to say, reported 'a staggering victory'.

One sergeant, taken prisoner, described how his unit had been ordered forward to relieve a position cut off by the Royalists. After a four-hour approach march along the wadi bottom, his platoon had suddenly been attacked by tribesmen: he himself was wounded above the left ankle and in one buttock, and saw three of his comrades killed before the rest ran away.

Among the victors' spoils were one T-34/75 tank, six armoured personnel carriers, four trucks and a jeep, besides numerous weapons and a great deal of machine-gun and mortar ammunition. The battle left 3 miles of the road, at the wadi's narrowest point between Harf and Hazm, firmly in Royalist hands. Another 5 miles of the road were denied to the Egyptians by Royalist artillery.

Bernard's schedule obliged him to leave before the fighting was over – but he had played a vital part in the Royalists' preparation. In Najran he reported to Prince Mohamed Sudairi that the battle had taken place, and in Jeddah he briefed Kemal Adham, head of the Saudi intelligence agency and brother of King Feisal's wife.

Adham was an important member of the Saudi hierarchy. A highly intelligent and crafty operator, of Turkish-Albanian descent and a graduate of Cambridge University, he looked like 'a pensive mandarin', with his 'small, carefully-trimmed fair beard, his drooping moustache, melancholy eyes and withdrawn expression'.[7] He was always extremely careful about his own safety. When a senior member of Mossad once said that he would like to meet Adham, Jim – who strongly believed that the heads of intelligence services should maintain contact with each other – arranged a rendezvous at the Dorchester Hotel in London. The Israeli awaited the encounter in his room; but at the last moment Adham became very nervous and said, 'What if he attacks us?' – whereupon Jim told him not to be ridiculous and assured him that his opposite number was a thoroughly civilised person.

Within a week of the Humeidat battle, Bernard was back in the Yemen, revisiting the scene. He spent one night halfway up Black Mountain, and got no sleep because of marauding camels; next he went down to the bottom of Wadi Humeidat to lay more mines, denying the Egyptians any further use of the road. By then many of the spoils had been looted, but he inspected the shot-up Egyptian tank, a lorry, a jeep and several armoured personnel carriers, as well as disabled heavy machine guns. In the evening, on the way up the steep side of the wadi, he was fired at four times. 'Private Yemeni war,' he noted. 'Cliff climbing without a moon is NOT FUN.'

A report on the battle said that the Royalists had enough heavy ammunition to hold up further Egyptian attacks for three or four days, but that fresh supplies were urgently needed. There was a risk that if the Royalists could not sustain their attack, enemy morale – at present very low – would start to recover, and the Egyptians might get a chance to negotiate with possibly hostile tribes. A second danger was that after a battle idle soldiers, especially Bedouin, were inclined to go home or back to their herds – and once that process started, all the Royalist successes could dissipate overnight.

The Egyptians sought to strike back by flying extra troops down to Hazm, and on 19 May they put in a strong counter-attack, reinforced by one battalion of parachute troops and another of their Saiqa special commandos. By then Hussein had given away many of his heavy weapons, so that when the enemy came over the top of the escarpment onto the plateau, there was little to stop them. The Egyptians captured Red Mountain and got a toe-hold on Black Mountain, but after heavy fighting for three days the tribesmen held out. At a critical moment the Prince showed his mettle: in an act of great courage he roused his troops, led them forward and drove the Egyptians off. The Royalists put their own losses at twenty dead and missing, those of the Egyptians at 200 dead. On 20 May it was reported (falsely) on Radio Sana'a that the Prince had been captured – whereupon Abdullah bin Hassan, in the Khowlan, put out a defiant statement:

> Although the Egyptians may capture our leaders, the Second Royal Army will fight with all they have. Even if we only have *jambiyas*, we will push the Egyptian invaders into the sea.

Confused fighting continued throughout May and June, but the victory at Humeidat turned out to be one of the most crucial of the entire civil war, for the gorge remained under Royalist control until the end of 1967, and the Egyptian garrisons in the east and south, on the lower slopes of the mountains and in the desert, had to be supplied entirely by air. Huge bribes in the form of money and rifles were offered to local tribes, in the hope of getting them to harass the Royalist forces, but to no avail.

In the wadi, as in numerous places elsewhere, dead bodies lay unburied, progressively desiccated by the burning sun. The mercenaries kept coming upon gaunt reminders: a skull half-buried in the ever-shifting surface of the desert, a human hand protruding 'like a warning from its owner's sandy grave',[8] or what the eccentric Irish peer Lord Kilbracken memorably called 'an arm reaching from the sand, to grasp at nothing'.[9]

In Jim's absence abroad, Tony Boyle had written at length to Mac McSweeney, confirming that he was to become the organisation's man in Aden when Franco (Rupert France) moved to Jeddah. 'I, personally, am very glad indeed that you will be the liaison between here [London] and the field,' Tony wrote. He had been greatly impressed by Mac's proficiency in radio work when they travelled together in the north, and by his 'powers of friendly persuasion', which would certainly be needed in his new post. A flat had been rented for him in Plot 115B in Khormaksar, but a note in his file warned that the address was 'Not to be used on mail or told to anyone going to Aden'.

Grin, meanwhile, was on his way home, and in his memoirs, published eleven years after the event, he recorded that as he passed through Jeddah, Prince Sultan and Shami asked him 'to take command of all the mercenaries in the Yemen'. Jim Johnson and Roger Faulques, he wrote, 'agreed with this proposal', and after discussing it with his wife he 'accepted the offer'.[10] As reported to members of the BFLF, the news was that Grin had become 'field commander' – not overall commander – and it provoked a waspish response from Faulques:

I hand over to D.S. as field commander? Please make my position clear if I not competent. Billy told different story. Answer ASAP. Please no ballerinas or prima donnas. This not the case.

Most of the mercenaries, though admiring Grin's record as a soldier, were irritated by his ceaseless peregrinations, and by his tendency to do things his own way. Soon they began to complain that he gave very little direction and there was no effective command. Their principal loyalty was to Jim, who remained their master and commander – and, as one of them put it in a letter to him from Jeddah, 'We are seen as a rudderless ship.' On the ground it was Johnny Cooper who increasingly took the lead in decision-making. At least the mercenaries were spared Grin's attentions for a few months, for in the autumn he went down with bilharzia in Scotland and was out of action until the second half of October.

Feuding among the Brits was as nothing compared with the recriminations that flew between Royalist leaders. Changes of mind and failure to carry out agreed plans often raised tempers, but above all it was shortage of money that made rows blaze. 'You have deprived me of Yacht [an air drop],' said one furious message. 'You [the] reason for breakage good plan in this war. I will not cooperate with you. I not responsible now for anything. I do not guarantee your safety. Today AA [Prince Abdullah] took away our last two staff by order . . .'

By the beginning of June 1965 Franco had completed his move to Jeddah, and informed London that 'after considerable haggling' he was well installed in the company's house, with free accommodation and car and one month's leave every six months: 'Nothing in writing so am keeping my fingers crossed.' The Saudis had also agreed to pay for the accommodation of some of the mercenaries passing through, provided that extra persons in transit stayed at the Red Sea Hotel and did not hang around.

In fact most of Jim's recruits stayed in the new house – a spacious, modern building on three floors, with seven bedrooms, a cook (a well-educated, well-spoken Saudi) and a cleaner. In the hot weather people slept out on the roof, and the premises had no form of security; but as the site was well tucked away in a residential area of the city, its openness presented no problem.

In the eastern Yemen the Royalist forces scored one success after another, capturing Sirwah early in June, then Qaflan, the historical capital of the Hashid tribes, and finally, on 16 July, Marib. By then dislike of the Egyptians had become so widespread that some of the princes believed that sheer hatred offered a basis for collaboration between Royalists, disaffected Republicans and others, and in July, they staged a conference at Taif, in Saudi Arabia.

Also in July, Tony Boyle made a return visit to Aden to check the BFLF's arrangements there and in Beihan. He went in some trepidation, aware that his activities during his final days as ADC to the Governor had made him 'socially a leper' in the colony, and not sure what the locals' attitude to the BFLF might he. He was startled when a customs officer asked him if he was coming back to Government House, yet in the event was agreeably surprised by his reception:

> Everyone I met who I knew before invited me to stay or eat or drink with them. This is an enormous relief. The whole attitude towards us is first class. Any help that can be given, will be, and we are certainly on the right side of the fence. The exception of course is the attitude of the few high-ups out there who are unable to acknowledge us.

On the other hand, he was alarmed by information that he gathered from local Political Officers, who feared that Whiskers, the Sherif of Beihan, chagrined by lack of action from the British Government, was about to leave the Federation and align himself with Saudi Arabia. This (Tony thought) would destroy the Federation and leave the way clear for the Egyptians to take over. He reported that Michael Crouch (one of the Political Officers) 'and most of the others, are fed up with HMG's attitude'.

They all blame the Egyptians fully, and consider really strenuous action should be taken against them. They mutter about resigning. He is longing for an opportunity, official or unofficial, to crack back at them, and asked if there was any way to co-operate with us. Also asked if he could have a job if he resigned.

In Aden itself, violence had been steadily increasing: bombs and outbursts of gunfire were becoming everyday events as Nasser orchestrated subversion through the NLF (the National Liberation Front), which was dedicated to evicting the British, and which in turn was fighting for supremacy with a second terrorist organisation, FLOSY (the Front for the Liberation of South Yemen). Terrorist incidents rose from an average of three a month in 1964 to twenty-four a month in 1965, to forty a month in 1966 and to 248 monthly in the first nine months of 1967.

Tony was dismayed by the condition of his old stamping ground. 'Aden state is pathetic,' he wrote: 'Lorries barred; troops, curfew and road blocks trying to head off the activities of the dissidents; while the vast majority of the population still enjoys a relationship of cheerful banter with the British Forces.' On the other hand, he was much reassured by the way the mercenary operation was going, and by the general state of the war. His trip left him satisfied that his decision to help David Stirling two years earlier had been correct: senior people in Aden whose opinions he valued now endorsed the BFLF enterprise and offered their support. 'We now have the initiative in the Yemen, and unattributable support from HMG,' Tony wrote. 'Can the Royalists seize this fleeting moment?'

He was impressed by a new recruit to MI6, known to the

mercenaries as Clancy. 'There is a very good one,' he wrote. 'Sound, erudite and amenable to fact.' When Clancy stressed the importance of keeping the Khowlan team provided with enough cash, Boyle entirely agreed, but pointed out that the problem was 'a bottomless pit', and that the inward move-ment of gold and silver was sluggish in the extreme:

The lead time for changing the budget has to take account of Jim persuading Shami, Shami convincing Sultan, Sultan giving Shami the money, Jim getting it from Shami, and then, after converting it into locally acceptable currency, getting it through the Egyptian lines and through ambivalent tribes who are looking out for any windfall they can engineer before it gets to the team who are spending it – possibly up to six months.

Clancy invited Tony to stay with him in Nuqub, and agreed in advance that when they both flew from Aden to Beihan, they would not recognise each other on the aircraft. Then on the flight they found they had been allocated adjacent seats – and the MI6 man, abandoning their earlier agree-ment, opened the conversation by saying that as they were forced to sit next to each other, they might as well use the time profitably. He told Tony that he had recently carried out a personal survey of the Harib airfield, which had been neglected for so long that shrubs had grown on it and mounds of sand had built up around them. He estimated that 300 man-hours, or one day with a bulldozer, would be needed to clear the strip.

There was news, also, from Marib, which at that stage was still occupied by the Egyptians. When Grin had arrived on a reconnaissance visit, the locals roundabout had run out firing salvos of joy, and the Royalists in the mountains behind loosed off more volleys in reply. The Egyptians in the town, thinking that a large-scale attack was being mounted, started shelling the area with mortars. Within a month Marib was in the hands of the local tribe. A few Egyptians remained on the airfield, but they had burnt their hospital and guest house, and two tanks, and it seemed that the place had been evacuated rather than captured, as a result of pressure from the Jahm and Abeida tribes.

Returning to London, Tony went straight to the Johnsons' house to have dinner, then to the House of Commons to see Amery, who 'quickly absorbed the seriousness of the Aden situation and brought in Duncan Sandys, who was his usual aggressively confident (and unpleasant) self and appeared to ignore everything we said.'

Early in June 1965 Jim had invited none other than John Woodhouse to visit the Yemen and make a personal assessment of the situation. The Colonel's decision to show himself above the parapet in the covert operation caused some surprise, for, at the age of forty-three, he had only recently retired from commanding the SAS. In a note to Jim dated 12 June he wrote: 'I shall be in London on Wed. 16th and will call on you that evening if this is convenient? I am signing off with my present firm on that day so hope I am still wanted!' A laconic message from London told Mac McSweeney that he 'joins us in mid-July as second-in-command in the field of operations' and that he would 'lead the Khowlan team'.

Woodhouse's purpose – in his own words – was 'to organise guerrilla operations around Sana'a with the aim of forcing the Egyptians to abandon the airfields there', and his personal ambition was 'to compel or persuade the Egyptians to withdraw from [the] Yemen'. It may also have been that, as usual, he was looking for a theatre in which the regular SAS might legitimately be deployed and thought the Yemen looked a promising candidate. But he stressed that he acted 'on his own initiative in a private capacity throughout this period'.

He planned to remain in the country for a few weeks, at most. He flew to Aden on 25 July, left his passport there for safe-keeping, reached Nuqub three days later and went on by truck to the border, then by camel or on foot. A stickler for recording times of day, departure, arrival and journey length, he noted salient facts about his travels in short, staccato diary entries:

Arrived West the Khowlan 0100 31 July (nine hours). Remarked camel's sure-footedness.

Left without warning 0050 hours 1 Aug. (Ali Hantash inefficient organiser at night). Camel until 0345 to foot of escarpment (at well) arr. 0830 (7½ hours). March to base 1515 hours, arriving 1845 (3½ hours). Max height 7,400 ft. Base 6,600 ft. Total times: truck 7½ hours. Camel and foot: 21 hours.

The first highlight of his trip was an Israeli air-drop, which he witnessed on the night of 14–15 August. The moon (he recorded) was two days past full, and the weather was 6/8 cloud at about 2,000 feet above ground-level. The aircraft came in from the direction of Sana'a without any radio contact, and was overhead at 0055. Seventeen boxes, each on three parachutes, landed within 150 yards of the T-shaped light formation, and by 0315 the DZ party had collected them all. 'Items received' included twelve Bren guns, ten bazookas, twelve Sten guns, fifty-two anti-tank mines, three different types of firing device (one kind chemical), 26,000 rounds of .303 ammunition, 200 bazooka rockets, twelve pistols, 250 pounds of plastic explosive, 500 yards of cortex fuse, and safety-fuse delays, besides cans of fruit, carrots, baked beans, peas and beer, and three bottles each of cognac and whisky.[11] Woodhouse was so impressed by the skill of the pilot that he later sent him a little framed account of the occasion as a memento.

In a report for Jim written on 19 August he said he had been struck by the 'total absence of any organised intelligence' in the mercenary ranks, and also by the need for a good interpreter. The team would never be able to 'persuade, cajole and insinuate' unless a fluent Arabic-speaker was present.

His other major excitement was a reconnaissance of the Sana'a front, made from Mustang, the mercenary station in Wadi Heera'an, which runs east–west, at one point only 35 miles due north of Sana'a, but separated from it by formidable mountains. At Mustang he fell in with Gassim Monassir – not a member of the royal family, but the most aggressive of all the Royalist commanders, and a leader of exceptional ability, much admired for his courage.

Tall and taciturn, with a swarthy complexion and the curly hair of Negro ancestors, Gassim emphasised his military bearing by wearing a British Army pullover under crossed bandoliers. Having once been a sergeant in the Imam's bodyguard, he had won the unquestioned obedience, affection and respect of his men by his example and his dominating personality. Woodhouse thought that he had 'no personal political ambitions, but is a simple, intensely patriotic soldier with considerable ability in guerrilla operations'.[12] Other Westerners saw him as an Arabian Robin Hood and recorded that, unlike some commanders who appeared to chew *qat* all night and sleep all day, he was setting a fine example.

At first the local commander-in-chief, Abdullah bin Hassan, made difficulties about going forward to meet Gassim, claiming that his camels were sick and that the tribes en route were hostile; but after a few days' delay the expedition went ahead, and from an observation point 8,000 feet above sea-level the party looked down on the Egyptian forward positions covering the capital. Woodhouse recorded:

> Walked to Gassim Monassir. Arrived 1030. Typical reaction of front-line soldier. Dubious – weighing us up – what use might we be? He had no way of expecting our arrival. Showed us who was boss from the start. Small arms fire heard soon after our arrival.
>
> He had walkie-talkie radio to his forward positions. Ate grapes while he decided to show us round. He rode a pony, we walked, preceded by barefoot bugler calling at intervals – splendidly feudal. Walked for 1¾ hours at speed to forward positions. Long talks and first-class view at five miles' range of Sana'a from NNE and Sana'a North airfield to the west of us. Eight MiGs and a few transports, one large.

In the middle of the day Woodhouse sent out a radio message to Aden and London saying that five MiGs were lined up side by side, and asking for the exact length of the runway, so that he could fix the range to the target. Back came the answer: 'the runway measured 3,330 yards'. At 1530 hours he enjoyed a 'delicious meat stew' eaten communally with Gassim and his forward soldiers:

Respect and affectionate humour mingled. He left to go to a wedding. We stayed in a section bunker, heavily scored all around by mortar craters, scarred by guns, rockets. How alike soldiers all are. Inside, a friendly, crowded muddle of kit, weapons hang on the stone walls. These soldiers laughed and talked like any others. Chewing qat, offering their sleeping spaces to us.

After nightfall he viewed the lights of Sana'a, identifying the prison, the radio station, Sallal's headquarters and vehicle park. As the party walked back in the dark, the guide lost the track and Woodhouse took refuge in a hut, where he shivered until the moon rose at 0200. Then he walked on to Gassim's headquarters, arriving at 0400 hours, and after a sleep and breakfast of a 'delicious broken omelette with tomatoes', he bade farewell to the Yemeni commander, promising to send him a radio, a medical man and a Stirling sub-machine gun.

In a handwritten message, which took two weeks to reach Mac in Aden, Woodhouse hinted to Jim how eager he was to get his hands on some 120mm mortars, which had long been promised, and which alone of all the weapons available to the Royalists had the range to bombard the Sana'a airfield. He asked for periodic reports on the progress of the heavy weapons, asking to know exactly when they, and ammunition for them, might arrive. Back in the Prince's headquarters on 22 August, he sent signals destined ultimately for Potato (London), saying that his initial reconnaissance had been successful, that the airfield was within range, and that the possibilities of sabotage and arson in Sana'a were great.

Clearly he was hoping to carry out an immediate attack; but his hopes were frustrated by external political developments. A few days earlier Nasser had crossed the Red Sea on his yacht *al Horriya* to hold peace talks with King Feisal, and President and monarch had together made a short pilgrimage to Mecca, to pray for the success of their meetings. The result was an immediate ceasefire and the 'Jeddah Agreement', announced on 22 August 1965 – the very day that Woodhouse signalled London.

By the terms of the agreement, which amounted almost to a surrender, the Egyptians would withdraw their troops from the Yemen within ten months of 23 November 1965; the Saudis would cut off all military aid to the Royalists and deny them the use of Saudi territory. Further, a national conference of Yemenis would assemble in the north-western town of Haradh, to agree a new system of government for the Yemen, and a joint peace commission would be formed by both sides.

Nasser appeared to have been humiliated: after innumerable boasts over Cairo radio that he would annihilate the Royalists – that he would never withdraw from the Yemen, even if the Nile ran dry[13] – he was about to start creeping away. The Egyptian Army had already lost nearly 20,000 dead and Royalist casualties were also appalling: 5,000 military dead and 30,000 civilians.

The ceasefire created a crisis for the BFLF, since the Saudis were naturally reluctant to continue paying the mercenaries. On 26 August, faced with the possibility that the war might suddenly be ending, Jay and Grin, in London, sent out a radio message to all stations warning of imminent closure:

CEASE FIRE ALL HOSTILE ACTS PARACHUTING ENTRY OF
CUBS AND FURTHER REINFORCEMENTS HEREBY STOPPED.
YOUR SALARIES PAID TILL END OF OCT . . . MEANWHILE

NO FURTHER OPERATIONAL AREA MONIES WILL BE PAID
ME OR YOU SO CEASE IMMEDIATELY ALL GUARDS
CARAVAN KINI MINI PAYMENTS AS FUNDS YOU HAVE
ARE ALL REPEAT ALL AVAILABLE YOUR OWN EXFILTRA-
TION INCLUDING LOCAL AIR FARES HOTELS EXCESS
BAGGAGE TO LONDON . . . CONGRATULATIONS TO ALL
AND WILL DO OUR BEST HERE REGRETS JAY GRIN.

Two days later Jim asked Mac, in Aden, to inform Bernard
that the Israeli drop planned for next month had been cancelled.
The drops would be subject to review in two months' time,
Jim wrote, and might be reinstated if Nasser had not fulfilled
his part of the agreement. He and Grin had just had two
meetings with Shami, who was adamant that he would not
give them a penny more than the salaries for September and
October. Jim asked Mac to make it clear to the outstations
that they must 'live off their hump', leaving themselves enough
money to extract themselves from the country. In the worst-
case scenario, Mac would be the final survivor in Aden: 'After
the last people have gone through you, if that becomes necessary, you will have to square your final bills by selling the car,
wireless set, medical kit and secretary!'

For the rest of the month hopes continued to fluctuate.
Jim was anxious about Woodhouse, still at large in the Yemen,
and flew yet again to Jeddah, hoping to arrange further operational finance; but for once he failed in his mission, undermined by news from Cairo, where the newspaper *Al-Ahram*
announced that Nasser was planning to withdraw 10,000
troops from the Yemen every month for the next seven months,
beginning in December. The Saudis saw no need for further
outlay, and Jim returned to Aden empty-handed. At 1130 on
7 October he put out a signal to all stations:

A. Regret announce financial death of Rally Films.
B. You all fired 31 Dec.
C. All stations close all personnel on leave 1 Dec. approx Aden/Jeddah.
D. Do utmost to save or evacuate stores/radio in case new firm starts in new year . . .

His gave as his reasons for closing down the facts that the men were due leave at the end of the year, and that it would be imperative that they were out of the country, should a Republican government be established. Further, his latest contract with Saudi Arabia would run out on 31 December, and at the moment there was no sign of it being renewed. All the same, he told everyone to stay put until the Haradh peace conference was well under way in November, so that premature departures did not undermine the Royalist-Saudi position. He finished the message in characteristic fashion: 'Genuine congratulations from face-less chairman who invites you all to Christmas punch-up at Hyde Park Hotel. Jim.'

The mercenaries had already begun preparing to pull out – and the threat of losing them provoked Mohamed bin Hussein to compose a letter, written in English in red ink:

To Mr Jim,

I send you my best regards.

We all don't agree to let Sayf [Sayf bin Abdullah was Bernard Mills] and friends to leave our area. This is final. Pleas respect our wishes because they must stay for many reson. Thank you.

There was still hope of a reprieve, and now it lay with Grin, who had recovered from his bilharzia and wrote to Jim from Jeddah on 19 October to say:

the fact that the British are leaving by December 12 is gradually beginning to dawn on the Yemenis, and it is throwing some of them into a state of alarm and despondency. Yesterday I heard that Mohamed bin Hussein is flying back from Beirut to raise the issue with the Saudis.

Smiley himself was preparing to go and beard Prince Sultan in Riyadh in an attempt to secure new financial arrangements; but first he saw Kemal Adham, and found that the intelligence chief had already got the King to agree that all the British operators should be taken on for another six months with effect from 1 January 1966.

On the subject of what our people are expected to do if they stay, and at what locations, I will get firm directions from Riyadh. They may well be paid for six months for doing nothing, and the chief enemy will be boredom, however good the pay. On the King's side, we are a good insurance policy, in case the situation worsens. We can be used as eyes and ears on local affairs, and keeping up the W/T comms [wireless/telegraph communications] is invaluable.

While Grin's letter was in transit, Shami and two other Royalist ministers had arrived in London, where they met George Thomson, the new Minister of State, at the Foreign Office. The Yemenis said that they had come to Britain to thank HMG for not recognising the Republican government and to seek assistance, especially medical aid and food, to counter the effect of the issue by the Republicans of new Yemeni paper currency. They also stressed that they sought self-determination for the Yemen. People (they said) 'had to experience Nasser before they learned to distrust him'. They felt that even if Nasser did withdraw his army, he would try to continue exercising influence in Yemen. 'The main danger now was not Egypt's army, but rather their activities in the fields of propaganda, diplomacy and Yemeni politics.'[14]

While the mercenaries' future hung in the balance, Woodhouse was still at large in the Yemen, and he remained there a good deal longer than he had intended, perhaps hoping that a renewal of hostilities would give him a chance, after all, to attack the Sana'a airfield. While waiting around, living in a cave, he passed the time playing Battleships with David Bailey, using scraps of paper to represent the rival fleets. In the event he did not start his camel journey down to the southern frontier until late in October. Then he made his way to Marib and Harib, where he met Abdullah bin Hassan, who warned him that famine was imminent, because the autumn rains had failed, and asked Britain to supply him with a large amount of money. Recognising Abdullah's patriotism and powers of leadership, Woodhouse thought that 'the expenditure of up to £20,000 for him might be a justifiable risk'.

His enforced wait must have borne in on him the disjointed nature of the war, and the difficulties under which the mercenaries were operating. On the first day of his exit trek, 21 October, five or six shots were fired at his party from a distance of some 400 yards, slightly wounding one of his guards. He did not regard this as a serious attempt at assas-

sination, but saw it as 'a joke in rather poor taste'. To his
escorts, however, it was a clear sign of annoyance that
tribesmen had not been paid, and they were keen to get
Woodhouse safely out of the area.

He finally returned to the UK at the beginning of
November, and in a manuscript note added to the end of
his diary twenty years later he wrote:

Considerable feeling of relief [at being on the move] as
very bored waiting from Aug 26 to Oct 21. Only conso-
lation was my pay of £750 a month in cash. Jim Johnson
organised this operation. It was overseen by the SIS.[15]
The Israelis carried out the air supply.

In an article entitled 'Highly Irregular', which he began
but never finished, he hit a descriptive vein:

Silence, empty landscapes grand in their lonely, spiky
mountain tops. The camel gives a sliding, backward-
forwards motion as he pads slowly on. It can be sopo-
rific under the brilliant stars of the still Arabian nights.
I find by day the camel rider can keep a sharper watch
on the rocky, bare hillsides than he could if he was
walking. My feelings, by now, were more prosaic and
physical. My bottom was sore, very sore.

In a more substantial report he reiterated his belief that
an attack on Sana'a airfield was entirely feasible, and that
enemy positions would be easy to penetrate at night because
of the wide dispersal and poor quality of Egyptian troops. In
particular, the prospects of a successful ground raid on the
northern airfield, 'if British planned and led', were very good

– and even without British leadership, important results could probably be achieved by advice alone. He anticipated that a night raid by six men, 'using a number of expedients to induce confusion and alarm', would cause panic, enabling heavy damage to be inflicted on aircraft and installations.

He thought that in the Khowlan the tribes' loyalty to the Imam had been strengthened by Egyptian intervention, and that even though the ruler himself might be expendable, no political solution would secure the support of the area unless the royal family retained a prominent position in the National Government. On a more positive note, he reckoned that the political advantages of providing medical assistance, as the mercenaries had been doing, were considerable and inexpensive to HMG. He considered that the recent introduction of modern medicine into the Khowlan had brought about a revolutionary change in the hitherto fatalistic attitude of the Yemenis to disease and injury: some at least of the tribesmen now saw that wounds could be healed and diseases cured. 'The taste for medicine, once acquired, grows ever stronger.'

In November 1965, before the promised peace conference, the Imam emerged from hiding again and made a triumphal tour of the north. The meeting was duly held at Haradh, a town of 300 mud houses, without electricity, an eighteen-hour drive to the north-west of Sana'a. Grin, who had been asked to represent the *Daily Telegraph* and went along as a journalist, found to his disgust that the delegates were corralled in a large tented camp surrounded by barbed wire, with machine-gun posts at each corner, some 2 miles out of town. At first Royalists and Republicans were accommodated in the same quarters, but they quarrelled so much that they had to be separated. At film shows in the evening the Republicans applauded Nasser wildly, and the Royalists cheered Feisal.

The Royalist delegation was led by Shami, but the conference, which opened on 23 November, held only three formal sessions before it degenerated into chaos. After a week Prince Abdullah Sudairi, the Saudi who presided over the formal sessions, quietly warned Smiley that the Egyptians knew of his connection with the mercenaries; so he slipped out of the camp at dawn one morning and made away across the border to Jizan, deciding that the conference had been nothing more than a manoeuvre by Nasser to gain time.

The accuracy of his view was confirmed by a statement later given by Shami at a press conference in Riyadh:

The stubbornness, willingness to falsify things and obstinacy were shown by our brothers who came from Sana'a only during the official sessions, while outside these meetings our encounters were cordial, and they often confided to the Royalists that they could not express all their views – a fact that reinforces the news that they had signed a document in Sana'a before coming to the conference, pledging not to abandon the existing regime in their area.[16]

On 19 November – just before the conference opened – Jim had had a serious disagreement with Prince Sultan in Jeddah (the proceedings of the meeting were referred to by Tony as 'fireworks'). Details of the row have not survived, but it was certainly about a future contract, and when Jim could not secure satisfactory answers, he threatened that he himself would pull out. In Grin's view, Jim was tactless and rude; reports of his outburst sent shockwaves through his organisation, and dissension spread among the mercenary force. When Tony went out to Jeddah yet again, early in December, he was met by Franco and Grin, with whom he talked until 1.30 a.m., recording in his diary:

[Johnny] Cooper is apparently contacting people to ask them to join him with the Imam if all else fails. This is highly undesirable and could jeopardise the relationship with Saudis and HMG we have so carefully nurtured. The Jim/Sultan row was the main topic. I believe there is a solution if Jim backs down a little – the alternative, that he leaves the operation, would be a disaster. Jim must be persuaded accordingly.

Writing at length from Jeddah, Tony did not hesitate to tell his boss where he had gone wrong. Jim (he said) had overrated the importance of the mercenary organisation to the Saudis. His offer to withdraw the group had been a mistake. He could not expect the Saudis to make any long-term contract until the results of the Haradh conference had become clear. If he himself withdrew:

One of two things will happen: either the sharp-end boys will accept the Saudi terms direct, and the problem of finding a figure known, trusted and respected by everyone concerned to replace you will loom large and practically insoluble. Inevitably our organisation would be deeply divided, and for this reason alone this possibility is not acceptable.
    Alternatively, and this is the second possibility, the boys will reject the Saudi terms and the organisation will disintegrate into small groups contracted to individual

princes . . . This would be undesirable, as the princes are notorious for their inability or unwillingness to pay . . . Such a move would alienate the Saudis, who would be unlikely to provide a rear base . . . In short, our work over the last 2–3 years to improve Saudi and Yemen relations with Britain could be expunged overnight.

The final possibility is that you concede the Saudis' point and accept monthly payment until the Haradh conference results have been effected, on condition that they will then consider a longer term contract . . .

To summarise, the whole thing now depends on you, Jim. If you can bring yourself, albeit reluctantly, to shelve your personal feelings about Dracula [Sultan] and to dilute your demands on the Saudis by agreeing to this formula, I believe the situation can be retrieved; if you can not, I see no alternative to an awful shambles, and the harm that could be done within the next few months will probably eradicate all our previous achievements, and it would be better if we had never started. Anticipating this chaos, I want you to know that if you do drop out, I, for one, while disagreeing with your reasons for withdrawing, will drop out with you.

Now my second point is as important, but not quite so urgent, as the first. As you know, November 15th didn't do your reputation here any good, I believe Billy then did it further harm. David, by not interrupting and disagreeing with you at the meeting, was loyally supporting you, yet in the eyes of the Saudis he is definitely closely associated with Billy, and Billy has apparently declared himself anti-you. So the Saudis have successfully driven two wedges to split the triumvirate. I would think that the split between you and Billy, on a personal basis, must be nearly irreconcilable; even if that is so, you and Billy and David should at least meet and decide on a specific division of duties . . .

When I saw Zaid [Sudairi] last night I emphasised on your behalf that you had not meant any offence to Sultan and that if you had offended him you were sorry for it. He replied amicably, and said that it was not in Sultan's nature to bear resentment. He added that he hoped when you meet again the matter could be treated as a joke, and that he (Zaid) hoped you would be able to attend the meeting on the fifteenth.

Tony added that Sudairi had spoken 'rather freely' about the Yemeni royal family, and had left him in no doubt that the aim of the Saudis was to rule the Yemen through the tribal sheikhs, without the benefit of the Hamid ud Din dynasty to assist them. A few weeks later, in another conversation with Boyle, Sudairi reiterated his remark. 'He made it quite clear the Saudis are interested only in ruling Yemen through the sheikhs direct. The Royalists merely provide a rallying point for the purpose of expelling the Egyptians. After that they are expendable.'

Even as Tony was composing his broadside to Jim, the talks at Haradh were failing. A communiqué signed by Shami stated that the Royalists were unable to persuade the Republican delegates to accept the terms of the Jeddah Agreement, and that there would be no further discussions between the two delegations. The conference ended inconclusively on 21 December 1965.

The close of the year found Tony Boyle back in the Yemen, and invited by the French to a celebration dinner on Christmas Eve. When he passed through their base at Ida'a, between

Amara and Najran, at lunchtime, he found 'a fever of activity – chickens, goats and sheep were being slaughtered in every direction, and many cauldrons were bubbling over open fires', in preparation for a feast that night. Returning at 11.30 p.m. (his driver having lost the way), Tony thoroughly enjoyed the party, at which nine nationalities were present:

> Christmas day was heralded with bursts from every gun on the establishment [he told Jim]. It was rather diffi-cult, later, in Jeddah, explaining away the reports of a large Republican attack on Ida'a on the night of 24th December!

His description of the festivities did not quite square with an account on which Jim dined out for the rest of his life. In this version the French chefs told Tony that they had caught and fattened up five desert partridges – and he ate the rich casserole that they gave him with great enjoyment. Only when he remarked that Yemeni partridges tasted rather stronger than English birds did his hosts let on that there had been an unfortunate accident: a week earlier the partridges had been killed by a feral cat. With a sinking feeling Tony asked, 'So what have I just eaten?' – and back came the answer, 'The cat.'

The leaders of the rival factions both left the field for the time being: Sallal was called to Cairo, where Nasser put him under house arrest for almost a whole year, and the Imam went to Taif in Saudi Arabia for treatment of kidney trouble. The Egyptians did start to withdraw troops, and from a high point of 70,000, numbers steadily dropped. For a few weeks it seemed that real progress had been made towards ending the war.

But then – for the mercenaries – everything changed, and this time it was Smiley who swung things round. 'News that Grin has pulled off four-month contract from 1st January,' Tony scribbled in his diary. 'So much for predictions, the most unexpected always happens.' Writing to Jim on 29 December, on board a Saudi Airlines flight from Jeddah to Riyadh, Grin triumphantly announced, 'Have got a cheque for £10,000.' Shami, he reported, had become 'very confident', and had said that although the Haradh talks might appear to have failed, they had given him the opportunity to see all the important Republican sheikhs, and he had boasted, 'I have them all in my hand.' He had added that the Saudis' attitude was very good, that he expected the mercenaries to be needed for at least a year, and that he wanted to discuss an increase in numbers with Jim on his return, the following week.

At the beginning of January 1966 the Royalist princes seized the opportunity of leaving their flea-infested caves for a while, and met in strength in Riyadh for a conference about the future of their relationship with the Saudis. 'After that,' Tony told Jim, 'if they are unable to find further excuses for delaying, the Princes will probably return to Yemen, but their excuse-finding ability is legendary.' In their absence the Royalist army dispersed to its homes with its guns; to rebuild it would require new guns, full payment of back-pay and the opportunity of loot. Unable to imagine these three essentials becoming available in the near future, Tony feared that if Nasser renewed his attacks, he could 'walk through the country'.

While the princes were meeting, Jim visited Jeddah three times. At the third attempt he persuaded the Saudis to agree: they restarted the flow of funds and, with the arrival of the

first cheque in the middle of the month, the mercenary operation got going again. Jim wrote:

> We now have people back with the Imam and Uncle
> Stan at Amara, and two parties on their way into the
> Khowlan, all having gone through Saudi Arabia . . . The
> moment Mac has got his radio installed happily with
> Abdullah [bin Hassan], he will go down alone through
> Nuqub to re-open the Aden flat.

Also in January, under cover of the British Yemen Relief
Committee, Jim sent out a doctor called Williams to make
a survey of the equipment left behind by the International
Red Cross in the hospital at Uqd, which had been abandoned in November. He found the mobile hospital still intact
and containing medical equipment 'of definite value'. In the
surgical field there were more than 300 operating instruments and about 600 packets of suture material. For dressing
wounds there were 20,000 gauze squares, 8,000 cotton band-
ages, 100 large packets of cotton wool and more than 1,000
dressing packs of Swiss Army design, as well as considerable
quantities of intravenous fluids, infusion sets, intramuscular
penicillin, ophthalmic ointment and Terramycin ointment.

All surplus medical material had been taken to Najran and
placed under guard in the care of Mohamed bin Hussein –
who, however, had no means of administering the medicines.
Dr Williams had also been briefed to make a 'medical reconnaissance' of north-east Yemen, but in mentioning all the
prevalent diseases – leprosy, trachoma, bilharzia, malaria, to
say nothing of war wounds – he appeared to be daunted by
the problems of terrain and language. His report struck a
rather despondent note, saying that if any doctor was sent

out, the most suitable person would be someone who had just completed a short-term army commission. He would have to be young and fit, and would probably have experience of 'living under difficult conditions'.

Early in February Jim told Franco how worried he and McLean were by the prospect of the Defence White Paper that HMG was about to produce. 'It may require some realignment in our position,' he wrote. 'Personally I am very depressed and think there may easily be a firm date given in the Paper as to when we are to withdraw from Aden.'

His forecast proved all too accurate. The Defence White Paper, published on 22 February 1966, announced not merely that the Aden base was to be closed, but that no military support would be provided for the new Federation of South Arabia. The closure of the base was of no great concern to the Federal Government, but the denial of defence support after independence certainly was, as it gave the Egyptians the scent of a swift victory in the region and put paid to their declared intention of withdrawing from the Yemen.

Senior British officials had all strongly advised against HMG announcing the decision on the base at that moment, arguing that it was a breach of British undertakings, that it would fatally weaken the Federation, and that it would impair Britain's ability to honour other commitments in the Gulf – but the warnings were ignored. The American Consul in Aden reported to Washington that the decision and announcement 'amounted to throwing the Federation to the wolves' and to losing South Arabia for the West in the Cold War.[17]

In Aden and the Federation the news was greeted with rage and dismay, succinctly expressed by Sultan Saleh al-Qu'aiti in the Federal Supreme Council:

For many years we have borne the abuse and vilification of most of the Arab world because we believed that the British Government was our true friend and that, until we were able to defend ourselves, it would protect us against the consequences of our unwavering support . . . we cannot believe it is your wish that we shall be sacrificed just because, after many years of repeated promises to the contrary, the British government finds that it suits its own self interest to desert its friends and leave them in the lurch.[18]

Two days after the White Paper's publication, Jim wrote to tell Smiley that Shami had been very hurt and annoyed by the announcement, and now realised it really was 'a race against time' to get Nasser out. The Yemeni Foreign Minister suddenly flew to Riyadh, having said that he might be away for any period between ten days and twelve weeks – the length of his stay depending on whether or not he could get the war started again.

Less than six months after the Jeddah Agreement, Nasser again demonstrated his mendacity by reopening his Yemen campaign, sending aircraft to bomb and strafe the mountain villages – and this, naturally, reactivated the Saudis' support for the Royalists and their allies. MI6 agents reported that they had resumed the delivery of arms and ammunition to their border towns of Jizan and Najran.

The Saudi leaders were concerned not merely about the Yemen: they feared also for their own safety, alarmed by the possibility that they, too, might be attacked, especially as their army was so weak (it had been deliberately kept that way to minimise any chance of a military insurrection against the regime). The Wilson Government sought to allay their anxiety by agreeing to speed up the programme for equipping the Royal Saudi Air Force with thirty-five supersonic F.53 Lightning fighters, six T.55 Lightning trainers (all built by the British Aircraft Corporation, BAC), and twenty-five Strikemaster trainers, and for installing Thunderbird surface-to-air missiles on airfields.

The sale of the aircraft and the entire defence system – the biggest arms deal ever achieved by British firms, worth £1 billion, known as 'Magic Carpet'– had been engineered largely by Geoffrey Edwards, a wartime RAF pilot now acting as a freelance agent, who had been working all-out to secure the contract for the past three years, and had won it in the teeth of intense competition from the Americans. The Government had given him minimal support, except to promise the Saudis that, if the contract was awarded to BAC, the British would stay on in Aden for two more years – a promise that they had neither the intention nor the ability to fulfil. One certain fact was that the mercenaries' efforts to block Nasser's conquest of the Yemen had helped Edwards win time to clinch the deal.

In Stirling's view, Edwards was 'far [and] away the most knowledgeable individual on Saudi Arabian affairs' and had 'a vast range of genuine friends at all levels'. A big man – a larger-than-life entrepreneur – he was backed by money from the takeover of a family steel business, and made prodigious efforts to secure his deal, flying back and forth from London to Jeddah more than ninety times. A single Lightning, taken out from England by BAC's chief test pilot, had created a powerful impression, especially when the aircraft, with its silvery, unpainted skin of bare metal, went through the sound barrier during a demonstration.[19]

Early in 1966, however, there were only two of the fighters

in Saudi, and, in the absence of native pilots, the aircraft were being flown from Khamis Mushayt by former RAF pilots now employed by Airwork Services, another commercial firm involved in the deal. These civilian pilots were authorised to fly only within Saudi air-space, and the vital question of whether the early Lightnings could be used for combat missions had yet to be resolved. (Later, in 1967, when five Lightnings and five Hunters had arrived on the airfield, a Foreign Office memorandum said that HMG had 'raised no objection to their being employed in operations', but characteristically added, 'We made it clear to the Saudis that we could not publicly acquiesce in any such arrangements.')[20]

In a letter to Judy from Jeddah, Jim wrote:

Got here to find that Big David [Stirling] and Geoffrey Edwards had gone quite a way down the line with Tourist [Prince Sultan, the Defence Minister]. The big deal obviously being that Tourist would sign their enormous deal if *we* could guarantee to hold everything together long enough for their bits to get here.

This, being interpreted, meant that the Saudis hoped that mercenary activity in the Yemen could continue to distract the Egyptians sufficiently to prevent them launching any attack on Saudi Arabia before the Kingdom's new aircraft and defence systems were functioning fully. Nasser inadvertently encouraged this hope when, the day after publication of the White Paper, he proclaimed that he would stay in the Yemen for twenty years, if that proved necessary to preserve the republic. Presented with a new chance of seizing Aden, he soon began rebuilding the strength of the Egyptian Expeditionary Force. In May 1966 the EEF had shrunk to 20,000 men, concentrated in the triangle between Sana'a, Hodeihah and Taiz; but in the second half of the year it rapidly built back to a total of 60,000 and Nasser threatened that if foreign troops invaded the Yemen, he would 'destroy the bases of aggression' – the Saudi towns of Jizan and Najran.

11

In the Balance

The war resembled a moorland fire, which can smoulder away underground in the roots of the peat for weeks, without any visible sign of life, and then suddenly flare up in a different place. The Egyptians would mount an attack, and the Royalists would retaliate; the Royalists would lay more mines, and when these were detonated by tanks or trucks, the Egyptians would strike back. Then everything would go quiet for a while as both sides withdrew to lick their wounds – only for hostilities to break out abruptly somewhere else.

By January 1966 Bernard Mills had become bored and went off to Jordan and the Lebanon in an attempt to improve his Arabic, having told Jim that he would come back if really needed. Yet far from being stood down, the other mercenaries – who by now had been rebranded the 'European Advisory Group' – were suddenly back in action, and the first months of the year brought an increase of activity on all sides. 'We stretched absolute limit on ground urgently need at least two reinforcements,' Johnny Cooper cabled Jim, 'as war seems imminent.'

On 25 February a telegram from Bosom, the mercenaries' network control station in Jeddah, reported that

Roger Faulques had secured a new contract for his French team: 'Business looking up all round.' But both sides in the war were under strain. On the 26th a newsflash revealed that ninety-five members of Sallal's bodyguard, including four named officers, had deserted with their rifles, all from the Beni Matar tribe – but that same day Franco cabled from Nuqub, reporting that after several heavy actions during the past three weeks Royalist supplies of ammunition had run very low, and that every day brought Egyptian air and artillery attacks. Roger Faulques had arrived in Nuqub that morning, armed with a three-month contract for six men and plans to move back into his original cave. 'He has completely fallen for Fiona [who had returned to the London office],' Franco told Jim, 'but is too polite to say so.'

Jim, meanwhile, had being lobbying in Westminster, and on 4 March he sent out a message, to be dropped to the 'the Khowlan teams', which showed that for once he was being positively encouraged (albeit covertly) by MI6 and the Government:.

Dear Shareholders,

Our Friends have let it be known that the Government would like *any* difficulties which could be put in the way of the Egyptians inside the Yemen during the next eighteen months, as this would take the heat off the Federation, and the British Army during its withdrawal.

The Saudi Government appears at last to have come face to face with the truth and realise that their only chance is also to make trouble for the Egyptians in the Yemen immediately. The Mango Production Co.

'An unlikely-looking guerrilla sheikh, small-boned and delicate': Prince Abdullah Hassan.

Imam al-Badr was an indolent and ineffective leader, yet commanded immense loyalty and respect among his subjects.

The self-styled Brigadier-General Abdurrahman Bruce Alphonso de Bourbon-Condé (*left*) – a combination of titles weird enough to make any British officer uneasy.

Johnny Cooper in conversation with Abdullah Hassan.

Troglodyte living: Dandy (David Bailey) and Kudu (Kerry Stone) at home in the mercenary base at Mustang.

Ancient rifles were highly prized, and many of the Yemeni tribesmen could hit a Maria Theresa silver dollar at 50 paces.

The safety of every mercenary depended on the loyalty of the bodyguards assigned to protect him.

Loading a camel in a sandy wadi.

Even small boys of ten were carrying a Mauser and 50 rounds.

Casing of a Russian gas bomb, dropped by the Egyptian air force.

Captured Russian heavy machine gun, jacked up on rocks for use against aircraft.

John Woodhouse (in turban) with Gassim Monassir and followers
on a high point above Sana'a.

He could dig faster than a mole: Jimmy Knox enlarging a cave.

Anti-aircraft position set up above the entrance to one of the headquarter caves.

The bulging cheek of a *qat* chewer contrasts oddly with his Canadian military jacket.

Tribesmen and their camels break the journey, camouflaged among the rocks.

Going in: a camel-borne party sets off into the High Yemen from the Beihan border.

naturally are keen to stir things up as soon as possible
. . . It is essential that we get the war going again, as
soon as possible . . .

I realise that you personally will probably be taking
quite a lot of the brunt of the anger and disillusion-
ment from our Arab friends [because of the White
Paper], and it will be very difficult to reassure them
of Great Britain's good intentions. There are however
a lot of people in the country here, who carry great
weight, who heartily disagree with the Government's
policy and will continue to bring pressure . . . to have
the decision reversed. This I think is the best I can
offer you to help explain away a bitterly embarrassing
position.

This message in effect gave the mercenaries carte blanche
to do whatever they liked. Once again the Saudis welcomed,
and were prepared to pay for, any action that would retard
hostile moves by Nasser and reduce his chances of attacking
the Kingdom.

At the same time, however, George Brown, Harold Wilson's
erratic Foreign Secretary, had taken to telephoning Nasser
and asking him for advice on what to do about Aden. Nasser
would feign ignorance, saying that he had no agents in the
colony, and suggesting that Britain's best policy would be to
get out as quickly as possible. In the view of some Arab
observers, Britain now had a government that was not loyal
to the country.[1]

Because Aden was becoming ever more dangerous, and
the future of the colony was clearly limited, Jim decided to
move his Middle East headquarters to Jeddah. To explain
why the organisation would no longer need the Aden flat,

he put out a fictitious report saying that Mac McSweeney had unfortunately been killed in a car crash while on leave in England.

Meanwhile Stirling, having met Prince Sultan twice early in March, sent him suggestions for the future in a letter from London, launching a bold attempt to bring the regular SAS into action, initially to train selected Saudi recruits for a Special Force that would carry out raids and harassing sorties. Sultan did not rise to this bait; but Jim also wrote to him with detailed suggestions for increasing the efficiency of his existing operation:

Your Royal Highness – Greetings and respects.

In view of the changed situation in the Yemen and on the Saudi/Yemen border, with the probability of greatly increased activity in the near future, and even a possible escalation leading to open war between Saudi Arabia and Egypt, the following are our recommendations:

a. Our present base in Aden to be closed down.

b. A similar base to be opened in Jeddah.

c. The establishment of radio stations in Saudi Arabia at Najran and Jizan, and later on Bishra airstrip.

d. An increase in the missions in the Yemen from the present six to eleven (including the French).

e. The London base to continue as before.

There followed a list of the officers and signallers who would be needed. Jim, one British officer and one secretary would remain in London. Ten British officers, seventeen signallers (one French, two Saudi), fifteen British soldiers (Striking Force) and twenty-six French . . . The headquarters in Jeddah would require a furnished house, two servants and two cars, and the transport would have to include nine Dodge Power Wagons or Ford four-wheel-drive trucks, as well as nine Land Rovers or jeeps. The letter recommended the urgent issue of 120mm mortars and their ammunition as soon as possible: 'The pre-stocking of 1,000 bombs each at Jizan and Najran should commence immediately.'

In a private letter from Jeddah, Jim told Judy that he had 'nearly concluded' a new contract with Sultan, and that if all went well he was about to buy a seven-bedroomed house, to act as the team's new base, together with a station wagon and a Chevrolet sedan. As usual Jim was on the lookout for experienced operators, and on 1 April 1966, from London, he wrote a cryptic letter to Bernard Mills, explaining that he had 'been given every encouragement and told to increase our effort in all directions'.

You said if ever there was real need for you again, you would consider coming back to us. Well now, there is a need for you, Bernard. Unfortunately the relationships between your late area boss and ourselves have not been good, and in view of his increasing importance I hope you will see your way to coming back, as he has asked for you by name . . .

Love from all of us here, Jay.

Bernard duly returned, and on 3 June flew to Jeddah, then on to Najran. Even though Jim's private army had grown so much, its existence was still cloaked in secrecy; and when Chris Sharma, who had left the organisation (having not had his contract renewed, and having lost all his kit on the way home), asked if he might write an article about his experiences, Jim firmly put the idea down. For months he had been receiving vitriolic criticism of Mansoor's 'megalomaniac inefficiency and general immaturity' from Jack Miller, but now he was too tactful to mention such defects, and he merely deflected the request by more subtle means. 'I have no real objection to you writing an article, provided of course no mention of us, the firm or parachuting,' he told Sharma in a letter.

However I would have thought that you would be very unwise to write an article either signed with your real name or your Arab *nom de guerre* as, after two years, the Egyptian Intelligence Services must have a large file on both these names, and in view of the fact that they are now paying hard cash for killing civilians and members of the armed forces in Aden, it would not be beyond their powers to get you or a member of your family at your home address.

Also, as you would be the first person in the group to have written an article like this, you would naturally bring the Press about your ears very quickly, and once this happened, it would be impossible to remain hidden from the EIS [Egyptian Intelligence Services]. I am sorry to be rather a damp blanket on this scheme of yours, but the EIS has a very bad reputation, as you know, and we are dealing in other people's lives apart from yours, here.

Grin was still nominally in command of the mercenaries, and early in 1966 he set off on yet another tour, driving his new Toyota – a gift from Feisal – into the semi-desert country of the Jauf, where the few villages consisted of tall houses built from mud rather than the rough-hewn stone that prevailed in the mountains. He found that in some places the Egyptians had changed their tactics from bombing to bribery, and remarked that 'It is now a war of gold.'

Yet his authority – such as it was – had begun to falter. The men in the field thought little of him: he was too much of a loner, too old, too pleased with himself. In the words of one, 'Jim was always the boss, no matter how far away he might be.' Jim himself had begun to regard Smiley as a rather loose cannon, and tended to ignore his advice; and in May 1966, as a potential replacement, he brought in Lieutenant Colonel Bob Walker-Brown, an officer with a formidable record of action in the Second World War.

Having been wounded and captured in the Western Desert, he had escaped from an Italian prisoner-of-war camp – a feat for which he received the MBE – returned to Britain and joined 2 SAS. In September 1944 he parachuted as stick commander into the Forest of Châtillon, north of Dijon, and took part in an attack on the German garrison, which inflicted more than 100 casualties. Then in December he dropped into the Italian Apennines and led a conspicuously successful guerrilla raid, for which he was awarded the DSO. After the war he served with both 21 and 22 SAS, and finally commanded 23 SAS.

Earlier he had earned a reputation for intolerance, and even now, at the age of forty-seven, although he had mellowed, he was known as 'the Toy Soldier' or 'Wobbly', because every now and then he was liable to throw a burst of temper. Jim, writing to Franco and his team, gave a muted warning:

He is, as you know, a very positive character and has of course more experience of SAS than any of us. He has changed since we last knew him and the trouble that he had with his stomach when commanding 23 has now all gone (let's hope so anyway, as you will remember he sacked twenty-two out of the twenty-three officers in his regiment last time).[2]

Because Walker-Brown spoke no Arabic, for his first trip into the Yemen, Jim provided him with an interpreter in the form of Dr Philip Horniblow. Between 7 and 22 May, together with one French mercenary, they made a short tour of the Jauf and the Khowlan, which enabled Walker-Brown to write a perceptive – if rather depressing – report on the military and political situation.

In the Jauf he found Mohamed bin Hussein unhappy at the lack of central leadership, and plagued by subversion among the local tribes. 'The situation appears to be held together by Saudi payments,' he wrote – but some tribes were accepting money from the other side as well. What his report did not say was that he started telling Hussein what he should do, and the Prince said he would prefer to take advice from his friend Bernard (who was then in London). The same thing happened when Walker-Brown met the Prime Minister, Hassan bin Yahya.

In the Khowlan, Abdullah bin Hassan's main problem was lack of money. He complained that much of his monthly budget was being stolen along the supply route, and he had scarcely enough to bribe Republican tribes. He was also 'somewhat ungracious' about the air-drops, which he thought had become redundant – although he had the nerve to suggest that the next parachutage should deliver a whole hospital, complete with prefabricated buildings.

In his report Walker-Brown suggested that although in the past the psychological effect of the air-drops had been considerable, the Prince was right in thinking that parachuting had become counter-productive, as the local supply of small arms appeared to have reached saturation point, and 'even small boys of about ten were carrying a Mauser and fifty rounds'. Weapons and ammunition, he believed, had become a substitute for currency, and many weapons were being sold to the Republicans. On the other hand, there was something to be said for increasing the supply of gold.

As for Gassim Monassir, his small, irregular force of about 300 men was occupying the same exposed position from which John Woodhouse had looked down on Sana'a; and although Walker-Brown formed a high opinion of Gassim's vigour and courage, he thought that he lacked imagination and basic military knowledge, and was overconfident, 'even having regard to the low calibre of the enemy'. Another problem was that Gassim's fame had aroused local jealousy: 'He has become a military legend, but this is by no means welcome to other leading personalities in the area.'

All went well with Walker-Brown's touring party until they reached Gassim's forward position. There, according to Horniblow, 'the Royalists decided this was a good moment to demonstrate their prowess and started firing their 81mm mortars'. When retaliatory shells came whistling in, the experienced Walker-Brown dived into a hole, but Horniblow merely got down behind a wall and received a sharp blow from a splinter in one foot. No great damage was done, but he decided to use his only shell dressing on his donkey, which had sustained a splinter in the backside, rather than on himself – reckoning that the most important thing was that the animal should be able to carry him on the first stage of the journey back to civilisation.[3]

Walker-Brown's trip left him feeling that in the Khowlan Royalist morale was deteriorating, because there was no central leadership or inspiration, and no overall policy. Many important Yemeni personalities had gone abroad, and the country itself was decaying, as men ceased to farm the land and sat around in caves accepting gifts of gold and rifles.

Walker-Brown's particular worry was that the four-strong British mercenary team deployed with Abdullah bin Hassan was not making any impact on the military situation. The men had supervised the reception of two air-drops, but for political reasons they were not allowed to be active against the Egyptians. Their relations with Hassan seemed quite good, but he was not using them 'to the full as military advisers'.

The French mercenaries were suffering from similar frustrations. Two 120mm heavy mortars with a range of 13,800 yards, and four 120mm medium mortars with a range of 8,000 yards, had arrived at their training camp near Najran, and there they gave an impressive demonstration of the weapons' fire-power, demolishing the target – a rocky hillock way out in the desert – with the first volley. It had already been proposed several times that these weapons should be used for an attack on the Sana'a airfield, but the Saudis withheld permission, fearful that they would be accused of breaking the terms of the Jeddah agreement. Besides, the reality was that any effective mortar attack on the airfield would be extraordinarily difficult to mount.

The only point from which the big mortar bombs could be launched successfully was Gassim's insecure position, and the task of ferrying weapons and ammunition to it would be almost insuperable: for the final approach march from the low ground of the Jauf, a force of 300 camels would be needed, and the journey might take a month. Even if the Saudi authorities agreed to release the mortars, Egyptian intelligence would get wind of the fact, and the likelihood of air-attacks on the camel caravan would be high. In any case, the principal targets – the MiGs and Ilyushins – might vanish, as the aircraft would probably be moved from Sana'a to Hodeidah.

In an attempt to launch a new initiative, Jim and Walker-Brown composed a joint memorandum to Prince Sultan, which Jim read to the Prince on 18 July. The paper's main recommendation – 'in the absence of HM the Imam al-Badr' – was:

> for the appointment of a strong military commander with responsibilities covering the whole of the Yemen. This person to be a member of the Bait Hamid ud Din family. He should be centrally based at a place where he can best control the whole of the Yemen. He should be advised by a small but influential Council of War which should include the commanders of the three principal areas . . .

The memorandum also spoke of the possibility of training a permanent military force, perhaps with the help of the Saudi army. But grandiose plans were one thing – their execution something else. The truth was that the leadership of the European Advisory Group was beginning to splinter.

Some of the mercenaries, bored by their enforced lack of action, wondered why Jim was still recruiting so enthusiastically. The answer seems to be that he was unquenchably optimistic, and believed that if he could put enough men on the ground, he yet might galvanise the Royalist commanders into a general uprising and get the Egyptians thrown out. So it was that he kept fishing, and among his latest haul was Alastair Macmillan, in his thirties, a member of 21 SAS, who had been working in public relations. Walking him through St James's Park, Jim suggested that he might like to earn more money, but he would not disclose the nature of the task until Alastair agreed to undertake it. Alastair was naturally cautious, and first established that the job was not in Africa. He then asked, 'Is it in the national interest?' To which Jim replied evasively, 'I think it's your duty to go.'

So he went, having told friends that he was off to sell oil rigs in the Middle East. From Jeddah he flew to Jizan, and thence he was driven south-eastwards towards his destination, El Qara. At the edge of the central massif, where the mountains rose almost vertically out of the plain, he was dumped, and from that point on he had to walk. A guide who met him immediately challenged him to a rifle-shooting contest. When the Arab put up two tin cans about fifty yards away, Alastair said, 'No, no,' and moved the targets out to a range more like a hundred yards. The Arab, firing first, missed twice, and was astonished when Alistair downed them both.

Eight thousand feet up the mountains he came to the complex of caves once occupied by the Imam, set at the foot of a cliff in an amazingly steep rock face. There he became part of the three-man British team manning the Broadway radio station and living in the caves. The inhabitants of the village had also taken to the natural rock shelters, and in some of them they had set up little shops, with a variety of hand-grenades and ammunition displayed for sale on shelves alongside domestic stores like rice and flour. Limited supplies of water came up by donkey and, as Alastair remarked, 'if you were a fool, you went down to see the place they was coming from'.

In the open, gun-positions fortified by rock walls were set out round a wide, semicircular ridge, the prize weapon being a Hispano-Suiza cannon dating from the Spanish Civil War, manned by a couple of fifteen-year-olds. In theory the period during which Alastair stayed there was one of peace and calm: there was little fighting on the ground, but bombing raids were frequent. For as long as these were launched by Egyptian pilots, they were relatively innocuous; but every now and then the accuracy of the attacks increased unpleasantly, and the team concluded that the aircraft were being flown by 'guest artists' – that is, Russians.

Like all the mercenaries, in the course of three tours Alastair moved around a good deal, mostly on foot, ferrying pieces of equipment to other stations, or temporarily replacing men going on leave. Every change of station meant hard walking, up and down exacting mountain tracks. One of his approach treks, going in from Beihan, took him past Marib and out into the wastes of the Rub' al-Khali, where he visited the remains of the building alleged to have been the palace of the Queen of Sheba: a great, grey ruin rising out of the desert, with flat-fronted pillars of stone, like upright ribs, built into the walls. Even though the place was in Republican hands, he and his companion went into the heart of the ruin and found a little *suq* in which they could buy food.

It was beginning to look as though the Saudis did not really want Nasser to be defeated. Now that they saw how much the Yemen war had weakened his army, and how it was draining his finances, they would prefer – it seemed – that his Expeditionary Force remained bogged down indefinitely. Yet at the same time they were reluctant to keep handing out gold sovereigns, which vanished like grains of sand into the mountains and deserts of the Yemen.

Jim's usual answer to a financial crisis was to head for Jeddah, and at the end of August 1966 he made yet another pilgrimage, reporting to Tony and Fiona on the 31st:

> All hell out here! Tourist [Prince Sultan] first of all said would we sign for one month. They are certain peace will be here in Oct. I said NO – must have at least two months. Finally settled for three months starting 1 Sept. I have the cheque, too. Roger has two months only.

So far, so good. But Jim also reported an 'enormous row' between Bookbinder (Bob Walker-Brown) and Bee (Bernard Mills) – 'all personal things'. The root of the trouble seems to have been that whenever one of the Yemeni leaders wanted military advice, he would turn to Mills, whom he respected most, rather than to the senior officer, and this made Walker-Brown see red. The main offender in this respect was Mohamed bin Hussein, whose faith in Bernard had been cemented by the part he played in planning the battles in Wadi Humeidat. Another cause of friction was the fact that Bernard had acquired some medication from a doctor in England who served as a medical officer with 21 SAS: one set of pills to keep him awake during long camel rides, and another set to make him sleep when he had a chance. When Walker-Brown heard about this, he told Jim that Bernard was on drugs, and Bernard was incensed to be branded an addict.

Having been assured by both that they wished to resign if the other stayed, Jim told Walker-Brown that he refused his resignation and would accept Bernard's. Jim wrote:

Consternation! The next thing I know, Bee has set it up good and proper. Sultan has left [Jeddah] and Khalid sends for me and says that Bee MUST stay and Bookbinder must accept this. I said, No – we were not Arabs. I would not sack my boss under any circumstances. This shook them, and I refuse to alter this. The row is all over Jeddah now.

Jim's temporary solution was to send Bernard on leave until he could see Sultan, and to keep Walker-Brown *in situ*. 'Don't be beastly to Bee on his return next week, but don't fraternise,' he told London. 'He has behaved very, very badly.'

By now Tony Boyle was acting as the mercenaries' field commander and political representative in Jeddah, with Mike Gooley (a recent recruit who had already done one operational tour) taking the role of Operations Officer. Writing to Jim on 10 October, Tony elaborated on the dissensions within the group:

He [Walker-Brown] said to both Mike and David [Bailey] that he thought both you and I might be mixed up in this for business reasons. He also had a complete fixation that the Friends were out to eliminate us – I have found no evidence to support this. I believe he also took as a personal insult any delay or postponement of a meeting, and the Arabs do not mean this – it is their natural behaviour.

While this row was boiling up in Jeddah, Jim had despatched Franco (Rupert France) to visit Hassan bin Yahya, the Yemeni Prime Minister, who was supposed to be terminally ill, in his cave at Ketaf, in the far north-east of the country. Franco was well set up for the journey, with three soldier escorts and a letter to the Naib (the local commander) at the top of the plateau, asking him to arrange onward transport. The party went by Land Rover as far as Nehouga, the camel-head at the bottom of the *jebel*, where an extraordinary organ-isation led by one man, with eight excellent camels and their handlers, spent their whole time lifting stores to the plateau high up the mountain. All the vehicles on the plateau had been raised section by section, and Franco's party passed a team of twenty-five men carrying up a vehicle chassis.

At 3.30 a.m. they reached Ketaf, in a long, narrow, fertile wadi, in the middle of which was the Prime Minister's head-quarters, called the *Hakooma*, or Government. 'My first impress-sion on meeting the PM was certainly not that of a dying man,' Franco reported:

Old-looking, yes, but alert, right on the ball, though very definitely tired. He apparently sleeps little, and works the rest of the time. His office had three commodi-ties only – *warraqas*, flies & odd pens & ink bottles, medi-cines etc. I have rarely seen so many flies in a building.

He immediately started discussing his problems, but I was not quite happy with his English and found it hard going, though I got the main points. We were invited to a jebel lunch about a mile away, and in due style we all walked, surrounded by guards, to the lunch RV.

On the way the Prime Minister talked incessantly, worrying particularly about the tribes' inability to retaliate against Egyptian aircraft. He claimed that Ketaf was not a secure place for a radio station, and insisted that Franco should move on to the military base at Khoudom:

On arrival at Khoudom we were housed temporarily for the night in a cave (ghastly one), but the following day we were given an excellent cave. We are half-way up a small jebel and have had a stitched cover of khaki material put right along the aerial to cut the shimmer which would give us away to aircraft. The guard system is good but noisy. Literally every five minutes whistles blow and sentries must answer or go in chains the following day. We have been allotted one guard-cum-orderly, but have four extra ones posted above and to the side of the cave each night.

Constant reference by the soldiers asking when we are going to start the war again and drive Nasser out of Sana'a. Contrary to all the views expressed, the PM has been kind and generous to us in all respects. The first impression I get of him is that the locals hold him in a combination of tremendous respect and fear. He is regarded as very hard-working (he sleeps very little) and just, but I don't see him as a popular figure. He is too withdrawn and ascetic in his ways.

Radio communication with Bosom and other stations good. Runners sent daily to neighbouring tribes. Local transport consists of six vehicles, including two three-ton lorries, all lifted bodily section by section up the mountainside.

The PM fully agreed that the British should leave Aden, but found their approach to the matter beyond his comprehension. He told Franco that although Egyptian bombing was not doing serious damage, it was having a bad psychological effect, because the Royalists could not strike back effectively, and this was worrying him considerably: he thought it would be a tragedy if the Egyptians could achieve from the air what they had been unable to do on the ground. The Prime Minister called for anti-aircraft guns, wanting 'to hit back and if possible down a bird or two'. Franco had to restrain his enthusiasm, and explain that hitting fast planes was very difficult.

Even though the situation was so volatile, Jim was still reinforcing his team. One new but seasoned operator was Frank Smith, who, having served in the Parachute Regiment and in the Middle East, had been in 21 SAS for ten years, reaching the rank of sergeant major. In civilian life he was a plumber, but when he tried to expand his business in Portsmouth by taking on a dozen men, he overreached himself and the firm went bankrupt. Urgently needing a new job, he turned to the territorial SAS, which was very strong in the town – there was a Portsmouth Squadron – and when John Woodhouse came down recruiting for the Yemen, Frank seized the chance. After an interview in London (he always remembered the big dolphin on the front door of Jim's house) he was away to Jeddah, and thence by road on a three-day journey across the desert to Najran in a convoy of five new Toyota pickup trucks destined for the French contingent.

After a short stay at the French training camp, now established in a wadi not far from the town, he went on to Amara, where Mohamed bin Hussein had his headquarters. Frank soon came to like and admire the Prince, but before long he moved on to his operational location, Mustang, the three-man outpost in Wadi Heera'an, which runs from Al Hazm in the east to Koulat Hamama (Pigeons' Bath), where the road ended, in the west, some 35 miles of the wildest mountain country north of Sana'a.

Compared with some of the other mercenary outposts, Mustang was paradise, in that a spring coming down the wadi flowed into a chain of oblong pools sculpted by centuries of spates, and in several of the hollows the water was chest-deep, so that bathing and swimming were a delight – the only hazard being the shoals of slim fish that came and nibbled at the hairs on people's legs. A hand-grenade lobbed into a pool yielded enough for a fry-up, but the fish turned out to be bony and tasteless.

The team's base was a cave in the side of the mountain. One bane of life was the presence of malarial mosquitoes, another the threat of flash floods: a tremendous storm, heralded by thunderous roaring and warning rifle shots from higher up the mountain, once almost swamped the camp. Although no rain was falling outside the cave, a raging torrent suddenly exploded past the entrance, flinging rocks with it and forcing the inhabitants to retreat up the sloping floor towards the back of their den. So violent was the flood that their Land Rover, 500 feet lower down the wadi, was swept half a mile downstream.

A more frequent threat was attack by MiGs: the aircraft came in so low along the valley that they were often level with, or even below, the encampment on the hillside; and although the detachment had two machine guns – one .5 and one .300 – set up in well-built nests, the Royalist tribesmen refused to fire them. When Frank stormed into the local commander, Prince Mochsin, and demanded to know why his men weren't firing, the answer was, 'It would make the Egyptians angry.'

'Well,' Frank answered, 'they're bloody angry already' – and got permission for himself and his colleagues to man the guns instead.

After a few attacks he noticed that the scream and crash of incoming 2-inch cannon shells preceded the arrival of the aircraft by several seconds. In the safe interval between the two there was just time to nip out of the shelter, man a machine gun and loose off a stream of tracer, mixed one-and-one with ordinary bullets, as the MiG started to pull up, exposing its belly. The Mustang team thought they hit at least one aircraft, and the sight of tracer looping towards the pilots evidently unnerved them, for the frequency of the attacks steadily diminished. One factor in favour of the men on the ground was the age of the ammunition that the planes were firing: it was Russian, dating from 1953, and many of the shells failed to explode.

The logbook of the Mustang radio was packed with reports of fighting. On 17 September 1966 – a typical day – it recorded:

1   Four nights ago a force sent by Gassim Monassir attacked Egyptian camp at Suq el Khamis, approx. 30 km from Sana'a on Hodeidah road. 25 Egyptians killed, 30 wounded. Two trucks, two tents destroyed. Encounter lasted four hours.

2   Two nights ago force sent by GM attacked Egyptians at Al D'Baart near Bahul. 1 x 75mm, 2 x 35 cal Czech MG destroyed. Encounter lasted 4½ hours.

18 Egyptians killed, 20 wounded . . . Cas[ualties] reported as one wounded only.

Gassim's initiatives apart, the Royalist war effort was almost at a standstill, because most of the army commanders had gone abroad, some to Jeddah, others to the lush pastures of Beirut. Mohamed bin Hussein, however, had departed on a serious mission. With the encouragement of King Hussein of Jordan, and in company with Billy McLean, he had flown to Teheran, where he appealed to the Shah for a colossal quantity of arms and ammunition: 50,000 rifles, 100 .5 machine guns, 130 recoilless anti-tank rifles, and much else. The Iranians agreed to train 100 Yemenis in Iran in techniques of sabotage and terrorism, and to send twenty instructors to train Yemenis in their own country; but nearly a year passed before they began to meet Hussein's ambitious request for weapons.

His initiative by no means pleased the Saudis or the Yemeni Prime Minister, Prince Hassan, who on 31 October sent out a querulous radio message marked 'For all Yemeni Princes':

1 Feisal angry Mohamed bin Hussein in Teheran without explanation or permission.
2 My situation bad as I must go El Qara, also remain here await Mohamed bin Hussein.
3 Ahmed Shami lost face with Saudis.
4 We may lose much from this.

In a paper marked 'UK Eyes Only' and dated October 1966, Jim gave an assessment of the general situation. He pointed out that the conflict in the Yemen had come to be seen as 'the tribal arena of a much bigger struggle between the so-called Progressive Socialist Arab block led by Nasser, and the traditional states led by Feisal'. 'The Americans think they can control Nasser,' he wrote. 'This I have the gravest doubts about.' The greatest danger, in his view, was that the Soviet Union would back Nasser more openly and move to fill any vacuum created by the British withdrawal from the area:

> Therefore I consider it is in the vital interests of Great Britain and the West that every clandestine effort should be continued to obtain the withdrawal of the Egyptian armed forces from the Yemen before we withdraw finally from Aden and the Gulf.

Jim was certain that Nasser would never win the Yemen war outright: he had failed to do so with an army of 70,000 men and a modern air force, and had nothing further to call on:

> Nasser can never defeat militarily the strong Zeidi tribes in their own mountains. The Egyptian army is bad, and won't work forward of 1,500 yards of its own supporting armour. It won't fight at night, and the infantry won't climb on foot up into the mountains.

The strongest possibility, he thought, was that the Egyptians would retain their present positions in the south-west – the Sana'a–Hodeidah–Taiz triangle – and simply wait for withdrawal of the British garrison from Aden in 1968. Meanwhile, they would talk and stall endlessly to avoid open war.

The best course for Saudi Arabia, meanwhile, would be to face up to the fact that Nasser had no intention of leaving the Yemen voluntarily, and to supply the huge amounts of money and arms needed to dislodge him. This would 'require the enforcing of discipline on the Royal princes and the massive backing of one or two of them'.

As for the European Advisory Group, which now had a strength of forty, Jim spelt out some possibilities:

In view of the apparent lack of interest by HMG in the problem, and the stated indifference to our activities by MI6, coupled with the absolute disinterest and lack of use of us at the moment by HRH Sultan, we appear to have three courses open to us:

1   To withdraw as soon as possible from the Yemen, before disaster overtakes us.
2   Convert ourselves into a pure intelligence-gathering organisation, due to the lack of other roles.
3   Hang on in our present role and organisation and hope we will be used sensibly again.

All common sense points to our adopting the first course. We have tried exceedingly hard over the last 3½ years to force the many parties concerned to do what we consider the right thing in this affair. We have discovered, trained and helped arm tens of thousands of tribesmen in previously unknown areas of the Yemen. We have built a nation-wide radio network and trained dozens of Arab operators, and continue to repair and keep running this service for them. Medical aid, MT maintenance and repair, military and technical advice and help generally has been produced wherever we have been able to do it. All this without [any] official Governmental encouragement whatsoever.

Far from it, in fact on many occasions we were actively frustrated and discouraged, and as this attitude has never really changed there is every pointer and reason why we should stop. There is no indication that HMG wants us to continue now . . .

As only one thing is ever certain politically in the Middle East, and that is that the unexpected always happens, I suppose we must hang on, on the chance that things the other side of the hill are even worse, and that although we have no hope of winning, it may be that they will lose first . . .

We believe:

Nasser is not going. He will sit it out with the minimum of expenditure of money and military effort till the British leave Aden.

The Saudis should change their policy to one of full support through the Hamid Ud Din family to the Royalists. This to include massive arms/money deliveries only to those areas still fighting the Egyptian army, and that this be done now.

That the Yemenis left alone will continue to drift towards disaster, and every effort should be made to pressurise them to unite and elect a leader, and have an overall military plan directed against the main enemy.

That we should continue with our present organisation and hope to help things as and when we can along the right lines.

Out in the field, some of the mercenaries were growing anxious about their future. On 2 November 1966 a radio message came into Bosom:

We require answers to following questions:
1 New contract November?
2 If not, reasonable guarantee for present work?
3 If not known please confirm to that effect, and inform present situation.
(It should not have been necessary to waste time sending this message).

Jim lost no time in putting out an answer to all stations:

Relax. Have never asked you to work for nothing. Contract for operational budget only is for me/Sultan to negotiate. Already hold your pay for two months ahead. Please trust me on your pay always. Jim.

In England Jim had continued to recruit volunteers with his unique methods. Once, having spotted potential in a young fellow on a train, he followed the man out into the corridor for a private discussion. The stranger was understandably apprehensive, thinking that he was about to be propositioned – and so he was, though not for the kind of activity that had immediately come to mind. 'We now have a target and a slogan,' Tony told Franco. '"A man a day, and Tourist [Sultan] will pay!" Jay has gone quite mad and is even picking up likely-looking young men in railway trains. He should succeed in reaching the target if he is not arrested first for indecent exposure!'

One newcomer was Kerry Stone, a wiry fellow in his mid-twenties who had served in the King's African Rifles in East and Central Africa. Returning to the United Kingdom, he had been able to find only menial jobs, first vulcanising aircraft fuel tanks, then driving a coal lorry and shifting 12 tons a day, for which he earned £8 a week. But he had also joined 21 SAS, and there one day 'a crafty old Master Gunner called Sandy Birkwood', who saw that he was in low water, slipped him a piece of paper saying, 'Kerry — ring this number.'

He called it and said, 'May I speak to the manager, please?' The voice at the other end (it was Tony Boyle's) said, 'Come and see us.' Kerry had a travel warrant for the train from Portsmouth to attend an SAS drill-night in London, but he was so poor that he could only scrape together 3s 6d (about 17p) in cash. Should he spend it on a meal or on cigarettes? Arriving in London on 5 July, he decided on cigarettes, tea and a bun.

At an address in Earls Court he found Jim and Tony in a starkly furnished basement office. The room, with no carpet or curtains — only a desk and a couple of chairs — struck him as 'not very prepossessing'; but after an encouraging preliminary talk, Jim asked him to go away, think things over and come back at 2 p.m.

'Well,' he said this time, 'what do you reckon?' Kerry said he would like to join — whereupon Jim turned to Tony and said, 'Would you give him an advance of pay, please?' When Tony handed over £150 in £10 notes, Kerry was flabbergasted. Finding the train home packed with rush-hour commuters, he took a first-class seat, and when the conductor came along, jauntily peeled a tenner off his great wad of cash, as though to the manner born.

He went to the Yemen via Jeddah at the end of July 1966, and over the next fifteen months was based in three different locations. The first was at Sirwah, which lies in a long, sandy wadi about three-quarters of a mile wide, in the Jauf, between the central mountains and the Rub' al-Khali desert, 60 miles north of the border of Beihan. The village consisted of some twenty small mud houses and a three-storey fort, and it was described by another mercenary as 'the most horrible place in the Yemen'. The local commander there was Abdul Karim al-Wazir, but as soon as Kerry arrived he disappeared to Beirut, never to be seen again.

Kerry described his existence as 'long patches of monotony and boredom, punctuated by moments of excitement whenever Egyptian aircraft attacked'. Normally they came at first light, so if people had to move around, they did so between 11 a.m. and 2 p.m. or at night. There was great excitement on 3 October, when an Ilyushin was shot down near Marib.

Two assassination attempts kept him constantly on his guard. He learnt never to trust any of the tribesmen except his own bodyguard, and when driving always had his automatic, loaded and cocked, concealed beneath a shawl. 'The trouble was, we had us, them and a third party. A soldier would get a rifle from the Royalists and sell it, then go across, join the Republicans and get another off them. Nobody was in uniform, so you never knew exactly who was who.' When bullets started flying, Kerry learnt that if they were passing well above him, they were designed to frighten, but if they were cracking around his ears, they were meant to kill.

Returning from a trip to Aden, he was lucky to get away with his life, for his Yemeni driver insisted on stopping in Harib, which was fiercely Republican. The pair were immediately surrounded by the local militia, and only when the driver managed to persuade them that Kerry was an American did they let them go.

Even if nothing particular was happening at Sirwah, the days seemed to pass quickly. Sleep, whether at night or by day, was punctuated by frequent alarms. The team, consisting of Kerry, Jimmy Catterall (Jingo) and Punchy McNeil (Nocturne), had three skeds (radio schedules) a day, sending signals to Bosom at 9 a.m., noon and 6 p.m., and all messages had to be encoded using OTPs (one-time pads) and a dictionary – a process so laborious that a long message could take several hours to complete. The team were always on the lookout, because they never knew what might happen next, whether it was an air-raid or just tribesmen constantly coming and going.

Food (*akl*) was a constant preoccupation. The men had no set meal-times, but ate whenever they could. The Arabs provided *khubs* – unleavened bread baked in great rounds the size of bicycle wheels, best eaten fresh, but lasting for a fortnight, by which time it would be green with mould, but still edible if dipped in tea. General supplies came in on trucks travelling at night up from Beihan or down from Najran, and the mercenaries were allowed one luxury a month. Kerry once asked for a sack of potatoes, but by the time it arrived the contents were rotten: nevertheless, he squeezed out some intact kernels and managed a small but very welcome plate of pea-sized chips. He could also get many things from the *dukka* (a little shop in the camp), including *basel* (onions, essentials for that staple of SAS diet, curry) and tinned pineapple. The Brits cooked over primus stoves in battered saucepans or rectangular mess-tins; the Yemenis also had paraffin stoves, but often lit small wood fires.

Hygiene was *not* the name of the local game. Defecation took place in the open desert, and no one made any attempt to bury the day's production. The sand was littered with turds which, within minutes, had been baked as dry as biscuits and crackled like cornflakes when walked over. Water was too scarce for any washing to take place: the best anyone could manage was to scrub sweat and dust off with a rag.

Water for drinking and cooking was brought up in a jerrican by Gaid, a lively lad of about twelve whose burning ambition was to own a rifle. Presently he was given one, but soon afterwards Kerry was dismayed to hear a great clanking, and to see the boy staggering along under the weight of a collar, shackles and heavy chains. Evidently he had threatened someone with his new toy − but it turned out that he was in no great need of sympathy. When MiGs suddenly put in an attack, spraying the camp with bullets and cannon shells, and everyone dived for cover, Kerry feared that Gaid had been caught in the open; but when he looked out, all he saw was a pile of chains, lying on the ground. The lad had slipped his shackles and popped into a funk-hole.

One night Kerry was asleep in a cave when he woke suddenly with the feeling that something was about to happen. It was a quiet, moonlit night, and although he heard nothing, the premonition made him reach for his automatic and tap his companion on the shoulder. Then a shadow fell across the mouth of the cave and a rather refined, low voice said in English, 'Good evening. May I come in?' The visitor was the explorer Wilfred Thesiger, who was spending five months in the Yemen as a guest of the Royalists. As usual he was on the prowl, partly for his own edification − he claimed, unconvincingly, that he was studying local dialects − but he was also acting as a messenger between the Yemeni leaders and giving a hand to MI6, for whom he was picking up information.[4]

Thesiger − who had served with the SAS in the Western

Desert during the Second World War – spent some time with the little group, and Kerry was moved to find that 'while this great Arabist and historian was with us, he was quite happy to accept orders and do as I told him'. He once delighted Kerry by remarking, out of the blue, 'The only thing my grandfather ever did was to lose the battle of Isandlwana'.[5]

Other mercenaries were amused, but also irritated, by Thesiger's affectations. 'Gentlemen do not travel by automobile in Arabia,' he would announce as he declined a lift – only to appear a few days later with a gash on his forehead, sustained when the jeep in which he had been a passenger ran into a French vehicle. Radio messages kept coming back to Jim in London saying, 'He's eating all our food . . . He's pinched my li–lo to sleep on . . . How do we get rid of him?' 'Try pop music,' Jim answered – and within two days Thesiger was on his way.

Normally it was impossible to warn other stations of imminent attacks; but one morning, when Kerry saw two MiGs heading due north, he radioed his colleague Don Wright (Woodcutter) at Ketaf, in clear, 'Two to you in two.' Don got the message instantly and took cover, but the aircraft rocketed his store, and his precious tins of milk, which had recently arrived after a long wait, finished up the size and shape of half-crowns.

For Jim the most galling feature of the situation was that, with the return of Sallal from Cairo to Sana'a in the middle of September 1966 and his appointment as Prime Minister of the Yemen, the Egyptians had resumed hostilities on a large scale. In the capital, doubtless on Nasser's orders, Sallal purged the Yemeni administration of what he called 'traitorous and criminal elements'. In the mountains the mercenaries' outstations reported a sharp increase in Egyptian air-raids, beginning on 18 September, and the office in Jeddah coordinated a summary of attacks witnessed by Europeans:

	September	October
Il–28 sorties	21	59
MiG	12	57
HE [high-explosive] bombs	152	183
Napalm	Nil	61
Earliest raid	0700	0530

'Air activity has been very heavy,' Tony Boyle confirmed from Jeddah. Besides all the attacks on Yemeni villages, the Egyptians had bombed Jizan and Najran, both inside Saudi territory; and although night-bombing of the Yemen had proved ineffective, a determined assault had been made against the Royalist staging posts along the Jauf supply route. On the afternoon of 18 October a deliberately murderous attack was made on Mahabsha by two Tupolevs, which dropped high-explosive bombs on the mosque when it was full of worshippers at prayer, killing eighty-one people. It is possible that this barbaric act was in revenge for the fact that the Imam had stopped for a while in the town during his escape in 1962.

The new Egyptian offensive was not confined to the air. One of Sallal's first actions on his return to Sana'a was to dismiss the Republican Prime Minister, General Hassan al-Amri, and his Cabinet, and place them all under house arrest. When Amri offered to go to Cairo, to see Nasser, he was forbidden to do so; and when he chartered an aircraft and tried to fly to America to appeal to the United Nations, he and his group were arrested again.

A 'Report on Yemen Situation', produced by the mercenary team in Jeddah, stressed that the princes must go back to their areas and make strenuous efforts to open motor roads into the centre of the country, setting up motorised transport services from Jizan and Najran to their headquarters. The document urged them to increase guerrilla attacks on primary targets, such as the roads from Sana'a to Hodeidah and from Sana'a to Taiz, and to insist that food could be paid for only with gold and Maria Theresa dollars – which would make the Republican paper riyal almost worthless.

12

Fresh Blood

During the summer and autumn of 1966 new recruits were still reinforcing the mercenary ranks. Among them was Mick Facer, a skilled mechanic who had known Jim for fifteen years in the territorial SAS and, as an MT sergeant, had specialised, among other things, in training people to drive across country. Summoned to appear at the office in Earls Court, he paraded outside and rang the bell – whereupon Jim appeared at the door of the basement below and demanded, 'What are you doing, buggering about up there? Come on in!'

As Mick had been earning £20 a week, and Jim offered him £80, he signed on at once and within a few days found himself in Jeddah, charged with the task of sorting out the group's transport. This was in poor shape – and when he looked underneath some Chevrolet trucks he found there were no split-pins securing the castellated nuts – only loose, bent nails, which could fall out at any moment.

His first deployment was to Najran. By far the quickest and least uncomfortable method of getting there from Jeddah was to fly: a bumpy ride of about four hours in an aged Dakota. But for Mick it meant an overland transit – and that was something else: a 700-mile marathon through the desert, which took a whole week. He made the trip in the company of twenty-one Frenchmen, who wittily split his cover name, Fathom, into two, and called him 'Fat Hom'. The drive was not for the faint-hearted:

> Every time we came to a new tribal territory we had to hand in a *warraqa* to the Sheikh, and he had to find someone he trusted to escort us on to the next area. Whenever we found good going, we didn't run as a convoy at all: we just spread out in a cavalry charge across the desert – and if anyone got stuck, you didn't stop or go back. Everyone had to get themselves out.

From his base in Najran, Mick made numerous sorties into the Yemen, going out with his toolkit to service vehicles or cannibalise broken ones, and often staying in the caves of mercenary encampments, both French and English. He was amazed by the emptiness of the country – the lack of people or habitations – although 'now and then a tribe would come out, with all the women singing and dancing on the mountain as a decoy'. He soon got the measure of enemy air-raids: if two Ilyushins appeared, one would circle round high up, while the other came in 'along the deck', and it was the high one that did the bombing, after its partner had carried out its low-level reconnaissance. As for the MiGs, by then they had heat-seeking weapons, 'so if you were in a vehicle with a hot engine, you'd jump out and run like blazes'. Years later Mick reckoned that from his time in the Yemen he learned 'not to make harsh judgements of anybody, and to look at both sides of the coin. Not "Who is being difficult?" but "What is the problem?"'[1]

Another mercenary who had a struggle to accomplish the journey from Jeddah to Najran was Frank Smith. Returning from leave, he set off in one of the trusty old Dakotas, only for the plane to turn back with engine trouble fifteen minutes into the flight. The problem was diagnosed as a lack of power in the port engine, and after half an hour the pilot took off again. The second and third departures both ended in the same way: a return after twenty minutes. That finished the day's manoeuvres. The fourth departure took place at 5.30 a.m. the next morning, and the fifth (after yet another about-turn) at 7 a.m.

The sixth and final departure appeared to augur well: both engines functioned normally for two hours – but then the port engine again began to falter, and because the pilot had passed the point of no return, he headed for Khamis Mushayt, the Saudi airfield some 150 miles short of their destination. There the plane was grounded until spares could be assembled, and Frank was hanging around, waiting for some alternative form of transport, when a well-dressed Arab approached him.

The stranger had also been stranded, but had procured a Chevrolet pickup truck and driver, and offered Frank a lift to Najran. Frank jumped at the offer and threw his kit into the back of the truck, whereupon the Arab asked him to give a hand with two extraordinarily heavy, bound and sealed wooden boxes. These, he insisted, were not to go in the back of the truck, but must travel in the cab. He then let on that he was a Yemeni official and was transporting the entire annual budget, in the form of gold sovereigns, for one of the Royalist armies.

The rest of the journey would have taken less than two hours in the Dakota; but by road, over the mountains, it lasted two days, and during that time, with £2 million beneath his feet, Frank's honesty was seriously tested. Miles away from civilisation, with a Russian automatic pistol on his belt and only the driver and official in the cab, he kept thinking how easy it would be to shoot them both, bury the gold and reclaim it later. But, being basically an honest fellow, he did not succumb to his fantasy.

Later, he was shocked to hear that while his pickup was crawling over the mountains, the repaired aircraft had flown to Najran and then taken off on the return journey to Jeddah, only to crash in the same mountains, killing everybody on board except one Red Cross doctor, whose back and legs were broken, but who managed nevertheless to crawl into the shelter of a rock. There he was found by some Bedouin, who stole his money, but rigged up a shelter to protect him from the sun, and left him bread and water. He survived, and Frank met him later. By a miraculous stroke of luck, a colleague of Frank's, Peter Bullivant, who was supposed to have been on that flight, missed it because he overslept.

No such disasters greeted Duncan Pearson, a Highland laird with a passion for deer-stalking, who had also served in 21 SAS. He had been working in the City, but, feeling he needed a break, had resigned and decided to go round the world, making Africa his first stop. In the hope that he might wangle a free flight to Nairobi, he rang Richard Marriott, then commanding 21 SAS, and asked if he had any RAF contacts. Marriott, however, immediately spotted another ideal candidate for Jim Johnson's private army and deflected him in that direction.

So it was that on 19 October 1966, after vague preliminary briefings, Duncan flew to Jeddah, having told family and friends that he had landed a wonderful photographic assignment in Saudi Arabia. That, in fact, was where he had been led to believe he was going to work, but the picture came sharply into focus when, at a more specific briefing, Tony Boyle told him he was bound for the Khowlan, and that if his team leader told him to take charge of a Yemeni ambush party, he would do so without asking any questions. Five days later, having changed his escape money into gold, Duncan and two colleagues, Neil and Jimmy, flew down to Najran, taking twenty new German 7.62 automatic rifles and 4,000 rounds of ammunition as 'personal baggage'.

After a tedious wait at Sirwah, and now code-named 'Gassim', Duncan set off with a train of thirteen camels, trekking up into the Khowlan to revive Fluke, the radio station first established by Johnny Cooper, which had been closed down two months earlier. He found everything in good order, and settled in to what turned out to be a surprisingly peaceful existence. His stay perfectly illustrated how compartmentalised the war had become. Not far to the north-west battles were raging, as the Royalists put in attacks and the Egyptians retaliated; but at Fluke there was no military activity of any kind. The team's main functions were to make daily radio contact with Bosom in Jeddah and to treat the sick and wounded, who came to them in droves. Once the daily sick parade was over, or visits to nearby villages had been made, recreational hiking, diary-writing and sunbathing were often the order of the day

A true Scot, Duncan was soon referring to their home wadi as 'the glen', and lamenting the fact that they had 'nae whisky or haggis or neaps' with which to celebrate Robbie Burns' Night. But his medical expertise increased rapidly. Breakfast one morning, he recorded:

was disturbed by a young boy, with his mother and sister in tow, waving around his John Thomas which he had just cut in a fall down the jebel. Everyone including the patient was highly amused. Jimmy put a bandage round it, and with peals of laughter the boy walked off down the hill, showing it to all passers-by.

Another patient easily dealt with was a small girl who asked for a pill because she was frightened of aeroplanes. A placebo sent her away happy; but congenital deformities and indescribable internal problems were more difficult:

I met for the first time a case of the 'evil eye' – a poor little lad with both legs wasted away and a horrid sore all down the right haunch to the back of his knee. The Arabs are so primitive in some things, yet so civilised in many others. Any disease that is unexplainable to them they feel is *min Allah* – from God – and they get into their minds that they are doomed, and nothing will change this view. The poor lad will probably die, but we did what we could – and it is no use us trying to make them think otherwise: we are unbelievers, and lower than the low.

Isolated though they were, high on a mountainside, the Fluke team were by no means cut off from outside events, which they could follow by radio. On Boxing Day they heard that their fellow stations Onion and Mustang were involved in a major battle in the Hamdan area, where Prince Ali bin Ibrahim was apparently the only Royalist commander doing any fighting. On 28 December they learnt that at lunchtime the day before the British cave at Amara had been burnt by incendiary bullets and rockets from a MiG; luckily none of the inhabitants had been present, but the attack had wrecked all their stores, wireless set, beds and other kit.

By 30 December the war seemed to have stopped for the time being, and at 0001 hours on 1 January 1967 the Fluke boys saw in the New Year with a glass of Gordon's gin, while over the radio Big Ben managed only nine chimes (because they were three hours in front of GMT) and the staff of Aden Forces' Network sang 'Auld Lang Syne' rather weakly. As Duncan observed, 'There can be few stranger places to see in the New Year.'

The big event to which the team looked forward was the return of their Prince, Abdullah bin Hassan, to his command. He had been away for months, dallying in Beirut, and now, although he was back on the border of the Yemen, he never came any nearer. Rumour had it that he was becalmed in Najran with forty lorry-loads of arms and ammunition, but that he could not move the consignment any further because the sheikhs of the Jacham tribe were demanding exorbitant amounts of money to allow the convoy through their territory. 'This situation is ridiculous,' wrote Duncan in his journal:

Here we have one of the leading Royalist Princes on his way to his area to make some attempt to fight the Gyppos, and he is held up by a tribe demanding money . . . If I was Abdullah I would rally my 'army' as he proudly calls it and knock hell out of the Jacham . . . I am afraid I get more and more sceptical about the ability of the Yemenis to ever again be able to make a concerted effort against the Egyptians.

On 10 January there was 'big excitement' at Fluke, when a message from Jim announced that Prince Sultan had granted him a further four-month contract; and when Ramadan ended the next morning, there was much rejoicing in Wadi Gara: people turned out in their finest clothes for the first day of Eid (the three-day festival after the end of Ramadan), and (according to Duncan) 'after a bit of communal praying everyone got stuck into celebration feasts'.

Jim's radio reports to the front did not, of course, mention the internal tensions that were threatening to tear apart the high command of his private army. In a long letter from Jeddah, written on 3 October 1966, Tony Boyle had told him:

> You cannot agree to Bernard [Mills] returning [here] without Bob [Walker-Brown]. The Saudis will *definitely* not accept Bob back without Bernard . . . There remains the alternative – that they both go. I know that Bob is not keen to return; I strongly advise you that if he returns here, we will not be re-employed.'

Jim gave way, and Walker-Brown did *not* return. He had not fitted in, and had found that there was really no job for him to do. In retrospect, his appointment appeared to have been a mistake. Bernard, who had left the organisation for the time being, was helping Stirling and Woodhouse set up a new organisation called Watchguard International, whose role was to furnish British Embassies with security and protect heads of government from violent overthrow. He then took a small team of former SAS men to Aden to train a Federal National Guard Special Force, but this project proved stillborn with the collapse of the Federal Government in the run-up to Britain's withdrawal. Later Bernard returned, was reconciled with Jim and went back into the Jauf, supporting Mohamed bin Hussein and supervising the training of the regular army that the Prince was trying to create.

In October 1966, in an attempt to stabilise his private force's situation, Jim flew to Jeddah once more, and a long letter to Fiona illustrated the range of problems that he was facing. On the one hand, he was practising diplomacy at the highest level, trying to retain the interest and financial support of the Saudi leaders; on the other, he was worrying about the safety of individual men living in caves in the Yemen, and at the same time grappling with dozens of small administrative tasks. 'The bombing in Yemen is getting more and more every day,' he told Fiona:

There are indications that the Wog ground forces are pulling back to Sana'a . . . Practically everyone has been bombed or rocketed, many a lot. Rupert has had a real plastering. He is closing his station today and coming up here with the PM, who has at last agreed to come out.

The Wogs have started gas again. It is being dropped from Russian aircraft flying direct from Egypt. They are also, for the first time in three years, bombing at *night*.

I have NOT seen Tourist [Prince Sultan], who is still at the Capital [Riyadh]. Meanwhile Roger [Faulques] and I wait here till the Yemenis and Saudis finally agree. However, the other side's problems really are worse now. Every day more Repubs get shot or arrested, and all under savage brutality too. At least I haven't started shooting our side, yet! Or being shot by them.

All our boys in good heart and send you love. I had no idea we had so many crushes on you. Nor exactly just how frightened some of them are of you!! Well done. It all came out the other evening when there were a dozen of them sitting here in the house talking.

Visas — well done, General Fiona!

There followed a volley of instructions for Fiona to discharge:

K. Stone — send £60 to Kerry's brother ASAP . . . Punchy [McNeil]: cable his wife DO NOT PAY ANY MONEY, LETTER FOLLOWING, NEIL . . . Uncle — December pay in dollars paid in Jeddah to BBME [British Bank of the Middle East] . . . BUY (a) 15 copies *Daily Telegraph* map of Middle East, (b) one copy *Daily Telegraph* world map, (2) two rolls of FABLON (max width) . . . .[2]

What else can one do but laugh and booze? The air conditioner failed during the night, & I think I may die.

On that trip alone Jim spent eleven days hanging around in Jeddah, waiting to see Sultan. Up to a point he enjoyed this kind of long-range sparring, playing the Saudis at their own game; but this time it became too much, and only by threatening to leave did he eventually obtain an audience. On 6 November he reported to Fiona that he and Tony had been to tea with Whiskers, his two sons and four or five Aden ministers who were in town to see the King and were staying in the Royal Palace:

Quite fantastic, all six times larger than life and eight times as vulgar. Blue walls, red ceilings, gold everywhere, slaves, guards, hangers-on and chaos all mixed up with ghastly Persian carpets and lovely, lovely Minton royal crested china.

The Sherif was very pleased to see us, especially Tea, and sat on the red plush sofa with us drinking his tea out of his saucer, mouthful by mouthful, but with very real dignity. He had dyed his hair and beard dark brown and was looking very well indeed. The London/Beirut nightclub life has done a lot for him.

We must conclude that:

Nasser's position as President of the UAR, and perhaps his life, depend upon his securing the oil royalties in Arabia.

Nasser intends to stay in Yemen until the British leave Aden.

Nasser intends to enter Aden when the British leave.

Nasser intends to use Aden as a base from which to attack or subvert the Arabian Gulf oil states.

The Russians have not armed and equipped Nasser's army for nothing, and we must expect a much stronger Russian dominance of Egyptian affairs after Nasser has entered Aden.

We believe that the only people capable of leading the Yemeni tribesmen to victory over the Egyptians are the Yemeni royal family. They may not be ideal but they are the only people we have met in Yemen who have enough control over the tribes to be able to unite them in a common cause against the enemy . . . We therefore strongly advise the Saudi Arabian Government to persuade the Yemeni royal family to unite and elect their best man as their military leader.

We therefore recommend that Saudi Arabia, through

the Yemeni royal family, give all financial, military and advisory support required by the Yemenis to drive the Egyptians out of the Yemen before the British withdrawal from Aden in 1968, and that all this should be started immediately, as time is now no longer on our side.

Much the same message was being given to the Saudis by David Stirling, who was lobbying tirelessly for measures to delay the British withdrawal from Aden and to strengthen the federal army in the south. One of his aims was to secure active support from the Shah of Iran, and he made several visits to Teheran, where he held talks with the Chief of Internal Security, General Nesiri.

On 14 November good news for all the mercenary stations came from London, relayed by Bosom:

Operational contract signed until New Year, plus your pay until end Jan.

New contract terms: after first tour and leave, 4½ months' tour and six weeks' leave. Jim

On that same day, in yet another attempt to galvanise the Saudi rulers, the European Advisory Group submitted a strongly worded document to Prince Sultan:

We feel it our duty to submit our report on the military situation in the Yemen which at this moment is extremely bad. During the last few months the Egyptians have withdrawn and concentrated their army into sensible military positions. They are now holding the southern Yemen with the minimum of financial and military effort. In our opinion they will continue to talk and delay without war as long as possible until the British leave in a year's time.

The only way to remove the Egyptians from the Saudi peninsula is to make it too expensive financially and militarily for them to stay, by restarting large-scale guerrilla war. This must be done quickly . . . If by the middle of next year nothing has been done along these lines, it is our opinion that Nasser will ultimately win.

Kerry Stone's second post was Mustang, the station in Wadi Heera'an. The road-head attracted frequent, heavy attacks by Egyptian aircraft, which strafed, rocketed and bombed with both high explosive and mustard gas and phosgene. Kerry reckoned that during his three tours, besides being mortared, he was strafed thirty-five times and bombed 100 times, seven or eight of them with gas.

Ordinary bombing was bad enough, and Kerry had one particularly narrow escape. As four Ilyushins approached, he took refuge behind a natural rock wall. Then he saw a bomb dropping straight at him. By a miracle it landed on a shelf about ten feet above and twenty yards behind him. The noise of the explosion was shattering, but the blast and shrapnel went over his head. Worst of all was being bombed at night. 'In pitch-black darkness you couldn't see the aircraft, but you could hear the bombs roaring down. The noise and vibration were like an underground train coming into a station, but ten times louder.'

On the evening of 16 November Royalist machine-gunners in the Wadi Heera'an had a rare success, when they downed two MiGs. There was some high-spirited argument about whose bullets had done the job – for the British team were now allowed to fire the guns. The pilot of the first aircraft did not eject and was killed. The second MiG crashed with one wing on fire: the pilot did eject, but was badly injured and had the misfortune to land among Royalist tribesmen. Although later rescued by the Egyptians, he too was reported to have died. The mercenaries' Bulletin No. 5 recorded that the wreck of his aircraft was being heavily guarded, and that an agent had been unable to get close enough to photograph it; but the team were confident that they had hit it with a .50 Browning while it was making a low run.

A later report confirmed that a machine gun reputed to be from an Ilyushin shot down near Wadi Marib on 3 October had been seen 'by British eyes'. It was a Russian 37mm, badly damaged in the crash, but not apparently by fire or explosion. The Egyptians were offering 1,000 MTDs for its return, and the tribesman who held it was hoping to trade it for a .50 Browning or heavy machine gun.

In the middle of November Prince Sultan invited Mohamed bin Hussein and other Yemeni princes to a conference in Riyadh, but the talks began badly with a fiery meeting between Hussein and Sultan himself. Hussein, after registering a protest by sulking for two days, was persuaded to return to the meetings, and in due course the Saudis agreed to channel their payments to the Royalists through the Yemeni princes. But at the same time the Imam – as usual – was wavering. Three weeks earlier he had nominated Hussein as the Crown Prince and formed an Imamate Council; but he was now being pressed to reverse those decisions, especially by his intriguing father-in-law and secretary, Yahya al-Hirsi.

While the Royalist leaders conferred, the Egyptians stepped up the military pressure, concentrating their assault on the

Haimatain, west of Sana'a: MiGs and Ilyushins kept up strafing and bombing runs all day, and tanks attacked on the ground, destroying many houses. Lorry-mounted rocket-launchers were also brought into action. A few days later Mustang radio reported that some of the sheikhs in the Haimatain area had been arrested by Republicans, and the people had been warned that unless they gave up their weapons, the sheikhs would be shot.

Considering the constant strain under which the mercenaries were living – the harsh conditions and the isolation – it was not surprising that their sense of proportion sometimes deserted them. At the beginning of December one head-of-station suddenly announced that he would be leaving his post five days early. When Tony queried this from London, saying he understood that the man would be remaining until the end of December, he received a sharp blast in return: 'I was. However because of lack cooperation this station's agreed roles, Ramadan, absence of Princes, I no longer consider my presence necessary.'

It was nothing new for operators to vent their frustrations on Tony, but when a feud broke out between two of his stations, who were supposed to be helping each other, he was not prepared to tolerate internecine strife; he told both antagonists to shut up, and soon afterwards went into the Yemen himself to spend three weeks with the man who had been the first to complain.

Fresh hostilities kept flaring up. On 6 December Egyptian tanks and artillery shelled positions in the Haimatain for four hours, destroying houses and livestock, but causing few casualties. Then on the 11th three devices exploded in Najran – on Saudi territory – one outside the house of the Yemeni Prime Minister, one under a water-tanker and one that

destroyed an anti-aircraft gun. The Saudis' immediate reaction was to arrest twenty people and forbid Yemenis to enter
their country from the Yemen, a move that started a witch-
hunt against all Yemenis in Saudi. As most of the unskilled
workers in Saudi Arabia *were* Yemenis, the ban threatened
huge repercussions – and after further harassing restrictions,
the mercenary organisation advised the Yemeni princes to try
to stop the movement of their people across the border.

While the Riyadh conference dragged on, decisions on
budgets and military supplies were repeatedly postponed. The
delay brought increasingly desperate calls for help from the
tribal leaders who, in the absence of the princes, were trying
to hold their ground against the Egyptian Army, and at the
same time attempting, with minimal resources, to stifle the
Egyptians' sustained psychological pressure on the tribesmen
to abandon the Royalist cause.

For Jim, one major worry was the instability of the Saudi
leadership. From Geoffrey Edwards, whose prolonged negotiations over the Lightning deal had given him inside political knowledge, Tony Boyle learnt that an anti-Feisal clique
was gaining strength. The group's aim was to overthrow the
King: already he was being deprived of important information, and his orders were not being carried out.

The danger of this development was emphasised by a letter
from Shami. The writer urged the Iranian Ambassador in
Riyadh to warn the Shah that Nasser's ambitions reached far
beyond the Yemen, and that his ultimate aim was to 'move
up to the oil fields of the Persian Gulf'. 'This movement
must ultimately be of vital interest to you,' Shami told the
Iranian envoy – and he offered to go to Teheran and discuss
the problem with the Shah himself, 'in order that we can
clarify our thoughts and work together on a united front'.

(In fact the Shah had agreed to send military supplies, and to train up to 100 Yemenis in Iran.)

In Riyadh, however, Feisal was still very much in command, and he did not like anyone telling him what to do. As Tony reported from Jeddah on 14 December:

> The King told the [British] Ambassador that while he appreciated the work Colonel Johnson and his men were doing for the Saudis and in the Yemen, and wanted them to continue, he was very vexed about a letter sent by Colonel Johnson to him. He considered that Colonel Johnson and his men were paid to do what the Saudis asked, not to advise the Saudis on what their policy should be.
>
> The Ambassador replied that he was not in contact with Colonel Johnson – but would Feisal like that message to be passed on to him? Feisal replied that he would.

In spite of all the difficulties, both political and physical, Jim's private army was in good shape. 'Mike [Gooley] has done very well here,' Tony reported from Jeddah on 17 December:

> and there is no doubt that in the third month of having an 'ops' set up here we are feeling the benefit. Requests from the field are being met, budgets and re-supplies are going in pretty well on time. The general sense of tightening efficiency here has, I think, reflected in improved morale in the field.

The year ended with vigorous fighting. On 23 December the Egyptians launched three major attacks, supported by tanks and artillery, pushing outwards from Sana'a into the areas of the Hamdan, Haimatain and Beni Hashaish tribes, and reconquering positions that they had abandoned three months earlier. Meanwhile, the talks in Riyadh were foundering on the Saudi proposal that the name 'Mutawakkilite' should be omitted from the title of the new political party, representing a united front, which they were urging the Yemenis to create. The princes refused to accept the suggestion, and the talks were undermined by the abrupt departure of Abdullah bin Hassan, who flew to Jeddah and threatened to go to Beirut, to publish an open letter to King Feisal, complaining of the overbearing attitude that the Saudis were adopting towards the Yemen.

The Imam was out of action, away in Saudi Arabia undergoing treatment, officially for a kidney complaint, but in fact for alcoholism. This was his second attempt at a cure, the first having been completed just before the revolution; but observers felt that it was unlikely to be any more successful than the first, as Yahya al-Hirsi, who lived with him and drank heavily himself, probably found the Imam more malleable when he was under the influence than when he was sober. In the Imam's absence, Shami met King Feisal for the first time, in Riyadh, and they talked in private for forty-five minutes. According to one of the regular Bulletins now being issued by the mercenary headquarters in Jeddah:

This meeting completely reversed the rather gloomy trend reported last week, and when King Feisal later met all the Yemeni Princes, he assured them that he agreed with their request to retain the name 'Mutawakkilite' kingdom, and to appoint two committees to coordinate and control the anti-Egyptian campaign in Yemen.

Another Bulletin reported mounting tension on the Saudi/Yemen border between Jizan and El Qara. In one incident Saudi soldiers shot dead four Yemeni tribesmen and took twenty prisoner, and quite large numbers of Yemenis were roaming without food or income on the Saudi side of the frontier. It was said that 200 Yemeni saboteurs had been trained by the Egyptians and despatched to work in Saudi Arabia – but the Saudis claimed to have arrested all except seventy of them, and to know the names of those still at large.

On 5 January 1967 the Egyptians carried out the most devastating air-attack of the entire campaign – a raid on the village of Ketaf. Although the target was almost certainly the Royalist headquarters, in caves a short distance from the houses, it was the ordinary people who became the victims. The raid began at 0730, when two MiGs dropped one smoke bomb apiece to assess the direction of the wind. Nine Il-28s, in formations of three, then dropped twenty-seven gas bombs upwind of the village. Each bomb made a crater about three feet deep and six wide, releasing a grey-green cloud that drifted over the houses. More than 200 people died almost at once. Most of them expired within fifty minutes of the attack; they died with blood emerging from mouth and nose, but without any mark on their skins. Affected survivors suffered no blisters or visible injury, but had difficulty breathing and coughed continuously. In the opinion of the International Red Cross doctors sent by Jim to investigate, the rest of those caught by the gas within a mile or so downwind of the impact-point were unlikely to survive. All the animals in the area perished, and crops and vegetation turned brown.

The attack provoked worldwide condemnation. Mercenaries who saw some of the victims were disgusted by the Egyptians' callousness. Bushrod Howard, a young American formerly employed by various oil companies in the Middle East, and now working as an anti-Nasser propagandist, managed to reach Ketaf just two days after the bombing; he collected accounts from survivors, got them to dig up dead animals, loaded them into a truck and took them to Saudi Arabia.[3]

Howard also helped organise press coverage, and on 21 January twenty reporters, including Richard Beeston of the *Daily Telegraph*, were flown to Najran. From there they had a twenty-seven-hour march with donkeys to the village – and when they arrived back in Najran, they were greeted at dawn on the 28th by an Egyptian air-raid, in which eight Il-28s and two MiG s bombed the town, killing four people and destroying numerous houses. Luckily many of the bombs proved duds, including a whole stick that fell along the main street, but failed to explode. A second raid with parachute flares and 500-pound bombs took place that night.

As Jim remarked, the journalists 'reported on the [Ketaf] incident from first-hand experience, and the world press is reacting enthusiastically. The Saudi Arabian Government is no longer able to overlook the fact that it is being attacked by the Egyptian air force.' And yet, in spite of the extensive newspaper coverage, the Egyptians persistently denied using poison gas, and claimed that Britain was exploiting the reports for the purposes of psychological warfare. The victims at Ketaf (proclaimed Cairo radio) had died of tuberculosis.

In London the Prime Minister, Harold Wilson, rejected suggestions that Britain should refer the atrocity to the United

Nations and, when asked an anxious question about the future of the South Arabian Federation, told the Leader of the Opposition, Edward Heath, to recognise the fact that 'we cannot, and should not, be asked to go on indefinitely maintaining an international peace role in all parts of the world when our monetary, manpower or physical resources will not permit it'. On 1 March U Thant, United Nations Secretary General, declared that he was powerless to deal with the matter.[4]

Many observers concluded that Nasser had become desperate to finish off the Royalist resistance; but in fact his murder-by-gas campaign simply increased his own difficulties. Spurred on by the Ketaf raid, the Saudi Government at last decided to reinvigorate the Royalist guerrilla campaign, and to abandon attempts to achieve a solution by political means – good news for the mercenaries, who were asked to revert to an aggressive role.

Jim had been in Jeddah on the day of the gas attack, and on 11 January he was still there, writing to Judy and Hannah Stirling:

It is now 3.45 and at last everyone has gone to bed . . . & I am nearly exhausted. Today after a full day and night Tourist [Sultan] finally agreed. We are to start up again in earnest – four months' contract and no mucking about.

I have spent the last three hours getting our Friends to agree to fly out a heart, lungs, clothing, earth and grass, all saturated with this gas from Ketaf. They will, I hope, be able to prove it at last . . . We must try to prove it and tell the world what's happening here. The Friends have pulled out their finger and will fly their man to London tomorrow with all our bits.

That same day Jim sent a radio message to Shami in London:

Excellent meeting Sultan. Four month renewal. Permission to restart operations including French mortars as
Saudi Arabian Government now admit no hope of political solution to problems.

The French had been awaiting this moment for months.
In training at their camp outside Najran they had found that
the size of the 120mm mortars made them formidably difficult to handle: a single base-plate weighed some 300 pounds,
and, to transport one across difficult terrain, they had to hoist
it on a sling between two camels. When the opportunity for
real action came at last, Frank Smith, who had carried out
a special reconnaissance, led the detachment up to a prominent launch-point that commanded a view of the new Sana'a
airfield, some 8,000 yards away, and early one morning the
French opened fire. A bombardment of some fifty rounds left
the runway pepper-potted with craters and put it out of
action for days.

The maverick Lord Lambton, then the Conservative
Member of Parliament for Berwick-upon-Tweed, had been
reporting 'Nasser's bestial little war' for British newspapers,
and under the banner headline THE ONE-SIDED WAR IGNORED
BY U.N., he published a vivid description of life in a Royalist
camp, where he had spent a night:

It lay on a mountain which looked like a huge pile of
stones . . . As the sun came up, out of crannies and
crevices came men and animals: little fires were lit, break-
fasts were cooked, and the whole scene was one of
animation. At about nine o'clock the front of the moun-

tain had the appearance of an animated beach, when suddenly the warning was given of aeroplanes. Within two or three minutes the space was empty – the rocks concealed everybody. The planes went on, and I could hear them dropping bombs . . .

The mercenaries' Bulletin No. 12, dated 11–17 January 1967, listed numerous actions in the war zone, including many raids with magnesium bombs designed to destroy crops. A more unusual news item reported that three women from the royal family had escaped from their incarceration in Sana'a and gone up into the Khowlan.

Bulletin No. 13 reported the preliminary interrogation of an Egyptian defector, Majdi Ali Hamed, service ID card no. 563161, who said that the Egyptians were transferring all gold and Maria Theresa dollars to Egypt, as if in preparation for a pull-out, and that the numerous spies planted among the soldiers in Nasser's army were shopping anyone who denounced the regime. All the operational pilots in the Yemen were Russian – Egyptian pilots not being trusted to fly in the mountains.[5] The gas and most of the high-explosive bombing attacks were being mounted from Egyptian aircraft refuelled in the Yemen. Gassim Monassir was 'a much-feared opponent. He prevents sleep and kills three or four Egyptians daily.'

A rapid build-up of mercenaries, French as well as British, was causing problems for Tony Boyle, who had taken over control in Jeddah, and on 22 January he told Jim that he had had 'a pretty hectic time for the last few days', as there had never been fewer than fifteen people in the house, and at one time the number had reached twenty-six. 'It has been like a terrible nightmare,' he wrote, 'when the house goes on getting fuller, and no matter how many you despatch to Najran, one or two more than you send off arrive on the next plane from Europe.'

To shift all these people to the Yemen border, he had chartered an aircraft; but the details had been left to his asinine liaison officer, M'saad – with farcical results:

We told him to tell Saudi Airlines there would be nineteen passengers and 400 kilos of freight. He came back and told us everything was all right. Would we please be at the airport at 5.30, as the aircraft left at 7? He would meet us there and would take us in the back way, and everything would be all right.

By 5.20 I was at the airport, where I waited for M'saad for fifteen minutes. Needless to say, no M'saad, so I took the first load of luggage in to be weighed. That came to 500 kilos. By this time Frenchmen and luggage were piling up outside the airport building, so I told them to go in. Of course at that moment M'saad and another load of luggage arrived.

M'saad, in a frenzy, said to bring all the luggage back again, and to put everyone into cars and drive round the side way into the airport. As the aircraft was about to take off, I wasn't too keen, but complied, so we pulled all the weighed luggage back to the cars and took it and all the people round to the front in relays.

By this time all the airport staff and half the military personnel had heard that there was a good performance going on, and had turned out to watch, and everyone was saying, 'Who are all these odd-looking people?' The whole point of going round to the front secretly was lost. In addition we had over 1,000 kilos of freight, and we had to off-load seven people to compensate, so we only got eleven away on the flight.

The incompetence of M'saad had featured frequently as a bad joke in letters ('M'saad has vanished again into space. He must be the most useless LO ever, bar none'); but by then he was about to be moved to a new post, and Jim wrote from London:

I do hope there is no gross malfunction when M'saad is fired into orbit. I am delighted to hear that he is on count-down. However, don't hesitate to light the blue paper even if I cannot get there to see it go off pop! He has done a great job and we are all proud of our boy, but please don't tell him my address in London, just mention Billy's name.

The beginning of March saw Jim in Jeddah yet again, sending Hannah Stirling a long list of administrative tasks: aircraft seats to be booked, visas obtained, cheques made out, telegrams sent. The organisation had built up to such a level that she was now handling 200 movements a year, and fielding some awkward requests — as when Tony asked her to research 'the best size hollow rubber springs to go between spring and frame instead of the bump stops on the 2½ litre short wheel-base Land Rover'.

'My dear Hannah,' Jim wrote on 4 March:

As we are now forty strong, and going on leave twice yearly, and the average leave pay request is £400 cash, this means a total of over £30,000 from the London petty cash account. This is bound to draw attention for tax & subsequent follow-up on individuals. Therefore think prudent henceforth only channel either in Sterling to Jersey or dollars to your BBME accounts Jeddah – but the latter always liable to seizure if the Egyptians arrive. Either way is legal.

The surge of enthusiasm shown by the Saudis at the beginning of the year quickly subsided. On 7 March the mercenaries' Bulletin No. 15 struck a gloomy note, saying that the hopes of substantial support from the Saudis were dwindling, as week after week went by without any sign of them following up the aggressive announcements provoked by the Ketaf gas attack. In the meantime, as the talks in Riyadh dragged on, the situation in the Yemen was 'rapidly approaching anarchy'.

By the beginning of April 1967 Jim's organisation was thoroughly demoralised. One report said that (with the possible exception of Mango drops) no offensive operation had been brought off during the last twenty months. Communications and medical support were the only fields in which any real contribution had been made. Jim's own burdens were increased by the death of his father, which took place in the middle of April.

Although short of meaningful tasks, the mercenaries were carrying on as best they could. On 3 February the Fluke team were galvanised by the arrival – at last – of Abdullah bin Hassan. To mark the occasion Duncan shaved off his substantial beard, but the Prince's reappearance proved disappointing, for he was in low spirits. The team talked to him from 8 p.m. until 1 a.m., but, as Duncan remarked, the whole discussion could have taken place in half an hour, for the Prince's options were limited by a dire shortage of money.

The Saudis had awarded him a budget of 500,000 riyals in January, but he had already spent two-thirds of it, and his tribesmen had not been paid for six months. He was in great need of gold, weapons and ammunition – and the Jacham tribe would not let his trucks through without payment. So desperate was he that he wrote out a note, in his peculiar English, for immediate radio transmission to King Feisal: 'All the tribes . . . are revolting and need strong commendores.'

With Abdullah had come Prince Hassan bin Ismail, described by Duncan as 'an amusing bird, very good-looking, a highly civilised, smooth individual', who until then had been Keeper of the Royal Wives in Beirut. This was the first time he had been into the Yemen, and from the way he behaved the mercenaries concluded that he had 'no more idea of commanding an army than a night-club operator'.

Two days later there was some excitement when, in the evening, dissatisfied tribesmen started shooting into the area of Abdullah's cave from the other side of the wadi. They were quickly driven off, but not until a good many rounds had been expended. 'They did not try anything in this direction,' Duncan recorded, 'so we just carried out normal drill when the glen is under fire – shut the door and turned up the wireless. Never any good to be heroic when you don't need to be. Seven o'clock is the popular time for shoot-ups.'

Next morning two local sheikhs came up the wadi, each with fifty or sixty tribesmen, to pay their respects to Abdullah, and no doubt wishing to get paid. A tremendous *feu de joie* took place:

The Digga force arrived at about midday, and the first we knew about it was two bullets whizzing over the top of the *bait* [house]. Accompanying their blazing-off, all the warriors were singing the Malakee war chant, and a drum was being beaten with no sense of rhythm. To add to the confusion a bloke sometimes tootled on a trumpet.

Sheikh Ali Abdullah arrived at about 12.30 with his gaggle, and again we got a touch of the 'crack and thump'. Just as they were all below us, and the noise was more like a platoon attack going in, Stan took advantage of the din to try out his German automatic rifle, and fired 20 aimed single shots into the rocks far above them. These rifles of ours are quite impressive for the fire-power they can produce, and Stan's little bit of controlled, brisk shooting put a stop to their antics for a few brief moments.

Grim news of events in Aden and Vietnam dampened the Khowlan team's spirits as they waited for news from Jeddah, to find out whether Tony Boyle had managed to prise more money for Abdullah out of the Saudis. 'No money, no action!' Duncan wrote.

On 17 April, in the middle of his stint in Wadi Heera'an, Kerry Stone went off on foot for a two- or three-day recce on the Arhab plateau in the mountains just north of Sana'a. There the Jebel Asama, which dominated the road leading from the capital to the northern airfield, was occupied by a company of Egyptian troops armed with mortars and recoilless rifles, supported by tanks.

The party of four — Kerry, his guard and two guides — set out on a misty morning with the aim of sniping at any target of opportunity that they spotted as they looked down from the *jebel* into the camp; unfortunately the guide led them into a zone commanded by enemy positions, where they came under fire first from mortars, then from heavy machine guns. The enemy were only 300 yards away, and above them. As Kerry remembered forty years on:

This woke me up. I had just been plodding along with my mind in neutral. Now, on looking about me, I saw that the mist had burnt off in the early morning sun. Not only that: for about two miles in any direction the ground was as flat as a witch's tit, and there wasn't a morsel of cover. For the next 1¾ hours we were machine-gunned and mortared, before we managed to get back to our lines, where I promptly spewed up.

The noise of battle had aroused the neighbourhood, and the locals observed the scene from afar. Sheikh Obeid [the Paramount Sheikh of the area] told me he had been very impressed, and that I was now to be known as 'Ahmed al Arnab'. I thought, That's nice. What does it mean? Ahmed the Magnificent? The Brave? The Great? I was a bit miffed when I found out that *Arnab* means 'rabbit'. How could I sit in a council of war alongside Abdullah the Courageous and Mubarak the Mighty with a name like that?[6]

On 20 April Stan told Jim, from Jeddah, that 'nothing firm has been arranged regarding David's future'. Grin, described in cables as 'penniless', but still enjoying the confidence of Sultan, had just gone into the Yemen yet again, to show Duncan Sandys and Billy McLean the British base and training school at Amara: one message described him as 'jubilantly playing Bob Walker-Brown's role', and he himself said that his particular brief was 'to find out why the war has not started, why the French are not playing their flutes, and why we are not helping more'.[7]

13

Exit Jay

For four years Jim's nerve had held. In the face of innumerable frustrations he had remained amazingly calm, travelling thousands of miles, tolerating delays and broken promises; but at the end of April 1967 his patience eventually gave out. Some scribbled notes left a skeletal outline of his final interview with Sultan:

> Military situation [in the Yemen] since last two–four months – BAD! . . . No Princes in West now . . . . Khowlan unsafe – Abdullah bin Hassan gone after four years . . . Egyptians in Marib, Barash, Elsalah . . . Impossible to move now, and only civil war if you did . . . No control or command . . . Never worse since 1962 . . . No time left before Brits leave Aden in six months now . . . Our military advice is 'Cancel us (+ one month's pay). Or, if you want to appoint someone else, we will hand over.'

Privately, Jim told colleagues that the Saudis did not really want the Egyptian Army to be defeated: they just wanted it to be progressively weakened and detained in the Yemen indefinitely, while Nasser's soldiers were being killed and his coffers emptied. At 0900 on 30 April a message went out from Bosom to all stations:

After many meetings Sultan accepts resignation Jim, Roger, Tony over basic disagreement conduct of war. Judge [Jim] offers hand over operation to Billy, Grin or anybody Sultan wants.

At 1200 Bosom came on the air again from Jeddah:

Sultan thanks you all and offers you new contracts same terms as now details to be fixed. If yes stay put, if no prepare to hand over rifles radios vehicles . . . but await final order.

That evening another message from Jim went out to all the boys in the field:

Sultan proposes coordinating committee of Mohamed bin Hussein, Shami, Khalid Sudairi, Zaid Sudairi, with Billy/Grin as advisers only. This committee to issue orders to our group, one of whom will presumably be appointed boss. Jay [Jim] releases you of all loyalty and sentiment, but you must decide Yes or No as contract starts tomorrow.

Rupert, Uncle, James resign. Jay departs tomorrow as he not believe Saudi will fight and unable serve as mercenary only or be morally responsible for you if you are − though he will not blame you.

In the event Jim did not 'depart tomorrow'. On 1 May, still in Jeddah, he wrote to London:

My dear Hannah,

At last Tony and I have resigned over their incompetence. I will be back on Thursday. Can you please ring Judy if she is in the country and tell her. It's too long to tell in a letter, so wait till I see you.

Love
Jay

Early on the morning of 1 May he sent out one last message to all stations:

I cannot thank you enough after four years, cannot say how sad I am. If there is to be any say, I have strongly recommended to Sultan that Migrant [Gooley] be appointed boss. If he is I hope you will all support him as you have done me.

On 2 May, as if in the hope of getting Jim to rescind his decision, the Mustang team sent in a strongly positive report:

Situation Aries [Arhab]. Hot war exists. Continual pressure maintained by Rake [Royalists] on Execrate [Egyptian] positions in and around Snail [Sana'a] suburbs with field pieces, company strength raids and sabotage. Egyptians ineffectively retaliate with aircraft and art[iller]y in Sharqa area. But reported losing heart rapidly. Only problems caused by shortage of everything due to unreliable and ineffective resupply. Personal impression Snail easy victory with right support from behind, this endorsed by those actively fighting. It seems that support is only sufficient to maintain pressure without actually defeating Egyptians. Rake morale and standard very high. Quite contrast to rear areas.

Jim, however, had had enough, and he left Jeddah on the 4th. Mike Gooley duly assumed command, but his appointment was by no means universally welcomed. 'I personally disagree most strongly with this,' radioed Kudu (Kerry Stone) on 4 April. 'I know Migrant. The only possible person for the moment is Dandy [David Bailey]. Berber [Billy McLean], please look further before taking any steps . . . Please ensure this and opinions [of] other stations to Berber personally.'

Most members of the private army felt bitterly let down. For as long as Jim had been in command, they had felt protected: even though they were living in acute discomfort, and under daily threat of air-attack, they had enjoyed a feeling of security. They knew their salaries were safe in his hands, and that he would do everything he could to defend their interests. Their dismay came out in a message from Bailey (Dandy) in Mustang:

Sincere apologies, Judge, we know what we should do [that is, resign]. But quite simply we can't afford to. We have to stay put and see what happens. If you have anything else up your sleeve, we are with you.

The majority soldiered on, and the radio network was full of their decisions: 'Following say Yes – Kingfisher, Woodcutter, Kudu, Alar, Parsnip, Roc, Pagan, Galaxy, Mimic, Wig, Jingo, Dolphin . . .' Others resigned out of loyalty to their long-term boss. 'Dear Jay,' one wrote on 1 May:

Well, they succeeded, I am sorry to say. I don't like the way they did it, and I don't believe they will make a success of it now that they are in control. I remember Grin's administration from before, so I would like to be relieved as soon as possible. In any case my tour finishes in three weeks but I would like to go before this.

Once all the teams are in this area it would a good thing if you could come here and talk to them, as a lot of them are really in the dark, and if they decide to stay, it's only fair they know what the score is . . . Whatever your policy is or line of action you take, I fully support you.

Jim had hardly arrived back in England when Mike wrote to him on 6 May from Jeddah, scribbling by hand in a state of exhaustion, to report that Tony was being 'a tower of strength and generosity as ever. Can only hope that his influence and ability can in some way still help the cause. This an opinion so far as I can judge universal from every faction and group concerned.' He enclosed a note to Hannah, asking her 'to continue her good work for us all'. On the other hand:

You will obviously be interested in the Billy situation. It is Tony's opinion and mine that he has completely lost out in every way . . . Billy is no longer a fear, even to me, and I think you can feel quite sure that he has lost another constituency and you've had a massive vote of confidence.

It was unfortunate, to say the least, that Jim fell out with the other two prime movers of the mercenary operation, for

McLean and Smiley had both played a large part in its success. Their constant travels through the Yemen had given them more influence over the princes than any other member of the organisation, and it was their diplomatic skills – developed years earlier in dealing with Balkan and Ethiopian tribal chiefs – that made them so successful in extracting money from the Saudis. Compared with them, Jim was a beginner at diplomacy, and perhaps was a little jealous of the comfortable relationship that the other two enjoyed with Feisal, Sultan and various prominent Saudis.

As if to demonstrate that Saudi Arabia had no adequate defence against air-attacks, the Egyptians intensified their assault, bombing Najran on 11 and 12 May, and Jizan on the 13th. By then a battery of Hawk ground-to-air missiles had been installed at Jizan, and the launchers were ready for action, but they failed to fire, apparently because of the Saudi operators' incompetence. When the Najran raids started, Hunters were scrambled from Khamis Mushayt, but arrived on the scene too late.

Renewed aggression hit the Yemen at the same time. On 11 May an urgent message went to Bosom from Mustang:

British team personally witnessed Egyptian gas bombing with eight Ilyushins at 0550 hrs 11 May on undefended, non-military villages of GAHR and GADAFA in ARHAB area. Fifty-one dead at GAHR no visible external wounds, twenty-four dead at GADAFA, only one of which had external wounds, Large number of survivors suffering from nausea, vomiting and respiratory/optic injuries. Have already requested Red Cross aid. Please take strongest possible action.

In response to this message, and an appeal from the surviving inhabitants, the Red Cross despatched a small convoy to the scene. On 13 May two doctors, a male nurse and other members of the team led by André Rochat[1] set out from Amara in two lorries loaded with food and medical supplies, but the Egyptians had discovered their plans, and bombed the convoy en route, destroying both vehicles and most of their contents.

The result was that when the team eventually arrived it had no equipment for taking samples. 'Rochat had no intention whatever of doing so,' said a furious message from Mustang. 'Three hours after arrival the whole bloody lot rushed off again, after slanging match with Dandy.' But the Red Cross did confirm that seventy-five people had been killed, some of them discovered dead in their homes, as if they had died in their sleep. Almost 200 cattle, sheep, goats and donkeys, as well as many chickens, had also died. The human victims had been buried in four large communal graves, and when one of these was opened, an autopsy performed on a corpse left no doubt that the people had been killed by poison gas. Within a few days Gadafa and the other villages were raided again, and 243 more people were killed. The mercenaries photographed women and children who had died in sleeping positions inside their caves, took samples of soil and vegetation, and collected an almost-intact bomb casing.

The Foreign Office, as usual, was doing its best to keep Britain out of trouble. It admitted that it had received confidential reports about the gas attacks 'from Royalist sources' – that is, Jim's mercenary teams – but claimed that it could not take the matter up with the United Nations because it 'had no quotable evidence', since its information had come 'from secret sources'. With King Feisal about to arrive in

London for talks, two 'defensive briefs' were drafted on how to deal with him when discussing Nasser's ever-increasing aggression. Under the heading 'Talking Points' some emollient initiatives were suggested:

We were shocked to hear of the latest wanton bombing of Najran. The King has our deep sympathy. We greatly deplore the loss of life and damage caused. We admire the King's patience in the face of repeated provocation. What in the King's view prompted this latest bombing? What are his intentions? We are sure that he will be right to resist, as he has in the past, the temptation to retaliate.[2]

Because the Saudi Air Force lacked enough aircraft and trained pilots to organise a proper defence (the brief continued), 'there is . . . a slight danger that King Feisal might ask for military help as he has done in the past':

The Americans undertook in 1962 to guarantee Saudi Arabian territory against unprovoked aggression. It is therefore to them that Feisal should turn. We do not have the forces available to defend Saudi Arabia against a major Egyptian attack and we can hardly contemplate becoming directly involved.[3]

As usual, the Foreign Office ignored the fact that Britain *was* directly involved, and had been for more than four years – albeit in a very small way. Even though Jim had stood down, his men were still in the mountains, and the London office was still functioning. On 19 May he wrote to Gooley in Jeddah, telling him that Hannah had banked a Saudi cheque for £10,875 with the Guarantee Trust of Jersey:

As you realise, things are very cloudy here, but basically the situation is as follows. The King [Feisal] has come here, encouraged by Julian [Amery] and Duncan Sandys, with the intention of trying to persuade the British Govt to change its mind. He has been made to believe that they may delay their departure from Aden and that they will then give some sort of defence agreement up to three years after the departure.

This he is rapidly being disillusioned about, and Mr George Brown [the Foreign Secretary] and Lord Shackleton [Minister of Defence for the RAF] have both privately told Tony Boyle in the House that the Brit Govt intends to stick to the following three things. Independence by November 1967, with if possible British troops out by January 1968, [secondly] a defence agreement for six or nine months maximum, consisting of a carrier force over the horizon. The wording of the agreement is so cynical that they admit that it can never be enforced, as it would only cover open aggression by the Egyptian army itself. And thirdly that at the end of the six or nine months there will be nothing whatsoever, and they don't care what happens in the area, Nasser or the Russians.

Obviously this is not what the King expected on arrival here, and far from strengthening his will to fight, it will tend to encourage the present vacillation of Saudi policy. The King is due to see the PM and the FO again next Tuesday and will fight hard obviously and will use the bargaining power of the [Lightning] air deal . . . . On the other side of the hill Mr Brown is indulging in a private correspondence with Nasser, with a view to re-establishing diplomatic relations and getting an agreement to call FLOSY [Front for the Liberation of South Yemen] off and let us get out of Aden quietly . . .

I regret that Foster Productions went out of business and no longer exists.

Two days later Mike wrote to Jim:

Things here have been absolute murder. Without any exaggeration, it has been 18–20 hours a day . . . The Royalist position is very poor at present. They are really in need of some positive encouragement and support . . . Mochsin at Heera'an is of course the last outpost, and they have made nine gas attacks against his area. This is enough to demoralise the stoutest hearts, and the death roll, I think accurate, is more than 250 souls. Really the Gyppos are cowardly, inhuman bastards, and at least that gives us all a motivation to even the score a little.

We see and hear from the world press/news that the gas story has been given good prominence . . . I'm sure that they [the Egyptians] used the tension on the Syrian/Israeli border to hope that it wouldn't even be noticed. The Middle East is sure hotting up.

On 24 May the Imam managed to cable Harold Wilson, appealing to his 'human conscience' to stop 'this horrible holocaust' and 'to take a drastic action to put an end to the Egyptian aggression . . . The Yemeni people put this responsibility upon your shoulders before God and history.'[4] To this impassioned plea the official files contain no reply.

At the end of May a small team of mercenaries – David Bailey, Kerry Stone and Mick Facer – was detailed to recover one of the gas bomb-casings and take it with them to Jeddah when they went on leave.[5] They found that the black cylinder was about the size of a small dustbin, with walls an inch and a half thick, and that it weighed nearly 200 pounds. They brought it out to Najran in the back of a Land Rover Sherpa pickup; but, seizing the chance of a lift, six or seven Yemenis swarmed into the back of the vehicle and travelled with the bomb, half-hidden under Kerry's *futa*, rolling around among their feet. In due course MI6 took it over and sent it on to England for examination at Porton Down. Samples were also taken from the hearts and lungs of victims – the desecration of the bodies inevitably upset the Arabs – and sent for analysis; but although the poison was identified, no clear evidence about it emerged.[6]

14

Smash Hit

Mike Gooley's words – 'hotting up' – were an understate-
ment. Throughout the first months of 1967 tension between
Israel and its Arab neighbours (Egypt, Jordan and Syria) had
been steadily building, with both sides intent on provoking
a showdown. The Arab nations were urged on towards a
major conflict by Nasser's propaganda, and on the other side
(in the words of the American historian Dr Eugene Rogan)
'The Israelis needed one good war to secure defensible bound-
aries and inflict a decisive defeat on the Arabs to impose
peace on terms with which Israel could live.'[1]

On 16 May Nasser ordered his army across the Suez Canal
into Sinai and stationed troops close to the Israeli frontier. On
the 18th he demanded the removal of the 4,500-strong United
Nations Emergency Force, whose function had been to act
as a buffer between Egypt and Israel. His final act of provocation, on the 22nd, was to close the Strait of Tiran to Israeli
shipping – a move that he knew was bound to lead to war.

For the next two weeks the Israeli Cabinet and High
Command feverishly debated their next actions. On 4 June
they took the decision to go to war, and in a surprise attack
launched at 7.10 a.m. next morning Israeli jets took the

Egyptian Air Force completely by surprise, destroying 286 out of 420 combat aircraft on the ground while their crews were still at breakfast. Sweeping in off the Mediterranean under the radar, sometimes only 50 feet above the sea, fighter-bombers wrecked thirteen air bases, besides twenty-three radar stations and anti-aircraft sites. Next, in mid-morning, the Israelis hit bases in Jordan and in two waves knocked out the entire Jordanian Air Force. In all these raids they lost only nine of their own aircraft. By midday the Egyptian, Jordanian and Syrian air forces had been eliminated.

It was these brilliant, pre-emptive strikes that turned the conflict in Israel's favour. The Egyptians had done no serious war planning, and they had no contingency plans. Robbed of its air cover, the army in Sinai was at the mercy of airborne predators and was quickly overrun. Its tanks, trundling across the desert in daylight, were easy meat for the Israeli fighter-bombers: 80 per cent of them were destroyed, and some 15,000 men were killed and 4,500 captured. Mendacious Egyptian propaganda, portraying defeat as victory and claiming amazing triumphs in Sinai, induced Jordan and Syria to join in the war; but within six days the Israelis had captured the Old City of Jerusalem, the West Bank and the Syrian Golan Heights, besides the whole of the Sinai Peninsula and the Palestinian Gaza Strip, defeating all the Arab armies and doubling the size of their own territory.

Forced to admit defeat, on 10 June Nasser announced his resignation on television, claiming that he had decided 'to withdraw totally and for good' from any official post or polit-ical role, and 'to return to the ranks of the masses'. True to form, within twenty-four hours he retracted his decision, in deference (he claimed) to the immense show of support that his first announcement had provoked.

It was the first, devastating air-strikes that turned the war in Israel's favour, but the fact that perhaps 50,000 Egyptian troops were absent in the Yemen – one-third of the entire army – contributed substantially to their country's collapse: Eugene Rogan reckoned that 'Egypt lost the '67 war in the Yemen'.[2] In any event, it was this shocking and unexpected defeat that made Nasser lose face with the Arabs as champion of their cause.

The victors wasted no time in thanking friends who, they considered, had given them sterling (if indirect) assistance. A few days after the war had ended, at the instigation of Mossad's Nahum Admoni, Jim and Tony Boyle were invited to Israel. They were both surprised, for they did not reckon they had done Israel any great service. On the contrary, it was the Israelis who had done *them* a considerable service by flying the arms drops. The leaders of the mercenary campaign had run it purely to help the Yemeni Royalists expel the Egyptian Army from their country, and so to protect British interests in southern Arabia. The fact that their efforts had also proved of benefit to Israel was entirely coincidental. Nevertheless, they were glad to accept the invitation – which was the only recognition they received for four years of often exasperating effort.

Travelling on Israeli passports via Paris, where Admoni joined them, they flew to Tel Aviv. In the middle of dinner on their first night there, a telephone call came through with the message that General Moshe Dayan, the Israeli Minister of Defence, would like to meet them. A car took them round to his house, and the General's first words were, 'I'd like to congratulate you.'

'Why?' asked Jim. '*We* came to congratulate *you* on a stunning victory.'

'No,' said Dayan. 'Every prisoner we've taken has been so terrified by what you did to their army in the Yemen that the whole lot surrendered.'

Thinking that Jim and Tony 'deserved to see the fate of the Egyptian army,' Admoni arranged for them to be flown over the battlefields in a Pilatus Porter light aircraft. Skimming low over Sinai, they saw pockets of Egyptian troops making their way on foot across the desert, and smoke still rising from the wrecks of tanks, armoured troop carriers, lorries and artillery pieces. Shattered vehicles choked the Mitla Pass, a V-shaped rock formation with a winding track going up the middle, through which fleeing combatants had tried to escape towards Suez. So desperate had some of the tank drivers become that they had tried to scale the vertical walls on either side of the pass, and the wrecked vehicles were packed so tightly together that there was no room for humans to walk between them.

The observers were appalled by the extent of the destruction – but there came one moment of comic relief, when they landed on the captured air-strip at El Arish, near the northern coast of Sinai. As they taxied to the end of the runway, a plump and scruffy Israeli corporal ran towards the plane, waving frantically. At first they thought he was warning of mines or booby-traps – but his anxiety turned out to be very personal: nobody had brought him his rations while he was on guard duty, and he was desperate for something to eat. Luckily they had lunch boxes on board, and handed a couple out. Taking off again, they flew down the Jordanian front from Jerusalem to Bethlehem and up to Nablus, where someone took a photograph of Jim and Tony posing on a burnt-out tank.

After their battlefield tour, Dayan invited them to his office, where he cracked open the beer and thanked them again profusely for everything they had done to help Israel. For the rest of his life Jim relished the story of 'the fat corporal of El Arish' who got his lunch, and he retold it with delight every time he and Admoni met.

The catastrophic defeat at last forced Nasser to abandon his ambitions for the Yemen, and he began to withdraw his army. Yet for the Royalists and their allies the struggle was by no means over. Seizing the opportunity created by Israel's victory, Stirling got Bernard Mills to compose a Top Secret document for the Saudi leaders. Headed 'A Proposal from Watchguard International for the Formation and Deployment of a Task Force in the Yemen', it ran to a dozen neatly typed foolscap pages and urged immediate action to clear the remaining Egyptians out of the country.

In effect the paper outlined a substantial upgrading of the mercenary team. It proposed the immediate establishment of a powerful strike force, commanded by Stirling himself and furnished with specially modified jeeps, which could carry out sabotage patrols and repeatedly block the road between Sana'a and Hodeidah, thus cutting the Egyptians' main supply line. The paper aimed high, asking for an immediate initial payment of £73,000 – some £2 million in today's terms.

It is conceivable that, given a rapid mobilisation, some such vigorous initiative might have turned the tide in the Royalists' favour, but it was too late. In the south – in Aden and the Federation – terrorist activity had been steadily increasing as FLOSY and the NLF (National Liberation Front) jockeyed for position. On 20 June there had been a volcanic eruption of violence: native troops had mutinied and gone on the rampage, killing twenty-two British personnel and wounding twenty-seven – a massacre that led to weeks of bloody fighting in and around the city. On the same day the NLF drove out the two British Political Officers in Dhala and raised their own flag over the market place. By the end of the month the whole of the Federation was crumbling. Many of the rulers had ill-advisedly gone to Europe or the Middle East in the hope of arranging some last-minute compromise that would hold the Federation together, and in their absence their states were seized, one after another:

> Audhali and Lower Yafa soon fell to the NLF and on 13 August they captured the ruler of the Muflahi Sheikhdom. The following day Dathina was taken over, followed swiftly by the Fadhli Sultanate. As the collapse continued there was surprisingly little bloodshed, and despite the sultans' claims that they had good intelligence, the rulers themselves were surprised by the speed and efficiency of the NLF coups.[3]

Among the political casualties was the Yemen mercenaries' long-term ally, Whiskers – Sherif Hussein of Beihan – who went to Saudi Arabia, apparently hoping to persuade the Saudis to take his state over, only to find, when he tried to return, that the NLF had gained control.

High-level diplomats were still struggling with the question of whether or not they should impose sanctions on Egypt in retaliation for the gas attacks, and London, as usual, was lily-livered on the subject. On 2 August 1967 a secret telegram from the Foreign Office to the Embassy in Washington considered that 'a direct lead by Britain or the United States would achieve little and probably damage our interests in the wider problems of the Middle East', and feebly suggested that 'a Scandinavian initiative is a possibility'.[4]

In the Yemen, on 26 August 1967, the mercenaries suffered their most serious loss of the entire campaign. Three men – two of whom had only recently come out – were on their way from Amara, where they were based, to Abdullah bin Hassan's headquarters at Ketaf. Allen Havelock-Stevens (Adze), Tony Parsons (Parsnip) and Terry Falcon-Wilson (Taxi) set off in the Land Rover allocated to Frank Smith, without his permission, and took along just one escort – Frank's tea-boy, Ali, who was fifteen or sixteen. They should have had *warraqas* for passing through tribal territories, but they had not bothered to acquire any. Although Ali carried a rifle, he plainly should have had reinforcements, and when the party stopped for coffee with Bernard Mills and Jimmy Knox, Bernard was furious to find them so poorly protected. He knew Havelock-Stevens, who had served under him on an earlier assignment in Aden, and now told him, 'It's a long journey – about five hours. Take two or three of my bodyguard.' But, in Bernard's words, 'He didn't feel he needed any instructions from me. "Oh," he said, "it's quite safe"' – and off they went.

About 12 miles short of their destination, at a point where the track ran through a narrow defile with high ground on either side – a perfect setting for an ambush – they were stopped by three armed tribesmen. When the leader, who spoke a few words of English, asked where they were going and they said, 'Ketaf', he told them they could not carry on, because they had no permission: they must leave their weapons in the Land Rover and walk up to the village with him, to get *warraqas*.

Little Ali later told Bernard that he had tried to warn the

mercenaries by saying, '*Jimhouri* – enemy. Not go – dangerous.' But the British ignored him. Leaving their rifles in the vehicle, they started walking towards the houses, together with the Arab who had held them up. After only fifty yards or so he suddenly broke back and ran towards the Land Rover, whereupon gunmen concealed in the rocks higher on the wadi sides opened up with rifles, killing one man and wounding the other two, who were finished off by a grenade. Ali, who had refused to hand over his rifle, was saved by a girl who had been herding goats and bravely ran down, calling out to the assassins, 'He's only a boy! Would you shoot one of your own kind?' – whereupon she took him to her house.

Word of what had happened soon reached Amara. At first Frank could hardly believe that experienced soldiers would have done anything so foolhardy as to allow themselves to be separated from their weapons: they had Spanish self-loading rifles, each with two twenty-round magazines taped together for rapid reloading, and if a firefight had broken out they could have defended themselves ferociously. But as soon as word came back, he prepared to recover the bodies. Prince Mohamed told him not to go on his own, but he was so incensed that he set out nevertheless.

At the scene of the ambush Frank found his Land Rover still standing there, its dashboard and bonnet riddled with bullet holes. He could only assume that the tribesmen had shot it up to make sure the soldiers did not escape; but, as he said, it was a stupid thing to have done, as they had effectively destroyed a vehicle worth a great deal in that environment. The only other thing he found at the site was a set of false teeth, which had belonged to Falcon-Wilson.

One of the Prince's lorries brought the bodies back, hugely inflated by the gas that had built up since death, and Frank

and his colleagues had the grisly task of bayoneting the stom-
achs before they could wrap the men in blankets and send
them on to Bernard. By the time they reached him, their
features were so bloated that he had a job to identify them,
but he put tags on them, and Jimmy took them to the French
wadi near Najran, hoping to get them onto an aircraft and
fly them back to Britain. That, however, proved impossible,
so the French helped bury them, with a slab of concrete on
top of the graves.

Prince Mohamed, distressed by the murders, wrote a note
in his faltering English:

> Dear Frank, I am sorry for what happened. I have ordered
> strongly to Brigedier Sirag to do a certain action and
> hold the responsible for the accident and he will give
> complete report. Again I am sorry, In the future we have
> to be mor caution.

Next day he wrote again, asking Frank to give Sirag 'the
Denanyat [dynamite] and fuse to destroy the houses of the
kellers in the villages'. The identities of the murderers had
been discovered; but, as Frank pointed out, there was no point
in blowing up their homes, as they had already departed, and
explosions would only have left their families without shelter.

The disaster shocked everyone in the mercenary organisation, from Jim downwards. Reporting immediately after
the incident, Mike Gooley cabled:

> After every conceivable effort to move the bodies to
> UK, it has now been necessary to bury them at Najran,
> Saudi Arabia . . . I have promised ALL concerned the
> best possible effort at security in face of this tragedy . . .

All my men/stations here absolutely steady and stalwart. So far Saudi reaction has been heartening, and nothing has been spared to help us . . .

Cannot express adequately all our feelings here. This has been unexpected in some senses, as the men were in a recognised 'safe' area and on a routine journey. Indeed a stunning and tragic blow to all. May we do all humanly possible for the next-of-kin. My immediate duty to get the highest compensation figure. Negotiations in progress at present.

On 3 September Jim sent a message agreeing with Mike that if the press got hold of the story, the official line would be that the three men had been killed in a motor accident; in the event, no mention of their deaths found its way into the newspapers. A requiem mass was held in England on 12 September.

Forty-five years later Bernard Mills pointed out that no area in the Yemen should ever have been considered safe – and it was something of a miracle that during the entire war only three British soldiers and one Frenchman (Tony de St Paul) were lost. The main reason for the survival of the rest was the outstanding loyalty of the tribesmen assigned to guard them. Far from having any fight with the Yemenis, the mercenaries owed their lives to their escorts' courage and lack of veniality. The volunteers were literally in the hands of the Royalists, and could have been murdered for the gold in their escape belts at any time, especially when travelling at night.

Luck sometimes also played a part. David Bailey was once climbing towards a ridge to site a 75mm anti-tank gun, when he paused for a minute a few feet below the crest to retie a shoelace. As he bent down, an incoming tank shell blew the top off the ridge just above him, sending a hurricane of rock and steel fragments over his head: had that lace not come undone, he would have been annihilated.

The war went on. Later in September the mercenary organisation produced yet another ambitious plan: the top-secret Operation Day-Spring, designed 'to deliver arms and ammunition by air to selected Royalist Princes in the Yemen'. Three possible methods were suggested: landing aircraft at Najran, parachuting supplies into the Yemen, and landing in the Yemen itself. Of these, the last was recommended as potentially the most effective, and the brief suggested that a trial should be held in the Jauf, on a desert strip prepared to a standard fit for a C130 Hercules transport. The aircraft (it was assumed) would be provided by the Royal Iranian Air Force and flown by an Israeli crew. The landing would be at sunset minus thirty minutes, and takeoff either immediately after unloading or at any time up to first light.

The blueprint for the landings clearly reflected the co-operation not only of Israel, but also of Iran, where the Shah had become increasingly apprehensive about Nasser's aggressive ambitions. Yet this plan, too, failed to materialise.

During the autumn of 1967 the mercenaries' role finally withered away. On 1 November a one-word message went out from Bosom to all stations – TERMINATE – and that was that. Jim Johnson's war was over. Withdrawal was a huge disappointment to his team, especially as he had promised all ranks that one day they would take part in a victory parade along the main street in Sana'a.

Extraction, however, proved anything but easy. As soon as the tribes realised that the British were about to desert them, they turned hostile – and when Alastair Macmillan and his two colleagues tried to leave the Khowlan by walking out to the east, they were challenged and arrested three times. Each time they were stopped the tribesmen demanded, '*Chi, chi* – give!', pointing at their rifles to which they replied '*Abudan* – never!'; and they bluffed their way out of the encounters by saying (in Arabic), 'We're very good shots, and if you attack us, each of us will kill three of you.'

Nasser's ruinous occupation of the Yemen was almost over. Mohamed bin Hussein – who had become in effect Commander-in-Chief of all the Royalist armies – had been proposing to open a general offensive in November, and told Feisal as much; but the idea displeased the King, who (ridiculous as it seemed, after so much expenditure and bloodshed) was reluctant to provoke the Egyptians into further fighting, and now preferred to use financial incentives to ease them out of the country. Thus he promised Nasser that he would cut off the subsidies on which the Royalists had depended for so long – but not until the last of the Egyptians had departed. He also pledged to pay Egypt compensation for loss of revenue from the Suez Canal, which had been out of action since the Six-Day War – but only at the end of the quarter, if the withdrawal was well under way.

For months Egyptian troops had been pulling back from their outposts in the east and north, in what they called their 'long-breath policy', and now accumulating pressures at last forced Nasser to accept defeat. On 3 November 1967 his puppet Sallal flew out of Sana'a, heading for Moscow, where he hoped to attend the celebrations for the fiftieth anniversary of the Bolshevik revolution. But he got no further than Baghdad, and on 5 November, when he heard that there had been a *coup d'état* in Sana'a, he went to ground in Iraq.

In the Yemen a new government was led by a presidential triumvirate – but the Republicans' main allies were deserting them. For once keeping to an agreement, the Egyptians were pulling out down the road to Hodeidah and taking ship for home. At the same time large Royalist forces, roused by Mohamed bin Hussein, were closing in on the capital from three sides. In the words of the American author Dana Adams Schmidt:

> Prince Mohamed had taken personal command. He was reported at Al Arush, he was reported in [the] Khowlan, he was everywhere, directing the emplacement of guns, organising a growing force around the hard core of the semi-regulars he had been training since 1964. Town after town around Sana'a fell to the Royalists. They took Amran, fifteen miles north of the capital and occupied mountains fifteen miles to the south-west of the city. They brought sporadic gunfire to bear on Rahaba, the main airfield outside Sana'a. They cut the road from Sana'a to Hodeidah on the coast. They sent commando groups up to the walls of the city and even into its streets at night to harass the Republicans with bazooka shots at government buildings.[5]

Had Hussein pressed home his attack, he might have changed the course of his country's history. As it was, his resolve was undermined by the jealousy of fellow commanders, and by the collapse of British influence in the south: the dismantling of the Federation and the evacuation of Aden. As the military historian Jonathan Walker noted:

> By September 1967 George Brown [the Foreign Secretary] had clearly washed his hands of the South Arabian

commitment, confiding [to his Cabinet colleague
Richard Crossman] 'it can't be helped – anyway, we
want to be out of the whole of the Middle East as far
and as fast as we possibly can.' And there were members
of the Wilson Government who were delighted when
the Federation collapsed.[6]

On 13 November HMG formally recognised the NLF as
the successor administration in the former colony, and at talks
held in Geneva agreed to hand over all its assets. A powerful
naval task-force was assembled, in case further violence broke
out during the final withdrawal, but in the event the retreat
proceeded peacefully, and the last British soldier left Aden
on 29 November 1967.

In the north, Sana'a held out for seventy days: then in
February 1968 the Republicans, deserted by the Egyptians
but bolstered by a fresh infusion of Soviet weapons and instructors, managed to reopen the road from Hodeidah, and the
siege of the capital was over. In March 1969 Saudi Arabia
cut off the supply of weapons and money to the Royalists,
and they, no longer able to retain the allegiance of tribes
through bribery, quickly lost their ability to fight. At a conference held in Jeddah King Feisal brought together the leaders
of the rival factions, creating a coalition government of Royalists, Republicans and Third Party, but specifically excluding
members of the royal family from holding office. So the
Yemen Arab Republic (YAR) was born. In July 1969 Abdullah
bin Hassan was assassinated, and Mohamed bin Hussein at
last abandoned the cause for which he had fought so long,
going to live in Saudi Arabia.

One notable survivor of the civil war was Ahmed al-Shami,
who became the united Yemen's first Ambassador to London.

But the Imam went into exile in England privately, and died there aged seventy in 1996; his father-in-law, secretary and boozing companion Yahya al-Hirsi settled in Hampstead. After more than a thousand years, the reign of the Hamid ud Din dynasty was at an end – but its demise brought no peace to the Yemen.

Nasser died of a heart-attack on 28 September 1970, aged only fifty-two. In spite of all his failures, his disastrous initiatives and his patent mendacity, more than six million people turned out to watch his funeral procession move through the streets of Cairo. It could be said that he had won the war in the Yemen, for the Royalists had eventually been defeated; but the victory had been achieved at the terrible cost of more than 20,000 Egyptian dead.

Also in 1970, South Arabia became the People's Democratic Republic of Yemen (PDRY), the first Arab nation to turn communist, bolstered by aid from the Soviet Union and China, and offering sanctuary to terrorist organisations such as Baader-Meinhof and the Popular Front for the Liberation of Palestine. From the inception of the Marxist state, violence was endemic, and in 1986 the infighting erupted into a full-scale civil war, in which more than 10,000 people were thought to have died.

In 1990 the PDRY joined forces with the YAR to form a single country, the Yemen Republic, which became peaceful enough over the next decade to allow visits by tourists, particularly members of the British-Yemeni Society and others. But in recent years the country has become increasingly dangerous, with terrorist groups such as al-Quaeda established in training camps in the mountains, and frequent threats to the British Embassy in Sana'a. As a result, the Foreign Office discourages visits by British subjects.

15

Aftermath

Some time after the mercenary operation had closed down, John Woodhouse wrote a brief review of its activities and achievements. As always when discussing the SAS or its members, and being a perfectionist himself, he was outspokenly critical of anything that he considered to be a failure or poor performance.

In the early summer of 1963 (he recapitulated) three SAS NCOs were 'permitted to be absent without leave' from the regiment to accompany Johnny Cooper on his reconnaissance of the Sana'a area. 'This disclosed that the Egyptians had no hope of victory if the Royalists could be encouraged to go on fighting.' The initial presence of the mercenaries, though limited to about four weeks, 'caused an immediate and considerable improvement in the morale of the Royalists'. Though serving SAS soldiers were not again 'allowed' to go absent because of the risks involved, more ex-SAS were recruited, largely from the territorial army; but 'most were well below the average SAS officer and soldier, both in up-to-date technical knowledge, and general intelligence and ability'.

Woodhouse remarked that the mercenaries carried out a

considerable amount of weapon training, but while in the field they 'did as they pleased' and sometimes allowed standards to slip, being subject only to self-discipline. Cooper and Mills (both former members of 22 SAS, and therefore more highly trained than their part-time colleagues) organised successful operations, but others achieved little apart from providing medical assistance, fixing up radio communications and taking air-drops. The colonel criticised the organisation's level of security, which he denounced as 'always very bad', due to the fact that the mercenaries had received no training in this field. He might have added, in mitigation, that this was not their fault: it was only because he had not been allowed to deploy fully trained, serving members of the SAS that the part-timers had been drawn into service. Almost all the mercenaries were amateur soldiers – civilians who had done territorial service. He agreed, however, that the ability to give skilled medical assistance 'again proved of great importance in winning popular support' – even though the religious fatalism of the Arabs 'does reduce the effectiveness of this asset compared to other countries'.

Woodhouse reckoned that the amateur army 'could have inflicted much more damage on the enemy factions had it been energetically and efficiently directed in the field'. His verdict was typically severe, and made no allowance for the fecklessness and irresolution of the native commanders. He did not acknowledge the Yemenis' highly developed gift for procrastination, and the consequent difficulties the mercenaries had in persuading them to form coordinated plans. Nor did he point out that the number of mercenaries had been extremely small, that they were scattered over huge areas of extraordinarily difficult country, and that, in any case, they had no authority to issue orders. As Bernard Mills remarked, forty-five years later, 'No Briton or Frenchman could go and tell a Prince what to do, or lead tribes into battle. A Prince or a sheikh had to be in command.' What the mercenaries *did* do, on the other hand, simply by their presence, was to give moral support to princes or tribal leaders and increase their prestige: merely to have a British officer present was often a great help when native commanders were dealing with intransigent followers.

Woodhouse's own brief experience of the theatre had perhaps given him a false impression of what could be achieved by guerrilla raids. He was lucky to have joined forces with the most aggressive of all the Royalist commanders, Gassim Monassir; and there is little doubt that, given heavy mortars, he could have created havoc by bombarding the airfield and other Egyptian installations round Sana'a. But Gassim's redoubt was the only one from which such an incisive attack could have been launched.

In spite of his criticisms, Woodhouse conceded that the mercenary organisation 'played a decisive part in defeating the Egyptian occupation because it raised and sustained Royalist morale'. He could have added that the men living in the war zone were usually under severe strain, harassed by daily air-attacks and often, for weeks on end, in the company of tribesmen with whom they could barely communicate. In retrospect, it seems greatly to their credit that although one or two of them did become a little eccentric, most survived extremely well.

The colonel might also have touched on two wider issues of importance. The first was the fact that the prolongation of Royalist resistance substantially retarded any plans Nasser may have had for attacking Saudi Arabia, and the delay gave the Saudis time to strengthen their defences by the acquisition of new aircraft and equipment. In supporting the Royalists and financing the mercenary force, they had spent millions – but the money had been spent well, for it had bought them safety, at any rate for the time being.

By the end of September 1966 ten supersonic F-35 Lightning fighter aircraft had arrived in the country, together with Thunderbird ground-to-air missiles installed to protect the airfields. In the absence of trained Saudis, the aircraft were being flown by British pilots employed by Airwork Services; it was never made clear whether or not these men would fly in combat; but the mere presence of the Mach-2 jets gave the Saudis a feeling of security, as it reduced the possibility of a sudden Egyptian air-assault. An urgent training programme was put in hand, to equip native pilots to fly the Lightnings; but the instructors' task was not eased by the fact that their pupils were unshakeable in their belief that, no matter how many mistakes they made, Allah would ensure their survival.

The second and more far-reaching effect of the Yemen deadlock was its contribution to the collapse of the Egyptian forces in the Six-Day War. In the view of the historian Professor Clive Jones, the mercenary involvement 'proved to be the nemesis of the Egyptian army'.[1] It was never the intention of Jim or his private soldiers to render assistance to Israel; but that, as it turned out, was what they did, by helping to detain perhaps one-third of the entire Egyptian Army in a foreign country far from home.

The story that Nasser offered Jim seven years' free accommodation, in any penitentiary he cared to name, may well be apocryphal. But the Egyptian President certainly made an attempt to buy him off. Flying from Jeddah to London one day, Jim found himself next to a Palestinian who lived in

Saudi Arabia and said he had a message from Brigadier Shawkat, the Head of Egyptian External Intelligence. The message was an invitation to meet Shawkat in any neutral country, but preferably Switzerland, where he would offer Jim a sum in dollars that he simply would not be able to refuse. Jim replied that this was very decent of the Egyptians, but pointed out that they were exceedingly short of money, whereas he had the entire wealth of the Saudi oil royalties at his disposal – so he would make a counter-offer 'for Nasser to join us'. No more was heard of that initiative.

In January 1970 Jim was upset to hear that a former colleague was planning to write a book about the mercenary operation – even though all ranks had sworn never to reveal anything about it until he himself authorised disclosure. To spike the guns of the would-be author, Jim fed carefully selected parts of the story to Ian Colvin, one of the senior reporters on the *Daily Telegraph*. In three long articles, published on 4, 5 and 6 February – miserably displayed and illustrated, as was the paper's wont at that time – Colvin divulged a few of the campaign's secrets.

The first piece, under the headline SECOND LAWRENCE FOILED NASSER'S ARMY IN YEMEN, described Jim as 'an elusive City and West End club man', and covered the launch and early stages of the operation. The second article concentrated on the air-drops and, after putting up a useful smokescreen by mentioning the Rhodesian Air Services' early contribution, focused briefly on 'new aircraft, whose markings were less notorious', parachuting supplies into areas of the 'unmapped Yemen'. No mention was made of Israel, and Tony Boyle came out of cover only far enough to recall how he had flown on one of the missions, giving a false time for take-off to disguise the length of the flight and providing harmless details of the final approach to the DZ. He even revealed that the British had put out, as a cover story, the fact that the aircraft came from Israel – a claim so incredible that it was treated as a joke, both at the time and later. Colvin's third article described Nasser's attempts to bribe the Royalist tribesmen with gold, touched briefly on the murder of the three mercenaries in August 1967, and discussed the political consequences of the war.

Congratulations on the disclosures came from Bob Walker-Brown, who wrote to praise Jim's 'Napoleonic bit of strategy' and to say that his 'handling of the main hot potatoes was clever and highly convincing'. The release of selected information left many secrets intact, but it was enough to deflate any attempt at a rival account. Another potential author was Billy McLean, whose reports to Jim and to the Government had revealed him as an excellent writer with a flair for description. He made copious notes for the outline of a book on his involvement in the war, but never got round to writing it.

The disclosures in the *Telegraph* brought about a reconciliation between Jim and Bernard Mills, who by then was working as Field Director for the Save the Children fund in Nigeria, at the end of the Biafran civil war. Jim sent Bernard copies of the articles together with a covering note, so that he would be aware of the party-line – and the package reached him in the middle of the Niger Delta. Relations restored, Jim and Bernard ended up friends again.

Jim never boasted about the achievements of his private army; yet, looking back with forty years' hindsight, he still felt it remarkable that four officers – Stirling, Woodhouse, Franks and himself – had managed to ignore Foreign Office policy for five years and, while HMG remained supine on the issue, had gone a long way towards discrediting Nasser. As he said, 'In those days, you could do those things.'

After the Yemen conflict, the mercenaries' two leaders went very different ways. Tony Boyle, by his own account, 'declined an invitation to join the British Intelligence Service'. Once freed from any form of military discipline, he gave vent to the slightly eccentric side of his character. Never marrying, he bought and ran a forty-acre farm in Shropshire, with a house so decrepit that when Jim's grandchildren came to stay, Tony warned them that, to avoid precipitating a collapse, no more than one of them must go on the stairs at any one time; he also, to their delight, positively ordered them to scribble on the walls as much as they could manage. In the end the house had to be demolished – whereupon he supervised the design and building of a new one. As a sideline he invested in a scanner that enabled farmers to tell how many lambs pregnant ewes were carrying: a valuable device, now common, but then an innovation. He also made a duck-house from the remains of a double bed cast out by Jim.

During the 1970s he travelled round the world and compiled an illustrated account of his journey, which he distributed to family and friends. A *bon viveur*, he was always full of new projects, and had a lifelong interest in the exploration of space.

Jim carried on much as before. For a while he returned to Lloyd's, but in 1974, together with David Walker (another former army officer, to whom he was introduced by Peter de la Billière), he formed KMS (Kini Mini Services) Ltd. The company's first contract, from the Foreign and Commonwealth Office, was to provide armed guards for the British Embassy in Buenos Aires: costings were worked out on the back of an envelope and, as Walker recalled, 'in true entrepreneurial spirit the formal legal contract was signed on behalf of a company which did not yet exist'.[2] Soon KMS was providing the British armed security for all our embassies.

Next Jim was back in the Yemen, where the firm trained the President's bodyguard – and it went on to undertake major training tasks in several Arab countries, not least Saudi Arabia. There Jim was welcomed by, among others, his old friend Kemal Adham, Head of Intelligence, and Sheikh Yamani, Minister for Oil. In 1976 KMS was instructed by Sultan Qaboos of Oman to raise, train and equip a Special Force recruited from the wild tribes in the mountains of Dhofar, where the SAS had fought a successful campaign against communist-backed forces from 1970 to 1975. The Special Force developed into one of the finest Arab units, and Jim spent many months in Oman, occasionally summoning Fiona (formerly Fraser, by then Mrs Robin Allen) to come and sort out his paperwork. By the time he retired in 1989, at the age of sixty-five, KMS had worked in every continent.

To his great distress, his beloved Judy died of cancer in 1979, but in 1982 his friends were delighted when he married a wonderful successor, Jan Gay. Once again he had found a perfect partner. In retirement he went to live in a cottage near Marlborough – and at his funeral in August 2008 his friend and former colleague David Walker concluded his fine tribute by quoting a Regimental Sergeant Major of 21 SAS, who once looked at Jim admiringly and said, 'Colonel, you're a man of many parts.'

David Smiley also returned to the Yemen, as a guest of the Government, who in 2003 invited him to Sana'a so that he could give them guidance on the official history of the revolution, which was then being written. Although, at eighty-seven, he had become rather deaf and lame, he enjoyed the trip, which he described in an article for the British-Yemeni Society's journal.[3] He was surprised to find that large numbers of men were still carrying rifles (mostly Kalashnikovs), and that numerous *qat* plantations had been established along the road leading east from the capital towards Marib; but he was delighted by the warmth of his welcome, and by the fact that he found no bitterness about the role the mercenaries had played in the civil war.

More than forty years after the event, memories of the Yemen adventure are still strong, and from time to time veterans of *Beni* Johnson have met for reunions – as when, in 1993, thirty years after the beginning of the campaign, Alastair Macmillan organised a lunch for all the survivors he had been able to locate. Generous subventions from Jim Johnson and Mike Gooley meant that the meal would be free to all comers, and in a letter of 11 September Alastair told Jim:

> As far as the buffet meal is concerned, I tried to pamper to your nostalgia by ordering tinned mackerel flakes followed by boiled, emaciated goat, washed down by green, stinking water. You will be glad to hear that the Regiment's traditional caterer, Tim O'Neill, persuaded me that a Regimental Curry, or the alternative of a salad main dish, might be more popular.

Select Bibliography

Bower, Tom, *The Perfect English Spy: Sir Dick White and the Secret War,* 1935–90,Heinemann, 1995

Clark, Victoria, *Yemen: Dancing on the Heads of Snakes,* Yale University Press, 2010

Cooper, Johnny, *One of the Originals*, Pan Books, 1991

Cradock, Percy, *Know Your Enemy*, John Murray, 2002

de la Billière, General Sir Peter, *Looking for Trouble*, Harper Collins, 1994

Dorril, Stephen, *MI6: Fifty Years of Special Operations*, Fourth Estate, 2000

Fielding, Xan, *One Man in His Time: The Life of Lt-Col N.L.D. ('Billy') McLean*, Macmillan, 1990

Fiennes, Ranulph, *Living Dangerously*. Macmillan, 1987.

Gardiner, Ian, *In the Service of the Sultan*, Pen & Sword, 2006

Gibbons, Scott, *The Conspirators*, Howard Baker, 1967

Harding, John, *Roads to Nowhere: A South Arabian Odyssey, 1960–65*, Arabian Publishing, 2009

Hinchcliffe, Peter, Ducker, John T., & Holt, Maria, *Without Glory in Arabia*, I.B. Tauris, 1966

Hoe, Alan, *David Stirling*, Little Brown, 1992

Horniblow, Philip, *Oil, Sand and Politics*, Hayloft, 2003

Jones, Clive, *Britain and the Yemen Civil War*, Sussex Academic Press, 2004

Lee, Air Chief Marshal Sir David, *Flight from the Middle East*, Ministry of Defence Air Historical Branch (RAF), 1978

Mackintosh-Smith, Tim, *Yemen: Travels in Dictionary Land*, John Murray, 1997

Rogan, Eugene, *The Arabs: A History*, Allen Lane, 2009

Schmidt, Dana Adams, *Yemen: The Unknown War*, Bodley Head, 1968

Smiley, David, with Peter Kemp, *Arabian Assignment*, Leo Cooper, 1975

Von Horn, Major General Carl C., *Soldiering for Peace*, Cassell, 1966

Walker, Jonathan, *Aden Insurgency: The Savage War in South Arabia 1962–67*, Spellmount, 2005

Notes

1 Clubmen Unite

1 Later in life, when sufficiently well primed, Jim would sometimes break into fluent Italian – or something that sounded like it.

2 Personal interview, Mick Facer, January 2010.

3 Personal interview, 25 March 2010.

4 In July 1956 Nasser seized control of the Suez Canal. In November a combined force of British, French and Israeli ships, aircraft and troops recaptured the canal, but financial pressure from the United States and threats from the Soviet Union compelled the allies to make a humiliating retreat, leaving the canal in Nasser's hands.

5 *Altareeq ila Tel Aviv Yamur abr Al Khaleej wa Al Riyadh* – 'The road to Tel Aviv lies via the Gulf and Al Riyadh'. Personal communication, Sultan Ghalibn al-Quaiti, May 2010.

6 Lord Home of the Hirsel (1903–95) disclaimed his peerage for life on 23 October 1963, when he succeeded Harold Macmillan as Prime Minister, and was thenceforth known as Sir Alec Douglas-Home.

7 Dana Adams Schmidt, *Yemen: The Unknown War,* p. 119.

8 Julian Amery (1919–96) was Secretary of State for Air 1960–2 and Minister of Aviation 1962–4. In 1950 he had married Harold Macmillan's daughter, Catherine.

9 CAB 128/36.

10 Ibid.

11 It was claimed that in 1956 Horniblow had half-poisoned the entire SAS contingent by injecting them with the wrong combination of viruses when they were waiting to go to Suez – a charge that he does not altogether refute.

12 Duncan Sandys (1908–87), Minister of Aviation 1959–60, Secretary of State for the Colonies 1962–4.

13 Lieutenant Colonel Neil McLean (1918–86). During the Second World War he twice parachuted into Albania in attempts to bolster resistance to the Nazi occupiers, winning a DSO.

14 In *Greenmantle* Buchan wrote of Sandy: 'He rode through Yemen, which no white man ever did before. The Arabs let him pass, for they thought him stark mad and argued that the hand of Allah was heavy enough on him without their efforts.'

15 Interview with Bernard Mills, 10 May 2009.

16 Many observers, including General Carl von Horn, head of the United Nations Mission to the Yemen, believed that some of the pilots were Russian. Scott Gibbons, *The Conspirators,* p.111. Intercepts obtained by the United States National Security Agency revealed that Soviet pilots were flying Tupolev TU-16 jet bombers to the Yemen from Cairo, where the aircraft's markings were being overpainted at night with Egyptian insignia. Tom Bower, *The Perfect English Spy,* p.250.

17 Ibid., p.248.

18 Colonel Sir David Stirling (1915–90) created in 1942 the Long Range Desert Group, out of which developed the SAS. He was knighted only in 1990.

19 Personal conversation, August 2006.

20 Al-Shami had at one stage opposed the Imamate, and had been incarcerated in one of the notorious gaols at Hajjah; but he had been released on the orders of Crown Prince al-Badr, and in 1961 became his personal adviser, before being appointed head of the Yemeni delegation in London, and then Foreign Minister.

21 Ranulph Fiennes, *Living Dangerously*, p.79.

22 Cooper much resented this description, but it was accurate.

23 Stirling later sent Oldman another cable, in Cooper's name, saying that his mother's health had 'further deteriorated'.

24 Johnston, whose rather aloof manner tended to conceal his high intelligence and sense of humour, was married to the Georgian princess Natasha Bagration, and as a hobby translated Pushkin's *Eugene Onegin* into English verse. Tony Boyle got on well with him, but once undermined his own façade of respect when, as he left a meeting, he failed to close the door and was heard by those still in the room shouting down the hall to the Arab gatekeeper, '*Ya*, Abdul. God wants his chariot at the front door in ten minutes.' In June 1963 Johnston

was succeeded as Governor of Aden by the more aggressive Sir
Kennedy Trevaskis.

25 Johnny Cooper, *One of the Originals*, p.157.

26 Described by Jim as 'a fly-by-night character', the Prince had been
a wartime member of the Special Operations Executive, and had
parachuted into the South of France on D–Day. A few months into
the Yemen campaign, he disappeared with all his organisation's funds.

27 Faulques had so many bullet holes in his body that he claimed they
made him sink while swimming. He later opened an agency in Paris,
recruiting mercenaries for the Yemen. The French supported Jim's
effort because they, too, wanted to deny Nasser access to the country,
to prevent him threatening their enclave in Djibouti, on the African
coast.

28 Much store was set on the handle or hilt of a *jambiya,* which
proclaimed the status of its owner. Most were made of ordinary horn
or wood, but the most highly prized were those carved from rhinoc-
eros horn or studded with jewels.

29 *Daily Telegraph*, 4 February 1970.

2 Nasser's Wiles

1 An account of this confession is among Billy McLean's Yemen papers,
stored in the Imperial War Museum (IWM) at Duxford, near
Cambridge. Because the collection has not yet been catalogued or
numbered, it had not been possible to identify the precise sources
of quotations in this narrative.

2 In an undated memorandum McLean wrote: 'Apart from a great deal
of circumstantial evidence that Nasser in fact both prepared and
organised the coup, the arrival in the Yemen by sea of the advanced
elements of the Egyptian army with their heavy equipment on the
day following the *coup d'état* provided further proof of this.' IWM,
Duxford.

3 Fairey Marine Atalanta yachts, designed by Uffa Fox, were first built
in 1956, and remain in demand to this day.

4 The Javelin that he flew is preserved in the museum at Cosgrove in
Shropshire.

5 Bennett had been King Hussein's best man at his marriage to
Antoinette Gardiner, who became Princess Muna. He was later
knighted and promoted to Air Marshal as the head of the Sultan of
Muscat's Air Force.

6   This consisted of twenty-five feudal sheikhdoms and sultanates, which had treaties of protection with the British. With a total population of about three-quarters of a million, they were known collectively as the Aden Protectorate, which stretched for 900 miles from Aden itself in the west to Muscat in the east, and bordered with the Yemen and Saudi Arabia to the north. In January 1963 the Federation and the Crown Colony of Aden formally became a single unit.

7   McLean Papers, IWM, Duxford.

8   Ibid.

9   Personal communication, Bernard Mills, 24 June 2009.

10   *Qat* is the dark-green, narcotic leaf of a bush, containing caffeine and cocaine. Among Yemeni tribesmen it takes the place of alcohol and tobacco, and is reckoned less harmful than either.

11   McLean Papers, IWM, Duxford.

12   Ibid.

13   Ibid.

14   Ibid.

15   The point of cutting off prisoners' lips was to send them 'smiling back to Nasser'.

16   McLean papers, IWM, Duxford.

17   Xan Fielding, *One Man in His Time*, pp.135–6.

18   McLean Papers, IWM, Duxford.

19   Ibrahim al-Khibsi had still been a student in Beirut at the time of the coup. Short and wiry, he spoke excellent English and had vowed not to shave or cut his hair till the last Egyptian had been killed or driven out of the Yemen.

20   McLean Papers, IWM, Duxford.

21   Ibid. The precise nature of the gas was never determined.

22   Yahya al-Hirsi's powerful influence over the Imam was revealed by a report that the ruler had banked $22 million overseas *in his secretary's name*, so that his enemies could not accuse him of misusing state funds.

23   Lecture to the Royal United Services Institution, 20 October 1965.

24   McLean Papers, IWM, Duxford.

25   Ibid.

26   Feisal probably did not know that McLean had no authority to send the regular SAS into action.

27   *The Conspirators*, p. 38.

28   The garrison at Marib was housed in the old Turkish fort, and resup-

plied by two Dakota flights every morning. The aircraft took forty minutes to fly from Sana'a to a sand runway 2½ miles from the town, whereas a journey by the tracks took four days.

29 General Sir Peter de la Billière, *Looking for Trouble*, p.106.

30 In November 1962, trying to reinforce their garrison in Sirwah, the Egyptians had staged a disastrous paratrooper drop, in which Royalist marksmen had a field day, killing numerous parachutists, most of them in mid-air before they reached the ground.

31 Frankincense derives from the reddish-brown resin of a shrub-like tree, *Boswellia sacra*, and myrrh from the sap of another small tree, *Commiphora myrrha*.

32 McLean, who had met Hassan earlier, described his English as 'a language in which he was almost totally incomprehensible'.

33 *New York Herald Tribune*, 5 August 1964. Sanche de Gramont, of aristocratic French descent, later changed his name to Ted Morgan and became a naturalised American.

34 Ibid.

35 *The Conspirators*, p.26.

36 From his service in Muscat, Johnny spoke some Arabic, but of a different kind from the hill dialect of the Yemeni locals.

37 'Wog', short for Wily Oriental Gentleman, was a term commonly used to mean foreigners, principally those of Middle, Far Eastern or African origin; but it might be applied to almost any non-British person – hence the catch-phrase 'Wogs begin at Calais'.

38 This account of the ambush is taken from Vol. 6, Issue 61, of *The Elite* magazine, 1986. The bodies lay in the open for more than two years, until some of them were recovered by the Red Cross.

39 *One of the Originals*, p.165.

40 The American Central Intelligence Agency also obtained an Egyptian order of battle, through their agent James Fees, whom they had infiltrated into Taiz, the Yemen's second city, under the guise of a consular official.

3 Mountain Warriors

1 *Yemen: The Unknown War*, p 169.

2 *One of the Originals*, p.170. In his account Cooper disguised the identity of the Frenchmen by giving them different names – Peter for Philippe and Paul for Tony. Here their real names are restored. Tony de St Paul was killed in March 1965, the mercenaries' first casualty.

His remains were brought to Mohamed bin Hussein's cave on 1 April by his comrade-in-arms, Amiral.

3   Obituary, *Daily Telegraph*, 29 June 2000.

4   Later General Sir Peter de la Billière (1934–), Commander of British Forces in the Gulf War of 1990–1.

5   David Smiley (1916–2009). In April 1943, as a member of Special Operations Executive, he parachuted into northern Greece in company with Billy McLean, and walked into Albania, where his service with the Partisans won him an MC and bar; but when, after the war, he was seconded to MI6, his attempts to infiltrate agents into the country were frustrated by the treachery of Kim Philby, who passed details of his plans to the communists.

6   McLean described how in the evenings all the personnel at one Royalist camp chewed *qat* whenever it was available. 'They then became zombies and moved around with one cheek bulging hugely, like cows chewing the cud, with glazed vacant eyes.'

7   David Smiley, *Arabian Assignment*, pp.129–30.

8   Ibid., p.130.

9   Carl C. von Horn, *Soldiering for Peace*, p.351.

10   Ibid., pp.344–5.

11   Ibid., p.353.

4 Beni *Johnson*

1   Franks soon dropped out of the organisation, because his daughter, who was working as a secretary for the Deputy Director of the Security Service, found his name constantly cropping up in intelligence reports.

2   Personal interview, 4 March 2010.

3   The Political Officers were Colonial Office advisers to the Sultans, amirs and sheikhs in the various states of the Federation. Later they were supported by young army officers seconded to MI6.

4   *Arabian Assignment*, p.171.

5   Stephen Dorril, *MI6: Fifty Years of Special Operations*, p.684.

6   Rupert France's regime served him well: he took great pride in his physical fitness, and continued swimming in the public pool at Ipswich well into his eighties. Friends remembered him as exceptionally punctilious, and he always took pride in refusing to discuss his Yemen days, in spite of much gentle teasing.

7   In 1966, after he had left the army, Symons twice went to Jeddah on the BFLF's behalf.

8   Personal interview, 20 August 2009.

9   The term *siasi* derived from the SAS's deployment against the Mau
     Mau in Kenya during the 1950s, the Swahili word denoting the
     movement of a snake through grass.

10   The Maria Theresa dollar, or thaler, has been in continuous use since
     it was first minted in 1741. Since 1780, the coin has always borne
     that date: 1780.

11   The gold content of the Beirut sovereigns was said to be superior
     to that of British coins.

12   The oasis famous in Arab legend as the capital of Queen Bilqis, the
     Queen of Sheba. In ancient times the land round Marib was extremely
     fertile, thanks to irrigation from the colossal dam built on the river
     Adhanat in the 9th century BC. The dam was destroyed, probably by
     an earthquake, in about AD 570.

13   Many Egyptians feared that the tribesmen were cannibals, and ate
     prisoners.

14   It was on this day that terrorists tried to murder Sir Kennedy Trevaskis,
     the recently arrived High Commissioner Aden. They struck at Aden
     airport when Trevaskis was about to fly out for a conference in
     London, dropping a hand-grenade among a group of officials on the
     tarmac. George Henderson, a Political Officer, seeing what was
     happening, thrust Trevaskis aside, thus saving him, but was fatally
     wounded himself, and was awarded a posthumous George Cross for
     his bravery.

15   The letter which included these instructions, but never reached
     Cooper, was one of the five intercepted and published in *The Sunday
     Times*. See pp.175–83.

16   *The Conspirators,* p.66.

17   Personal interview, 20 August 2009.

5 Digging In

1   Bob Denard 1929–2007. Already, at thirty-four, he had served in the
     French navy in the Far East and in the colonial police in North Africa,
     and served a fourteen-month prison sentence for his alleged partici-
     pation in a plot to assassinate the French Prime Minister, Pierre Mendes-
     France. A vehement anti-communist, he was married seven times and
     eventually succumbed to Alzheimer's. The French at Khanjar had been
     having trouble – their former Commander, the Prince Bourbon de
     Parme, had run off with some months of their operational money.

2   The French and Belgian mercenaries, recruited and oganised by Roger Faulques, always outnumbered the British, and frequently cooperated with them.

3   *Arabian Assignment*, p.189.

4   From November 1963 to May 1964 Jack Miller kept a wonderfully detailed diary, which he sent back to base in instalments. When typed, it ran to ninety-nine foolscap pages – some 50,000 words. The Yemenis saw him scribbling so often that some of them thought he was a writer, and an old woman once addressed him as '*Ya Sáhafi*', 'O Writer'.

5   CAB 130/189 Gen 776.

6   Later Jack Miller remarked: 'HM will have to be informed that a sense of urgency is of use in wartime.'

7   *Sunday Telegraph*, 15 December 1963.

8   Jack was impressed by the doctor's skill and willingness to go anywhere, and suggested to Jim that his pay should be increased from £250 to £300 a month.

9   In his report Johnny gave the date of the attack as the 30th; but his first, staccato radio message – 'Attacked Jihannah. Seven hits out of ten. Many Egyptians killed. Panic. No counter-fire' – reached Nuqub on the 27th.

10   FO 371 174627 (BM 1022/59).

6 Manna from Heaven

1   In January 1965 Feisal told McLean that there was a secret agreement between Golda Meir (then Israeli Foreign Minister, later Prime Minister) and Nasser, whereby Nasser agreed not to attack Israel, in exchange for money from America and secret help from Israel. McLean Papers, IWM, Duxford.

2   Weizmann became President of the State of Israel, 1993–2000.

3   Personal communication, May 2009.

4   Johnny himself reported that the Israelis had 'muffled the engines', but this was physically impossible.

5   Nearly fifty years later Arieh Oz still reckoned that 'for daring, planning and execution, it was a masterpiece of a military operation'. Personal communication, 21 May 2010.

6   The Israelis gave Tony Boyle a backgammon set made of olive wood.

7 Shortage of Gold

1 John Harding, *Roads to Nowhere*, p.239.
2 Personal interview, 5 March 2010.
3 Ibid. Somebody else – probably John Woodhouse – had a similar idea, suggesting in a memorandum in the BFLF files that an SAS commando raid on the ships at Hodeidah could be carried out 'without undue difficulty'.
4 DEFE 25/129.
5 Ibid.
6 Victoria Clark, *Yemen: Dancing on the Heads of Snakes*, p.95.
7 This included a request for 10,000 .303 rifles, three million rounds of ammunition, twenty light anti-aircraft guns, 500 anti-tank mines, 1,000 hand-grenades and 2.8 million Maria Theresa dollars (approximately £1 million) for pay.
8 Hansard, 14 May 1964, Vol. 695, cc. 604–5.
9 Ibid.

8 Breach of Security

1 *One of the Originals*, pp.179–80.
2 Hansard, 21 July 1964, Vol. 699, cc. 267–9.
3 Ibid.
4 Ibid.
5 *One of the Originals*, p.179.
6 Clive Jones, *Britain and the Yemen Civil War*, p.105. DEFE 13/570 77705. Top Secret telegram No. 472.
7 DEFE 13/570 77705.

9 Business as Usual

1 Personal correspondence. Admoni frequently visited the Johnsons' house in Chelsea, and became very fond of Judy – so much so that after her death he organised the planting of a grove of pine trees on the western hills of Jerusalem, in her memory.
2 McSweeney suffered a grievous loss when, on leave, he took out his back-pay in cash and stored it, for safety's sake, in his mother's oven. Failing to notice that the oven contained a package, she lit the gas, with disastrous results.
3 While Camus was convalescing at his father's villa on the island of

Ischia, his fiancée was killed in an air-crash on her way to join him. Thinking there was nothing left in life for him, he returned to the Yemen, to die, but there recovered his zest and became an excellent operator.

4   Personal communications, 2009 and 2010.

5   Jack Miller recorded in his diary that the *gebile* 'have a weird addiction to tribal dances, including the use of knives therein, and their strange, high-pitched singing . . . might, in the distance, be likened to the droning of the Scottish pipes. Pipes here are in frequent use and even more barbaric in sound than their Scottish counterparts.'

6   Kilbracken had borrowed a cine-camera from the mercenaries, and knew a lot about their activities, but never mentioned them in his articles.

7   Later the Marchioness of Salisbury.

8   He had left after the discovery of financial discrepancies.

9   George, a Belgian, was a mortar expert; Amiral, a small, bearded Frenchman who liked to operate on his own, had won an amazing number of medals.

10 Eugene Rogan, *The Arabs*, p.332.

11 FO 371/179863.

12 FO 371/174638 BM 1041/369G Secret FS/64/133.

10 A High and a Low

1   Jimmy Knox had been in the merchant navy, but after an incident at Malta he was seized by the police, and the only way he could escape gaol was by joining the army.

2   *Arabian Assignment*, p.188.

3   Ibid., p.190.

4   McLean Papers, IWM, Duxford.

5   *Sunday Telegraph*, 25 April 1965. In his memoirs he wrote that he left Humeidat on 6 April, and so missed the battle, which took place on the 21st, (*Arabian Assignment*, p.190).

6   In August 1965, after the battle, when the Egyptians applied for help to withdraw troops from Hazm to Humeidat, through Dahm territory, they asked for members of the tribe to travel with them as a guarantee of safe conduct.

7   *Arabian Assignment*, p.182. Over the years Adham accumulated an immense amount of money through various deals, and in 1992 was fined $105 million by United States prosecutors for his part in the scandal involving the Bank of Credit and Commerce International.

8   *The Conspirators*, p.71.
9   In the commentary on a film that he made for the BBC.
10 *Arabian Assignment*, p.191.
11 In some respects the men in the field were better off than the diplo-
    mats in Saudi Arabia. The British Embassy had to import their drink
    as 'furniture', and one dinner party in the First Secretary's house was
    interrupted by a telephone call from customs saying that the 'British
    Embassy's furniture is leaking. Could someone please come quickly
    to collect it before the smell of alcohol wafting through the airport
    leads to arrests.'
12 Gassim eventually defected to the Republicans and was murdered.
13 *Lan ansahib min al Yaman wa lau Jaffat myah al Nile* – I will not with-
    draw from the Yemen even if the Nile's waters run dry.
14 Peter Hinchcliffe, John T. Ducker & Maria Holt, *Without Glory in
    Arabia*, p.70. FO 371/179858.
15 'Overseen' was not quite correct. The SIS were aware of Woodhouse's
    involvement, but did not control his movements.
16 Weekly *News from Saudi Arabia*, 11 January 1966.
17 *Yemen: Dancing on the Heads of Snakes*, p.84.
18 CO 1055/307.
19 Over Saudi Arabia, Brian Carroll, a former Lightning chief exam-
    iner, took one of the aircraft up to 87,300 feet, at which height he
    reported that control was 'on a knife-edge'. The Kuwaitis also bought
    Lightnings, but lacked the skill to maintain them.
20 PREM 13/1923 C417465.

11 In the Balance

1   Interview with Sultan Ghalib al-Qu'aiti, 14 June 2010.
2   Bob Walker-Brown was known to some of the mercenaries as 'Bob
    Danvers-Walker', after the presenter who announced the prizes in
    the television show *Double Your Money*.
3   Personal conversation, 3 November 2009.
4   When he returned to England in December 1966 Thesiger gave an
    informal report to members of the Defence Intelligence Staff. DEFE
    13/571.
5   Thesiger's grandfather, 2nd Baron Chelmsford (1827-1905),
    commanded the British force that was defeated by the Zulu army
    at the Battle of Isandlwana in 1879.

12 Fresh Blood

1   Personal correspondence, 10 December 2009.
2   This was for covering maps, to lengthen their life.
3   Mac was very suspicious of Bushrod Howard, 'who purports to lobby Americans in support of Royalist cause and demands large sums money in return . . . An unsavoury person.'
4   *Yemen: the Unknown War*, p.263.
5   This claim was later denied; but another source said that the Egyptian pilots were German-trained.
6   Personal interview, November 2009.
7   In his memoir *Arabian Assignment* Smiley described this visit to Amara and other places in the Yemen, but made no mention of the fact that by then he had been ostracised by the leaders of the BFLF.

13 Exit Jay

1   Rochat, a Swiss, was a smooth former hotelier then in his early forties. David Bailey had a blistering row with him over the Red Cross's supine attitude.
2   PREM 13/1923 C417465.
3   Ibid.
4   Ibid.
5   The gas bombs were designed to break open on impact, rather than explode.
6   In its issue of 7 August 1967 the American *Newsweek* reported that the gas had been identified as phosgene.

14 Smash Hit

1   *The Arabs*, p.333.
2   Private conversation, 10 May 2010.
3   Jonathan Walker, *Aden Insurgency*, p.271.
4   PREM 13/1923 C417465.
5   *Yemen: the Unknown War*, p.295.
6   *Aden Insurgency*, p.288. In Vol Two of the *Diaries of a Cabinet Minister, 1966–68*, p.384, Crossman noted: 'George Brown has been appallingly uncertain of himself about the Aden policy.'

15 Aftermath

1   *Britain and the Yemen Civil War*, p.72.
2   Funeral address by David Walker, 30 July 2008.
3   'Return to Yemen', in the journal of the British-Yemeni Society, August 2003.

Index